The Image of
Success

Make a Great Impression and
Land the Job You Want

BY LIZANDRA VEGA

D1456536

 AMERICAN MANAGEMENT ASSOCIATION
New York • Atlanta • Brussels • Chicago • Mexico City • San Francisco
Shanghai • Tokyo • Toronto • Washington, D.C.

Bulk discounts available. For details visit:
www.amacombooks.org/go/specialsales
Or contact special sales:
Phone: 800-250-5308
E-mail: specialsls@amanet.org
View all the AMACOM titles at: www.amacombooks.org

This publication is designed to provide accurate and authoritative information in regard to the subject matter covered. It is sold with the understanding that the publisher is not engaged in rendering legal, accounting, or other professional service. If legal advice or other expert assistance is required, the services of a competent professional person should be sought.

Library of Congress Cataloging-in-Publication Data

Vega, Lizandra.
The image of success : make a great impression and land the job you want / by Lizandra Vega.
    p. cm.
Includes bibliographical references and index.
ISBN 978-0-8144-1454-5
1. Employment interviewing. 2. Job hunting. 3. Success in business. I. Title.
HF5549.5.I6V44 2010
650.14—dc22

                                                                2010005831

About AMA

American Management Association (www.amanet.org) is a world leader in talent development, advancing the skills of individuals to drive business success. Our mission is to support the goals of individuals and organizations through a complete range of products and services, including classroom and virtual seminars, webcasts, webinars, podcasts, conferences, corporate and government solutions, business books, and research. AMA's approach to improving performance combines experiential learning—learning through doing—with opportunities for ongoing professional growth at every step of one's career journey.

Printing number
10 9 8 7 6 5 4 3 2 1

DEDICATION

This book is dedicated to my five pillars of strength and inspiration: my parents, Wilfredo and Elsa Vega, who have infused me with never-ending love, support, and the confidence to reach for the stars at a very early age; my daughter, Julianna, and son, Christian, who light up my world even in the dimmest of times and who add loving significance to the term "working mother"; and finally my husband, business partner, and childhood friend, Stephen Brown, whose unconditional devotion allows me to soar to new heights. Together we have made it!

In loving memory of Sharon Stutman, my mentor-friend; and my mother-in-law, Frances Brown: two women whose nurturing ways taught me patience, persistence, and compassion.

CONTENTS

Introduction

YOU'VE BEEN gainfully employed for seven years, performing your duties and responsibilities to the best of your ability. The positive evaluations throughout the years confirm this and have anchored your job security . . . or so you think. You've attended every boring social and professional office function, even if just to stay within the good graces of the powers-that-be. It has *never* dawned on you that you would get the dreaded interoffice phone call from the boss asking, "Do you have a moment for me?" Even though you have about a zillion things to do, you answer in your most polite yet fragile voice, "Of course I do" and you scurry your way into her office while rehearsing how to remain cool, calm, and collected.

"Maybe I'm getting promoted?" you whisper to yourself while your heart is pumping at 80 beats per second. You knock lightly, and the familiar voice ushers you inside; as you enter, the gaze in the boss's eye confirms every awful suspicion. It's clear from her stance and her tone that there are extenuating circumstances that have driven her to execute this unpleasant task. You zone out as she gives her long-winded explanation. All you see are her lips moving, but the volume is on mute. Finally, you tune in just in time to hear her say, "I'm sorry to have to let you go." It doesn't matter that you've been given "a package," or that some of your dignity's been spared by not being escorted out the door immediately, or even that she apologized for having to do the deed. The fact is that from the moment you heard the dreaded words of termination, you felt frazzled, vulnerable, and destitute.

When she's done, you haul yourself back to your desk, while resisting the urge to scream through the hallways, only to hear a reprise of the interoffice phone call in the office suite next door. In this instance, misery doesn't love company. It just means one more person to battle in the dog-eat-dog world of interviewing, where potential employers will want to see it all: education, talent, experience, ethics, and image. As the new fish in the shark pool of statistics, it's survival of the fittest. As you switch into survival mode inspired by fears of when you'll see your next paycheck, even a simple manicure or shoe shine seem extravagant.

How do you ever go about persuading employers that you possess that certain je ne sais quoi that they've been looking for when you are now on a tight budget topped with a morale that's in the dumps? Surely, your competition is bound to have a glowing professional and educational background. So what exactly *will* you have to do to leave a lasting impression on a potential employer who you're hoping will choose you for a job?

Surprisingly, there is no single winning universal quality that potential hiring managers look for; it's more of a multifaceted feature that each decision maker ranks according to his or her own perception and rules of scrutiny. Simply put, the intricacy of this element is based on how you choose to present the layers of what makes you distinguishable and unique: your appearance, behavior, and communication, otherwise known as your "image." These three layers encompass your most influential interviewing vehicle, but the vehicle will take you the distance only if you load it up with compatible fuel. It is when you make these three layers compatible that you are most sought after. (Image is not to be confused with your genetically inherent identity traits [DNA], although these characteristics do play a role in how you shape your image. Your height, for instance, is a part of your genetic makeup. How you alter your height with shoes is part of the image you choose to create.)

While it may seem unrelated or unfair to be judged by the cover of your book rather than your contents, the truth is that assumptions about your capabilities, sophistication, pedigree, intelligence, and performance *can* and *will* be drawn based on your image. The good news is that you have exclusive control of creating the image you want to project. It may take some tweaking within one or more of your three layers, but when all three are harmoniously aligned you will appear at your best. And with a little time, patience, humility, and some good old-fashioned self-analysis, you'll be able to achieve complete synchronization of your image.

Balancing the components of your image is an attainable and cost-effective way to gain a competitive edge while seeking a job. There is no premium for choosing appropriate colors, fabrics, textures, and silhouettes, nor is there one for exercising proper etiquette or communicating in a professional manner.

As an executive recruiter and certified image coach, I have guided thousands of candidates through metamorphoses that have been essential to their winning the interview wars. My counseling has helped individuals master the art of interviewing by using image as their most dominant asset. Let's face it, selling one's ability to do a job in as few as 20 to 60 minutes requires an entirely different skill set than actually doing the job. The sooner you're in on the inside information, the sooner you'll get that competitive edge.

For the past 15 years, I have diligently recorded, *confidentially,* the reasons why seeming *star* candidates have failed miserably at clinching a job behind closed doors. Overwhelmingly, the top reasons consistently relate to image. It pains me to get the much anticipated "feedback" phone call from a client who ends up offering the most crushing news:

"Thanks for sending Jane Doe, but I'll pass on her. She just doesn't fit our corporate culture."

I spent weeks or sometimes even months trying to identify the "perfect" candidate. I take all of the necessary precautions: prescreen, interview, background check, prep, re-prep—only to get a flat-out rejection! What falls under the umbrella of "doesn't fit our corporate culture"? For women, sometimes it's a suit that's so skin-tight that it is bound to stop circulation. Other times, it's an inappropriate hemline four inches above the knee (which can land you a different type of job altogether—one I don't represent). Other times, plump cleavage is peeking out like a pair of anxious puppies panting to be walked. For men, some of my personal favorite issues include asphyxiatingly strong cologne and chest hair that is unsuitably peering out of all sorts of crevices. Is it too much to ask you to wear a tie for this formal encounter we refer to as an interview? Apparently so, since wearing a tie for some would be like wearing a neon sign around their neck announcing they are looking for a new job. Then there are behavioral faux pas that designate that candidates may be better suited for a farm than an office. It has gotten back to me that a male candidate has stopped midsentence during an interview to check out a female employee strolling past the conference room's glass doors *(oink oink)*.

I am also often flabbergasted at what some candidates consider a proper handshake. But we'll discuss this much later.

As far as communication, sometimes candidates are so nervous or excessively eager that they blow the interview by not knowing when to zip it. Often, administrative support candidates use blatant "yuhs" (i.e., you) and "aksses" (i.e., asks) while going off on a tangent whenever "akssed" a simple question. Senior-level candidates are not exempt from blunders. Highly educated and experienced candidates are frequently eliminated from the interview process because they wrote bad or generic thank-you notes. Other times, writing a thank-you note is skipped altogether (which shows arrogance). In fact, there have been so many interview indiscretions that I've decided that it's my duty to job candidates everywhere to finally "tell all."

My professional credentials and the experiences that I've gained through my own development qualify me to speak with such candor about the makeover of your image. Born and raised in the Arthur Avenue section of the Bronx, the only and first-generation child of parents from Puerto Rico, I had a humble upbringing. Once upon a time, *I* was a person for whom communication was a challenge because English is my second language. Nonverbal communication was my savior, as my verbal skills were exceeded by my outgoing personality. I've been there. I have spent countless hours in front of a mirror practicing my pronunciation, while my facial features reflected my frustration.

Appearance was an entirely other transformation. My teen years were spent emulating the Melanie Griffith look from *Working Girl.* Jewelry choices ranged from gold nameplates and ankle bracelets to rope chains and "initial" rings—the more, the better. While my disposable income was limited, somehow I seemed to spend enough on cosmetics and perfume (also piled on) to feed a small village. During my college years at the ultra-liberal Wesleyan University, in Middletown, Connecticut, my encounters with students from diverse cultural and socioeconomic backgrounds opened my senses to a whole new world of possibilities. To date, I've experienced a complete transformation from Bronx chic to Preppy chic to Execu-mom-chic. It took some work.

This book's message is simple. Though its delivery may at times seem bold, I assure you, it's without malice or condescension. Call it an infusion of blue-collar influence meets blue-blood intellect. I write this book from the perspective of someone who has arduously built a successful image and business from the ground up. While my image has given me the authority and credibility to work with others on achieving similar positive results, I still consider myself a work in progress.

Years of speech, voice, and performance training in order to overcome my own communication barriers add personal insight to the communication portion of the book. As a beauty adviser for Elizabeth Arden Cosmetics (my day job while I pursued an acting career), I gained valuable hands-on experience with skincare and color as well as helpful practice assessing faces. My involvement in costuming during college initiated an affinity for wardrobe and accessories. These interests were later cultivated by attending the Image Certification Program at the Fashion Institute of Technology. My college experience as a senior interviewer for the admissions office at Wesleyan was later followed by a successful career in staffing and ultimately cofounding Perennial Resources International, a full-service temporary, contingency, and retained search firm located in Manhattan.

Even as a child, I had the foresight to coach and counsel. Persistently, I encouraged my parents to pursue better job opportunities only to find out that they were resistant to interviewing for internal postings. They both had identical qualms: "Better language skills are required for another job. We know we can pay the bills and save up for your education with the jobs we have." Although I was too young to understand the depth of their reservations about trying something new, I was old enough to learn about the discipline, loyalty, and pride it takes to keep a job.

My parents devotedly pursued positions with the exact skills and responsibilities they were originally hired to perform at Montefiore Medical Center—my father for 33 years in the transportation department, my mother as a dietary aide for 20 years in the nutrition department. Snow, rain, or sleet didn't stop them; calling in sick wasn't an option, unless they were on their "deathbed." It was their duty to ride the number 9 bus to work each day with a positive disposition and (I feel the need to mention) not a hair out of place. While their work attire consisted of uniforms, these were always freshly laundered, neatly pressed, and paired with expertly polished shoes. Their behavior on the job was exemplary, and their hard work and dedication were often recognized with salary increases and commemorative pins that decorated their photo I.D. badges. It all makes sense to me now, and I am proud of their accomplishments.

Excellent hygiene and grooming were required in our household. I am convinced that it was this meticulous attention to appearance and behavior that helped us assimilate into a culture that didn't understand our spoken word. I was well aware that if, like George and Louise in *The Jeffersons* (one of my favorite sitcoms while growing up), we wanted to "move on up," there were lots of things I needed to develop and change. Indeed, I did alter many things about myself, which has contributed to seeing life outside the walls of my quaint Southern Boulevard apartment with picturesque views of the Bronx Zoo. In a sense, this book contains semi-autobiographical tidbits as a way of leading by example (most of the time).

The birth of *The Image of Success* is meant to integrate the necessary ingredients for a full blend of your spiciest alphabet soup—your **ABCs** (**a**ppearance, **b**ehavior, and **c**ommunication) if you will. It is meant to minimize your interviewing anxieties and to encourage you to embrace the challenge as an opportunity for development and success in your job search. I have intended this book for those who are sick of being over-looked time after time for the position one or two notches above their present one; are bouncing back due to corporate restructuring or down-sizing; are returning to the workforce after years of caring for a loved one; have recently attained a college or postgraduate degree and don't have a clue where to begin; or are attempting to refresh their interview-ing skills as an experienced job hunter. Regardless of the job categories and industries covered, one thing is universal: Image matters even more than you think.

As you read through the chapters, you may find that some chapters are more pertinent for you than others. Feel free to read chapters consecu-tively or in order of their importance to you. Just do yourself a favor and read them earnestly and objectively. Challenge yourself to improve on your image and remember that keeping yourself looking, feeling, and sounding great is something that will benefit you to undertake as a lifestyle. Especially during tough economic times, don't shoot for instant miracles or you'll be disappointed and tempted to give up.

Take toddler steps and add on pieces of this book's advice as your com-fort zone expands. Before you know it, paying attention to your image will no longer be a choice; it will become an integral part of who you are. For some of you, working from the outer layer of your image and allowing the results to penetrate into the core of whom you want to project may come easiest. Others may naturally gravitate toward starting from the inner or midlayer. The choice is yours. However you choose to connect the pieces of yourself, make the image advice in this book a daily part of your routine. And then, should you ever get that dreaded interoffice call from the boss, you will be able to grab a hold of your emotions and dive right into the job-search shark pool with ample gear. Let your image become your winning asset. Before you realize it, it won't be whom you *know* but who you *are* that will move your candidacy right to the top of the list.

PART ONE

APPEARANCE

1

The "F" Bomb—Flair

An artist's flair is sometimes worth a scientist's brains. —*Anton Chekhov (Russian playwright, short-story writer, and physician)*

THE LUXURY OF a silver spoon may not have been mine at birth. Instead, I was blessed with a different sort of gift: I got "It" as part of my layette. It's as if someone from up above threw me a bone to offset my world of material deficiency. Except that growing up in my neighborhood I didn't see it as such. Rather, "It" became my curse as opposed to a talent. Once regarded by me as a burden to bear (since I was verbally harassed by schoolmates who thought I thought I was better than everyone else), I now recognize "It" as a powerful gift...the "F" bomb...aka flair. Style, poise, and panache are all synonymous with flair. Today, I can fully appreciate the competitive advantage that having flair has given me. Call it superfluous, but I am proof that flair will tip the scale in your favor, especially in your attempts to snatch a life-changing job opportunity. Let this book help you recognize and hone in on your inborn flair, or let it help you start building your flair one block at time.

Your interview attire must narrate a subliminal story; one that coincides with your behavior, intentions, and spoken word. Basically, if you lack flair, you are missing a huge part of what recruiters and employers want to see you exude . . . confidence, knowledge, and authority. (It's also one of the reasons some people are always a bridesmaid/groomsman and never the bride/groom). Other bonuses of developing flair will be less time wasted on making purchasing decisions, fewer bad expenditures, and less aggravation. I do admit to being a design junkie; however, I am well aware that flair is only mildly associated with who you are wearing. I ask you to look beyond the labels (though they don't hurt) in order to understand that in the grand scheme of things, they are merely *gravy*. Flair has much deeper roots, whose exploration entails a journey of self-discovery. My goal is to guide you through this exploration process. Your instincts will help you to adequately execute the winning professional appearance you may have visualized for years.

I can't promise that there is a single foolproof recipe to nailing a job, but I can say with confidence that if you came in to my office for an interview and you had flair, I would remember you even after a daylong "cattle call."

Nothing is more distracting than interviewing a candidate who is so painfully uncomfortable in his own skin that all he can do is squirm like a child who needs to "go potty." He could be dressed in Armani, but if he lacks flair, he may as well be wearing a burlap sack. I enjoy *People* magazine's Style Watch celebrity face-offs, where two stars are shown with one look. Though it is largely a popularity contest, I usually choose the celebrity who demonstrates the most flair. It's because flair is based on your individuality and your ability to bring a garment or accessory to life on the terms of your own creativity and know-how. The final product is almost an intangible criterion to be judged. That is flair. But what it takes to attain this triumphant aura we recruiters look for as a hiring credential can be explained in very tangible terms.

It's not easy to fend for yourself in a retail store where salespeople are circling you and trying their best to lure you into buying. After all, they have sales quotas to fill and mouths to feed. But no one need fall prey to the hungry piranhas because of ignorance. Instead, read on to discover what goes into developing your very own signature flair.

Be grateful for the lemons you've been handed . . . and make lemonade.

Assessing Your Physical Characteristics

You wouldn't be human if you didn't look at yourself in the mirror and nitpick some minuscule flaw only you can see. When you're out to impress, even the slightest physical blemish is bound to be magnified, resulting in a wounded ego, which flings your flair right out the window.

If you've decided to launch a job search on your own or if you've been given advance notice of your termination, you may have the time to, for example, shed any extra pounds you've been lugging around. But if you are one of many for whom the news of unemployment has been shockingly sudden, with little if any recovery time, there's no choice but to make lemonade with the lemons you've been handed.

You can never afford to sit back and wait for opportunity to knock on your door—and especially not during a recession. This is the time to get out from the emotional gloom you've been under and use your natural abilities to get your mojo back. In other words, strike them with your "F" bomb. If you don't have the faintest idea of where to start, I'm here to tell you that your physical traits are a road map to finding your flair. Looking your absolute best will add one more check mark next to your name when stacked against your competition.

When I refer to physical characteristics, I mean your body proportions, body type, lines, pattern, texture, scale, and color. Excuses like saying you're "color-blind" or "left-brained" are not valid here. There's too much at stake. Besides, if you can't be meticulous about yourself, if it's not important enough for you to exude flair, then how can an employer presume you will be scrupulous about your work? So unless you've got secret plans of going under the knife at a plastic surgeon's mercy, you've got to work with what you've got. Trust me: Whether you think so or not, you've got plenty to work with. You just have to learn how to use it to your advantage.

Make Nice with Your Proportions

I'm guilty of having had temporary jealous thoughts about the person in the fitting room next to mine who happens to be trying on the same suit as I am. It looks stunning on her and hideous on me. But I'm shrewd enough to know that her tall, svelte figure won't look nearly as good in every suit she tries on. Obviously, it's her lucky day in finding one that was designed using a model with proportions nearly identical to hers. My point is that if you're planning to buy a suit "off the rack" or "ready to wear," don't beat yourself up about not fitting into it properly. The fact is it's not your body's fault; it was the manufacturer's decision to target a different body type. Proportions serve as essential guidelines toward making adjustments that help you dress with buoyancy and flair.

Analyzing your body in "parts" will enable you to eliminate any disapproval you may feel over your entire body. It will help you isolate the "challenge areas" and allow you to work on creating an optical illusion to make it appear ideal. You may be surprised to know that the ideal body does not translate into a thin body. Actually, you may be parading around with an ideal body and not even know it. For your information, an ideal body is one whose height is eight times the length of the person's head. These eight heads are then divided within four sections of your body. If you discover that an area of your body is shorter or longer than the "ideal" number of head lengths designated to it, that's when your balancing act should begin. The magic code is 1–2–1–4. Adjusting break points to achieve balance is vital.

Unveil your proportions:

▪ **Step 1:** Measure your head's length from scalp to bottom of chin. If you have a double chin, be sure to include the entire chin in your measurement. Next, measure your entire body from the top of your head to the bottom of your feet with a ribbon, string, or measuring tape for precision. Divide your entire height by the scalp-to-chin measurement you obtained. If your full height equals eight of your head lengths, then you are the proud owner of an *ideally* proportioned body—that is, one that is easy to dress.

top of head

chin

waist

pelvic bone

knees

bottom of feet

Camouflage: If you find that your body is fewer than eight head lengths, your head is long in proportion to the rest of your body. Therefore, you may want to consider a hairstyle that is close to your scalp with bangs and without much volume at the top of your head to help minimize the length of your head. Conversely, if you find that your height exceeds the eight head lengths, then your head is short and you would benefit from adding volume to the top of your head with a hairstyle that is layered, pinned, or tied up in order to achieve proportional balance.

▪ **Step 2:** Measure your torso from the bottom of your chin to your natural waist (where you feel the break with your hip bone). The *ideal* proportion for this section of your body is two of your head lengths; shorter than two heads equals a short waist, while longer than two heads is considered a long waist.

Camouflage: We short-waisted folk can find harmony by wearing monochromatic colors around your midsection (see Chapter 2) to extend the waist. This can entail wearing a shirt and pants or skirt that are monochromatic. You may also opt for wearing a suit jacket that is slightly longer, which would lengthen your torso and specifically your waist. For those of you with long torsos, choosing pants or skirts with a waist that is slightly higher than your natural waist works well. Select wider belts in contrasting colors to break the extra inches that throw the "ideal" numbers off kilter.

▪ **Step 3:** Next, measure from your waist to the bottom of your pelvic bone (your rise). If this area is proportionate, the measurement equals one head length; anything shorter than one head length indicates a short rise, while a measurement longer than one head length indicates a long one.

Camouflage: Wearing pants with a slightly higher waistband will help conceal the area if you have a short rise, while a slightly lower waistband will conceal a particularly long rise. Keep your suit jacket closed to conceal your rise if you are self-conscious, except when sitting down.

▪ **Step 4:** Finally, measure from the bottom of your pelvic bone to the bottoms of your feet, and if that measurement equals four head lengths, then your legs are the ideal proportion; fewer than four heads reveals shorter legs, while more than four heads means your legs are disproportionately longer than your upper body.

Camouflage: If you find that you have short legs, wear pants with a vertical pinstripe or chalk stripe in a slightly tapered style; avoid cuffs. Socks or hosiery that are similar in color value to your skirt and shoes and are lighter in texture will also add length to short legs. If you have particularly long legs, choose a pattern like a glen plaid or windowpane to create a wider look. Long legs can also be balanced with pant legs that are flared. Hemmed cuffs will aesthetically dissipate the disproportionate leg length. However, as far as style, cuffed hems are too casual on interview pant legs. Socks and hosiery that are nude in color and of thicker texture will optically shorten long legs.

Bodies Come in All Shapes

The outside lines of your body, whether straight, curved, or a combination of straight and curved, form your silhouette. Your silhouette is the overall shape you see when you notice your shadow following you along a dark hallway. There are four body shapes that are gender-neutral, and two additional body shapes that apply only to a woman's body. In keeping with our ABCs, below you will see the letters of the alphabet that represent the six different silhouettes: "H," "O," "V," "A," "X," and "S."

H, O, V, A = GENDER NEUTRAL; X, S = FEMALE ONLY

▪ As an **"H"** shape, your shoulders, waist, and your hips have virtually the same dimensions throughout.

Choose suit jackets with a softer shoulder to minimize the appearance of sharp angles. The crisscross "inside" lines formed by a buttoned double-breasted jacket will give definition to the waist area, as the objective is to add definition to your waist by creating a "V"-like optical illusion. You might even opt for a jacket with a slightly asymmetrical one-button closure. Keep your suit jacket open and use a dress belt to create a converging

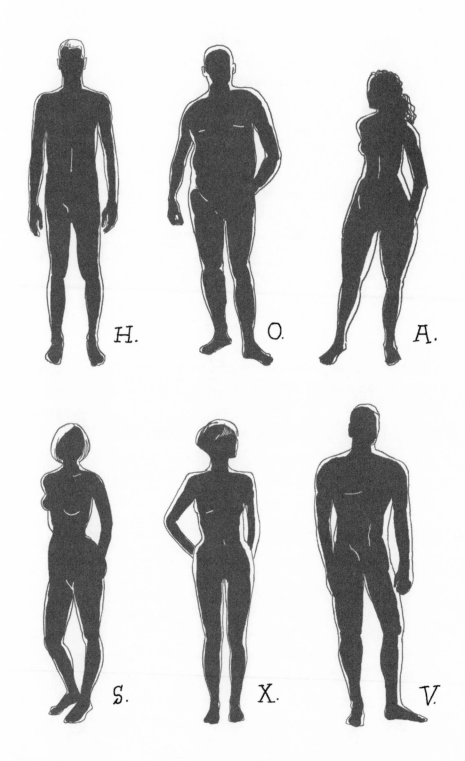

focal point with the buckle. Look for details such as darts and slant pockets near the waist to create an illusion of indentation.

▪ As an "O" shape, your rounded midsection is much larger than your shoulders or hips. Suit jackets and bottoms that are too baggy accentuate the "O" silhouette. Though you may think it conceals the roundness of the shape, the bagginess actually maximizes it. Choose suit jackets with peaked lapels to balance your look. Avoid cuffed hems and choose socks and hosiery of color value similar to your good shoes. Opt for vertical or diagonal patterns that are close together to narrow and elongate your frame. Use monochromatic colors and smooth textures that provide a slimming effect. Fabrics should drape well in order to allow room for the curves of your body. A double-breasted suit will be flattering, because of its diagonal inside lines. For women in this category, a hemline below the calf will create a slimmer-looking leg.

▪ As a "V" shape, you are funnel or conelike. Your shoulders are the widest part of your body, and you have tapered hips and thin legs.

Choose jackets that have pockets, hip yokes, and/or other details near the hip to help widen the area. Women should choose full skirts in crisp fabrics that enlarge the area. Trousers for both genders should have more fullness at the bottom to balance the wideness of the shoulders. Add volume to the lower portion of your body.

▪ As an "A" shape, your shoulders are considerably smaller than your waist and hips. Balance your silhouette by adding width and/or visual interest to your upper body. Achieve this with more pronounced shoulder padding, brightly colored ties, or scarves with decorative patterns. Spread collars and wider lapels can also balance narrowness. Jacket hems should adequately cover your hip area, and a slightly longer suit jacket should accomplish this. Choose trousers with tapered hems to minimize the disproportionate fullness of your hips, legs, and derriere. Skirts with a center pleat (not slit) create the illusion of a narrower bottom.

▪ **"X"** and **"S"** shapes are designated for certain women's bodies. Both silhouettes have indented waists with shoulders and hips of similar proportions. The difference lies in the "X" shape having angular lines along with lower hip placement, while the "S" shape is the curvier sister with a higher hip placement.

It doesn't take much to balance these shapes, as these are the two most naturally balanced silhouettes. The "S" or "figure 8" shape will need more fluid fabrics to fall freely around her curves, while the "X" shape can carry more taut fabrics around its sharper lines. Camouflaging these silhouettes may be necessary for interviewing as they are the most feminine and sensual looking of bodies. Wear tailored suit jackets without details that attract attention to what could be considered a "sexy" waistline. Detract attention from the waist by keeping the suit jacket closed so as not to overexpose the waist, and avoid jackets that are tight fitting around the waistline when fastened.

Reading Between the Lines

Your body, face, and hair are a series of lines (yes, wrinkles are included). Some may be straight, others curved, and others a combination of the three. The next time you disrobe to jump in the shower, take a moment to look at your body with an objective eye. The grass is always greener but no matter what your results are, there are ways to complement your body.

In his 1954 book *Atlas of Men*, American psychologist William Herbert Sheldon developed an interesting theory by which he classified human bodies into one of three "somatotypes" through which a person's mental characteristics could be derived. In the present day, employers will make stereotypical assumptions about your work ethic based on your body type: endomorphic, ectomorphic, or mesomorphic.

You are **endomorphic** if you have ample flesh covering up your bones. I'm on your team even at my thinnest. You and I see curves around our arms, shoulders, chest, stomach, buttocks, and legs. Employers may assume that you are not as agile as the "meso" or "ecto" competitors. Your endurance and stamina may be in question whenever you are considered for a job. Therefore, in order to create harmony with the curves found in our bodies, it is best for us to invest in finely tailored garments made of fabrics that cascade fluidly around the curves. Choose darker colors for your body and brighter colors around the head and face area. Garments with geometric patterns may offset some of the roundness in the curves, while ties or scarves with rounded patterns or circles will accentuate this body type.

You are **ectomorphic**, or "skeletal," if there is bone protruding from areas such as wrists, fingers, shoulder blades, chest, rib cage, elbows, knees, and toes. Sometimes, an ectomorph may be thought of by a potential employer as not having enough of a commanding presence for a job that requires a leadership role. This body type can easily drown in too much fabric. Opt for well-tailored clothing in textured or bulkier fabrics to add volume to your frame. This may also be achieved by layering garment pieces such as undershirts, button-down shirts, or a vest under a suit jacket. Patterns with curvy or paisley motifs offset the sharp lines in your body type. Use bolder color-contrast choices within your wardrobe and accessory pieces.

The **mesomorphic** body is a combination of skeletal and fleshy or thin and muscular. This describes those of you who may have angular shoulders and legs and a ample stomach or derriere, or vice versa. It can also describe those of you who possess athletic bodies. The typecast for this body type is the most lenient since you are not labeled sluggish or frail. (However, don't be surprised if the recruiter isn't wondering whether you will work on staying in shape during company time.) This type of body benefits from buying garments in which the top and bottom pieces are sold separately. While every body type could really benefit from custom-tailored suits in order to balance and camouflage, this body type would benefit the most because of the disparity in line direction. Since you are a hybrid of the endomorphic and ectomorphic body types, following the recommendations given previously for each of the categories will help you balance a particular area that exhibits too many of the traits of either body type.

Pattern, Texture, Scale, and Color . . .
More Road Maps to Discovering Your Flair

Think of yourself as a natural stone or a piece of marble with veins, imperfections, and beautiful movement in your skin. Pattern in skin refers to freckles, moles, or discoloration of the skin due to sun damage. Raised moles, scars, wrinkles, and stubble add even more irregularity to the touch. Your natural skin pigment comprises hemoglobin (red), melanin (blue), and carotene (yellow), which dictate the colors you wear (more on this in Chapter 2) to highlight or recede in your personal color palette.

Last but not least, you must consider your scale. I'm not talking about the scale in your bathroom that needs cobweb clearing. I'm referring to the scale that defines your mass or how much elevator space you take up horizontally. Scale is important because it relates to your overall size and how much or how little detail you can wear without looking washed out or overpowered. If you have a large scale, then you may be best choosing a large window-pane pattern over a small check since the small check print will magnify your size. The bulk of your accessories such as briefcases, totes, earrings, cuff links, and even shirt collars, pockets, and buttons on your clothing should be in direct correlation with your scale. A thin-strapped watch gets lost on someone with a large scale, while large eyeglasses on someone with a small scale will look awkward and comical. There's no flair in that!

Assessing Your Preferences

Preferences also correlate directly with flair. It's common to gravitate to things to which we have emotional ties. Often, we choose garments based on what we wore as children, or variations on what our parents wore. Certain colors or styles make us feel safer than others because we associate them with a certain familiarity. Since we can't bring our teddy bears or favorite blankies on an interview, we gravitate to what I call "hot fudge sundae" attire or dress that we associate with positive or comforting memories. On the contrary, certain styles will forever carry the stigma of being associated with someone in your past you do not remember fondly. Those memories will perpetually remain in your mind, and you will always link that particular style with that person's image, so you would never entertain adding it to your interview wardrobe repertoire. So how does this relate to flair?

The preferences you exercise are integral to your flair because they focus on your "gut" feelings regarding the message you want to convey to the world. Are you drawn to tailored or comfort-fit suits? Do you prefer light fabrics as opposed to heavier, texturized ones? Have your favorite colors changed since you were a kid? Depending on your body type and scale, your preferences may be sabotaging your flair.

Your preferences should be in synch with the goals you set for the message you want your flair to transmit. Are you trying to come across knowledgeable? Or perhaps less intimidating because the person who will be interviewing you is a peer and you don't want to overpower him? If you are a woman who is socially perceived as attractive, your goal may be to detract attention from areas that could be potential focal points of distraction during an interview with someone of the opposite gender. One thing is for sure, no matter what your preferences are for weekend or resort wear, you can be sure to kill an interview and divulge your lack of flair by sporting any of the following:

- Hat or gloves (worn during the interview)

- Tie-dyed or printed T-shirt

- Athletic wear, tube-top, or any beachlike top

- Button-down shirt displaying chest hair

- Low-cut shirt showing cleavage

- Miniskirt

- "High-water" hems

- Fishnet or highly decorative hosiery

- Open-toe shoes or sneakers

- Unpolished shoes

Expressing Your Personality

Personality contributes greatly to your flair, as it allows you to express your inner originality and distinctiveness even when the job sought is not in a creative industry. Personal flair is about aligning your behavior with the clothes you wear and establishing a consistency that gives you credibility as a potential employee. One of the easiest ways to demonstrate your flair is through the use of color, as described in Chapter 2. And, if appropriate for your body type, mixing patterns and textures will show a bolder, more daring nature as opposed to traditional solids and plain-weave fabrics.

Professional Industries and Job Level

Flair also correlates with your present or desired professional industry and the job level you are seeking within that industry. Back in the day when I was new to staffing, I used to play a game with colleagues in which we guessed candidates' designated professional sector or job level based on their projected style before we even shook their hands. We worked in a large bullpen where everyone interviewed at their desks, and for those of us who weren't busy with a candidate or cold calling, people watching was an entertaining perk. We didn't stereotype, though the groups were as easily identifiable as a herd of zebras.

Using flair to associate yourself with a specific professional industry can be the first step toward being accepted into *the club*. Convincing a human resources manager that you are right for the job is much like an actor convincing a casting director that he can play an important movie role. At the very least, you should look like you can play the role. Of course, you must back it up with the right experience and credentials once you get the part. In my career, I have observed so many candidates that I now categorize them by professional industry and job rank. Here are my assumptions about some norms of each "club."

Professional Categories
Enterprisers: Business/Finance/
Law/Accounting/Politics/Administration

Enterprisers have traditional flair. The silhouette or outside lines are straight, vertical, and structured. Fabrics are tightly woven in navy or gray as a staple. There's no bling-bling in details such as buttons, belt buckles, jewelry, or eyeglasses (usually wire-rimmed). Collared dress shirts for men with paisley ties or small-patterned scarves are customary, and women also wear collared shirts with pearls as a finishing touch. Oxford shoes for men and medium-heeled pumps for women are details that define enterprisers. Hair is cut short for men, with little to no facial hair, and for women it is either a bob or one-length style with natural-looking makeup, if it is used at all.

Advocates: Fashion/Cosmetics/Public Relations/
Real Estate/Corporate Sales/Interior Design

Advocates are usually the face of a corporate brand, and their flair must reflect this. Advocates exhibit the most fashion-forward flair because they are "in the know" about trends. Many advocates are commission-based within competitive industries where appearance is essential (this is so in all professions; they just have a more heightened sense of it). The silhouette is straight and exaggerated. Firm, smooth fabrics that have a slight sheen are common for this group. Colors are bold and jewel-toned, often using black and white as a dramatic backdrop. Advocates do like bling-bling in their jewelry, buttons, belt buckles, and anywhere else they can find high luster. Suit jackets have customized details such as hand-stitching, patterned, silk linings, peak collars, and pockets in interesting and sometimes nonfunctional, yet stylish places. Pants have more of a flare, with longer hems covering a high-heeled pump or spit-shined lace-up oxford shoe. Men will wear stylish cuff links, and women will accessorize with bold rings and oversized designer bags. Patterns are used as a focal point to keep the look clean and sharp. Hair is either layered or stacked in the back with angular lines in the front with bangs or on the sides with sculpted sideburns. Makeup application is contoured around the face and neck, with lips and eyes that are clearly defined through a combination of eye shadow, liner, and lush lashes with filled-in eyebrows.

Innovators: Technology/Publishing/Pharmaceuticals/ Music/Theater/Marketing/Advertising

Innovators are avant-garde or free-spirited, and because of this, their flair is a mixed bag of a lot of different looks thrown into one. It can range from grungy to bohemian to preppy to artsy. The silhouette is straight and curvy with diagonal lines all at once. Tightly and loosely woven fabrics will be incorporated by layering knitted pieces like a poncho over a loosely fitted suit in vibrant colors and prints that are associated with ethnic cultures. Innovators can wear clunky, hammered statement pieces of jewelry located in places like eyebrows, tongue, thumb, and upper ear. Yet there are also innovators who choose simple flat-weave fabrics in similar color values with inconspicuous silver-toned jewelry and wide-rimmed glasses. Innovators prefer not to wear matching suit jackets and pants. The male prefers to wear separates, and if he chooses to wear a tie, the pattern will correlate with his artistic nature of mixing bold stripes with a floral or bold geometric print. Scarves for women are similar in style, with stretchy pullovers instead of a button-down, collared blouse. Innovators love to carry their belongings in backpacks or messenger bags. They usually prefer shoes that are in a color other than black. They will very often resort to a boot or a thick-soled shoe with buckles instead of laces. Hair can be colored in rich hues like red, blue, or purple and cut short and spiky, or maybe color is avoided altogether, if they opt for the bald-headed look. Another innovative look is long and shaggy or long, braided, and dreadlocky. Makeup is either extreme and harsh or nonexistent.

Altruists: Nonprofit/Education/Medical/Insurance/ Hospitality/Activist/Clergy

Altruists are caregivers or "do-gooders." Comfort and practicality are their main criteria. The silhouette is very relaxed, and the colors are earthy and muted. Fabrics are not luxurious, opting for cottons, twills, and linen in either solid or small-pattern check, plaid, or thin stripe. Jewelry is used not as an accessory but as a necessity (i.e., a wedding ring to show devotion to a partner or a watch to be on time), and the luster is usually a matted metal or rubberized material so as not to attract attention. Bags are medium to large in size, and functional, not fashionable, in style. Footwear is composed of sneakerlike, round-toed, rubber-soled shoes. Hair can be kept long and pulled back from the eyes and face or cut very short for a wash-and-go type of flair. Makeup is . . . What makeup?

Job Rank

Pioneers: Interns/Recent College Grads/ Re-entrants/Administrative Assistants

It is so humbling to be a pioneer. Yet, there is something refreshing and invigorating about starting with a blank slate. Résumés are sparse in professional experience, so life experience and, you guessed it, flair count lots. This is the most competitive job level to be in because it's the one that requires the least amount of specialized credentials. Pioneers are not a proven entity in the world of business, so potential employers will get their pulse on you based on appearance, behavior, and communication. If there's one single thing pioneers learn from this book, it is that they don't get a pass from wearing an interview suit to an interview just because they never had to wear one before. Pioneers often make the mistake of going on an interview wearing noncoordinating separates without a jacket. That gets a resounding "NO THANK YOU" from recruiters like me. I should also share with you that the flair a pioneer had in college (shaggy hair, comfy sweats, and Birkenstocks) is not going to work for interviewing. Re-entrants should refrain from digging out the family photos from the diaper-bag-like totes.

Nomads: Temporary Employees/Floaters/Relocates/Expatriates

Nomads rarely walk around with a résumé, as all of their interim positions would take hours or days to discuss during an interview. Nomads are professional job hoppers (many by choice); temping is their "day job." They may have other long-term goals or commitments that prevent them from accepting a *permanent* position in the corporate world. Some of them are musicians, actors, or artists. As a nomad, the person to impress is typically the recruiter at a staffing firm or temporary agency. As long as they believe nomads will not set the place on fire or steal paper clips (nomads should be prepared for a background check), they'll usually have an assignment in 24 hours or less (in a good market). Other nomads use temping as a means of showing their talents on the job and getting employment through the hidden job market. If that is their goal, then every day they go into work at a job site is an ongoing interview. This is why so many clients and human resources professionals prefer to hire from a crop of nomads or offer a permanent position to a floater within the company. They get to witness a nomad's flair for longer than through the traditional interview method. Internal floaters have a job within a company. However, nomads' interview process continues as they float from department to department before they find the manager with whom they would be compatible. Again, they are still under observation, so they should be conscientious, diplomatic, and consistent in their flair.

For those relocating on their own, or those called expatriates (those who have been transferred to the United States through current employers' overseas office location), it is important to do some homework on the type of flair needed for a new destination. What worked overseas may not work in America. While your job may be pretty secure since it's your employer who is sponsoring you to be here, these pioneers may undergo a different type of scrutiny if they find themselves sticking out like a sore thumb. In this case, it's peers, superiors, and subordinates who will sniff out an outcast, and it could be crucial to whether or not this pioneer can cut it in new territory.

Natives: Internal Promotion Seekers/Lateral Changers

Natives often have a sense of entitlement because they have already been with the company for an extended period of time. They know all of the players, and because of this, they are apt to let their guard down and show little if any flair. They feel they've put in their time and don't need to impress. It's not surprising to me when I get a call from a native, the disgruntled native complaining about how he lost out to an external candidate. I can see by how the natives come in to meet me that they are far too laid-back in their approach, and the desire to impress is bleak or altogether missing. Natives are often disillusioned because they feel like their loyalty is not being rewarded or acknowledged, but in fact it is because they have not been fired. To combat this dejection, natives often interview for outside jobs just to get leverage and get noticed at their current company. They seek the "should be dreaded" counteroffer just to put their self-esteem at ease.

Natives need to be more proactive in their quest to climb the internal corporate ladder. Upgrading their flair is not a bad place to start. In fact, it is exactly the place to start. The reason they may not be advancing within their own company could be that it is harder to convince those who "knew them when" that they have now grown up with the company. For this reason, a visual transformation is the most attention-grabbing technique for getting noticed for a position with added responsibilities, status, and pay.

Proprietors: C-Suite/Executive/Partners

Proprietors are the high-rollers of the interviewing world. They don't walk around with a résumé because everybody in their industry knows who they are. Sure, there's only one or a handful of them in one firm, but when they confidentially put their hat in the ring, they can be sure they will be speaking directly with the decision makers. Often, they will bypass human resources and will meet only with someone from the department, though just to tie up loose ends. As proprietors, they have earned and enjoyed the highest income bracket and the flair that comes with it. That's not to say that because they are CEOs that they can automatically put an interview outfit together. In this case, it's the authority, power, and prestige proprietors bear that are the catalysts for their flair.

Color Blind
The Unprotected Group

Mere color, unspoiled by meaning, and unallied with definite form, can speak to the soul in a thousand different ways. —Oscar Wilde (Irish poet and dramatist)

HAVE YOU EVER seen people who look like they got dressed in the dark? They probably did. Many of those wacky-looking characters end up in my reception area. An interview later, I realize that the clothing and the colors they are wearing aren't really indicative at all of who they are. It turns out they are as normal as any person can be. I am truly baffled at how intimidating and confusing color can be. Trust me, once you understand and befriend color, your interview wardrobe will have the punch it so desperately deserves. Worn properly, color will confidently underscore your verbal and nonverbal communication. It will mirror your personality and shave pounds off your rear end. However, handled incorrectly, color will become your foe; it will go toe to toe with your distinct natural coloring and play nasty tricks on you. And color is gender neutral, as Donald Trump has publicly proven through his signature pink-shirt-and-tie getup.

On a dreary, rainy day, nothing kicks me into gear quite like wearing color. The energy I soak up from color's warmth empowers and inspires me to jump-start my day. Color is a couch potato's dream; It stimulates you without hours at the gym. The compound nature of color instigates a far more detailed prep. It's simply not enough to say, "Wear a dark-colored suit and light shirt or blouse and go on your merry interview." No way! You have to pull out all the stops and believe me: Color is a defining breath of fresh air. These days, landing a job is as competitive as getting your hands on a winning lottery ticket. It seems as if everyone is vying for the same job!

I absolutely cringe when "dress for success" articles and books describe color in obscure terms. Vague explanations leave *way* too much room for error and offer zero inspiration for using color as a visual instrument of success. So it's no surprise why I once had a candidate waltz through my doors sporting a dark-red suit without a second thought. What? It *was* a dark suit and what the heck did the color red ever do to deserve such scorn? The goal here is to have you embrace the right colors, not shy away from them or, even worse, ignore them altogether. So if red *is* the color you insist on wearing to an interview, you'll be fully aware of where to place it: On the soles of your shoes, of course . . . just as celebrated shoe designer Christian Louboutin does.

Color Fun Facts

Before we begin, you'll have to bear with me while I clarify the technical components of color. I'll try to make it fast and painless:

- Hue: Another word for color

- Temperature: Warmness or coolness of a hue or color

- Value: Lightness or darkness in a color (i.e., how much white or black is in a color)

- Intensity: Brightness or dullness in a color

Are you still with me? Good. I promise you'll thank me the next time you are getting dressed for an interview. Sir Isaac Newton's discovery of how light is broken into wavelengths, which create a rainbow (remember "ROY G. BIV" from science class?), is neatly laid out in a format known as the color wheel. Make time to (at the very least) take a peek at the color wheel. It will help you understand how to spice up the colors within your otherwise humdrum interview wardrobe. In the following paragraphs, you will find the terms of how colors relate to one another on the color wheel. I know, you're getting tired of all the definitions. Just bear with me. I can't be an angel on your shoulder telling you what colors to wear on the day when it matters the most . . . so read on. Trust me—it's for your own good.

Analogous colors, such as purple and red, or purple and blue, sit next to each other on the color wheel. Think of them as coworkers who sit on either side of you.

Monochromatic colors are colors of the same family with varying tints (color + white) and shades (color + black) or tones (color + gray), such as all blues, greens, or browns. They're like your morning coffee with varying degrees of milk.

Complementary colors are opposite one another on the color wheel. Think of them as the company across the hall from yours. Think of yourself as a color and the complementary as your counterpart from another division within your company.

Split complementary colors are made up of three colors: your main color choice and the two colors on either side of the complementary color. Think of them as your counterpart's superior and subordinate.

Intermediate colors (tertiary) are red-violet, blue-violet, blue-green, yellow-green, yellow-orange, and red-orange. Think of tertiary colors as the finished project you and the coworker sitting next to you collaborated on—the product of both of your efforts.

Triadic colors are colors formed by creating any triangle within the color wheel. Remember them as the triangle between yourself, your employer, and your new employer.

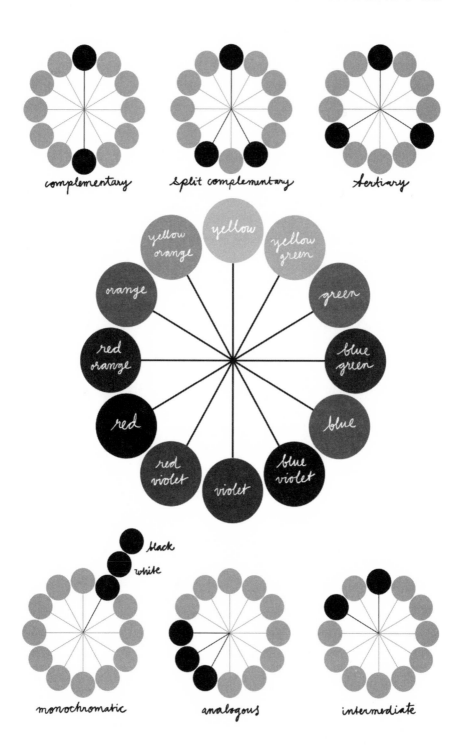

complementary

split complementary

tertiary

yellow orange — yellow — yellow green
orange — green
red orange — blue green
red — blue
red violet — blue violet
violet

black
white

monochromatic

analogous

intermediate

Now that you're up on some of the nuts and bolts of color, you are ready to move forward to create your "signature" flair.

Reasons for Seasons

Think back to your first box of freshly opened Crayola crayons. Mine was a small box (I know, get the violin out). I used my creativity to come up with some of the froufrou colors that I didn't have but were found in the 48- and 64-packs. No matter what the size your box was, the red, yellow, and blue crayons were always staples. Those are primary colors: the basic colors used to create all the other hues in your Crayola box. They're also the natural colors of which your skin is composed: hemoglobin (red), carotene (yellow), and melanin (blue). The ratio of hemoglobin, carotene, and melanin in your complexion, along with your hair and eye color, dictate your personal relationship to color. This relational color premise was coined in the 1980s as the seasonal color theory by Carole Jackson, in her book *Color Me Beautiful.* Divided into four categories of warm/cool and light/dark, the seasonal color theory is both accurate and easy to follow.

There are all sorts of multistep color systems that we image consultants use to personalize hundreds of color categories within each season. If you've never had a professional color analysis, it's a must to have one done through a certified image consultant in your area (contact www.aici.org for more information). You'll save thousands of dollars in shopping mistakes and it will take the pressure off buying your interview attire. For a quickie "do-it-yourself" approach, follow these three easy steps using natural light and a nice-sized mirror to help the process:

1. Reach for two pieces of wrapping paper or fabric: one in silver and one in gold. Place each under your chin. If the silver one looks best next to your skin, hair, and eyes, you are cool; if the gold one looks best, you are warm. If your skin glows next to gold and silver, you would be considered balanced, giving you the flexibility to wear a broader range of undertones.

2. Next, find a light- and a dark-colored shirt/blouse in your closet and place each one under your chin. If your skin, hair, and eyes glow next to the light piece of fabric, you are either a spring or summer. If it happens with a dark piece of fabric, you may be an autumn or winter.

3. Lastly, pick a garment or fabric that is bright and one that is muted or dull and repeat your action of placing each under your chin. If your skin, hair, and eyes shine next to the bright colors, you may be a spring or winter, or perhaps you are an autumn or summer if it occurs with muted fabrics.

Congrats, you have now informally color-coded yourself. Use the guide here to find out your results and see which iconic talk-show host's seasonal coloring you are most closely related to:

Spring: Warm + Light + Bright = Martha Stewart

Autumn: Warm + Dark + Muted = Conan O'Brien

Summer: Cool + Light + Muted = Ellen DeGeneres

Winter: Cool + Dark + Bright = Oprah Winfrey

Face Your Color (Mostly Females)

Truth be told, I was the reigning queen of bad makeup in the late 1980s and early 1990s. The multicolor eye shadow with the owl-framed liquid liner, Parisian pink blush, and overtly lined mahogany lips topped with cement cracking, matte lipstick in my favorite shade of burgundy were all part of my daily repertoire. Oh, and the eyelashes—don't let me get started on the eyelashes! I never thought for one second that my makeup was—well— awful! After all, it was all synchronized with the colors I was wearing. I wore every color in the spectrum because my natural coloring is an olive-y tan. I thought to myself, "Bring it on. . . . The more color the better."

The fact is that matching cosmetic color to clothing color is not self-sabotaging *if* you follow the seasonal-color rule of thumb. "Natural" colors for your interviewing face should not automatically be interpreted as light.

That is as general and as vague as saying "Wear a dark-colored suit on an interview." Light colors can look gorgeous on a summer. Don't forget "light" refers to only one of color's traits—its value. So, if you are a summer, flattering cosmetic colors would be ones that are light, cool, *and* muted. Don't snooze on how colors look directly on your skin, right next to your hair and eyes. By the same token, if you are a spring, you could handle wearing bright colors on an interview as long as they are warm and light. Do you get my drift? There is no universal color that is an all-around *natural* color for corporate appearances or interviews. Finding your "natural" color is a process based on *your* personal coloring.

And to my male readers (I haven't forgotten about you), a dab of under-eye concealer won't kill your reputation (I won't tell). As long as the base color matches the natural color of your skin (pink, yellow, or blue), you're in good shape. The trick is to always blend it r-e-a-l-l-y well so you don't look femme. I'll fill you in on application tips in Chapter 6.

Kick the Black "Habit"

Black habits are for clergy. So why does your closet bear a strong resemblance to those ordained for religious service? In the Big Apple, where my office sits, the majority of candidates prefer black. Don't get me wrong; I'm not anti-black. It's just so predictable when it comes to interview garb. In addition, wearing black on an interview is not always the best choice because of its exceedingly authoritative message—aloof or unapproachable.

Wishy-Washy Neutrals

I love neutrals: they're subdued colors that anchor a sophisticated look. It's only when you pile them on without any type of accent color that they really start to make me wonder about you. Dressing in all neutrals for an interview may classify you as dull, shy, or low energy.

Taupe, cream, beige, bone, camel—whatever the neutral is—can use a rich tone of green or a tint of blue to give it the jolt it deserves. Challenge yourself to come out of your shell.

Color-Challenged

These include my infamous candidate who wore the red suit all the way through to creative types who want to express themselves by wearing a tie-dye of color all at once. If you are among these color fanatics gone mad, I applaud your bravery but it's time to put a lid on your vigor. Be discerning with your color choices. Too many bright or dark, metallic colors tells me you are a bit unruly, not willing to comply with rules or take direction. Now that you're familiar with the color wheel and you've done a quick color analysis that has identified your season, my recommendations should not come out of left field.

- Springs: Tan, brown, rust, French or teal blue, turquoise; off-white blouse/shirt; accents of spring green or melon; metallic shiny gold

- Autumns: Olive green, brown, navy, gray; cream shirt/blouse; accents of rust-orange or aubergine or purple; metallic matte gold

- Summers: French navy, heather gray or brown/taupe suits; ivory or bone blouse/shirt; accents of pastel colors such as peach and lavender; metallic matte silver

- Winters: Charcoal gray, navy, black/brown, forest green suit; white blouse/shirt; accents of any jewel-toned color such as burgundy or cobalt blue; metallic shiny silver

Other Contributing Factors

Personality Plus +

You can wear *every* color in the world as long as the value, temperature, and intensity are adjusted to suit your natural coloring. Here is where factors like personality, preferences, and likes and dislikes become important. Who you are and what you gravitate to developed early in your childhood. Don't feel like you have to change who you are; you may just need a slight modification. For instance, I have been color-coded as an autumn (not all autumns are redheads), as I have olive skin, dark brown hair, and amber eyes with rings of green and specks of gold (I know, too much information). For business, I embrace autumn colors, but at home when I'm running around with my kids, I prefer warm, bright colors, so I dip into spring. My eveningwear/special events wardrobe consists of high contrast with jewel tones that give me the drama of a winter. The only season I veer away from is summer. Summer colors make me look tired and drawn—most unflattering.

Here are some of the seasonal observations I've made over the years. Don't give in to the characteristics of a season if they don't work with your natural coloring. Appreciate and embrace your season because the results will not only make you *look* fab, but they will also make you *feel* fab. Remember that even if the colors of a season look less than perfect on you, they may still qualify as your secondary season. The goal is to find your *optimal* colors so that you don't have to compromise.

- Springs are youthful and brisk in their manner, so they don't mind running around on interviews; they are spontaneous, which makes them open-minded about many different opportunities and scenarios.

- Autumns are firm in their demeanor, and their speech is authoritative, which makes them difficult to sway; they are very driven and goal-oriented, which usually makes them stellar candidates with great credentials on their résumés.

- Summers are laid-back or passive-aggressive, which makes them difficult to read and negotiate with; they are nonintimidating and nonthreatening.

- Winters are bold and striking and can go from one extreme decision to another with no middle ground; they are truly black or white in their way of thinking as in the high contrast they carry in their wardrobe.

Weather or Not

Looking younger is not necessarily a goal when interviewing for a senior-level position, as age can work in your favor. Maturity is associated with knowledge, experience, and responsibility. However, let's not confuse looking your age with looking haggard or weathered by using the wrong colors. It is important to revisit your colors as you age in order to ensure an updated look. As hair starts to gray, augment your coloring by increasing the intensity of your colors to avoid looking washed out. If you chemically enhance your hair color, choose one with a value similar to or within one or two shades of your natural hair color so that it blends with your skin and eye color. Few things are more unsightly than a bad dye job. It will make you look dated and positively unpolished.

Industry-Specific

Certain industries are more color-friendly than others. Don't make the mistake of ignoring color altogether when interviewing at in an investment bank. Financial firms are famous for their old-school navy suit, while creative companies have succumbed to the black-on-black epidemic. So where does that leave color? This is precisely where you can excel and differentiate yourself from your opposition. No matter what your season, the trick is to adjust the temperature, value, and intensity of your colors in order to achieve a happy medium of fitting in with your surroundings while staying true to the colors that most favor your individual coloring. You may want to play with accent colors through your accessories to gain some flair. If you happen to be looking for a job at a super-creative company where black-on-black is the norm but you are a summer, take a chance and try navy-on-navy instead.

Accentuate and Camouflage

Color has enchantingly magical powers. Light, bright colors accentuate areas of your body you may want to highlight, such as a small waist you inherited from Great-Aunt Martha or the broad shoulders you've worked on for years. On the other hand, dark and muted colors camouflage areas from which you may want to divert attention, such as saddle hips or a barrel chest. Color's talent for creating optical illusions works wonders on stretching and shearing pounds off your appearance when one color is used in assorted values throughout an outfit. This is accomplished through monochromatic dressing. Conversely, dressing in contrasting colors will shorten or broaden a body area.

Color as a Second Language

Color can be as pure as unplowed snow, as envious as a green-eyed coworker, or as healing as the light-blue walls of the office of the phony doctor's appointment you had on the day of your interview. Color, like sound, has a *voice* along with vibration, tone, and pitch. Remember this when you dress for an interview, and think of color as your alter ego. It will whisper things about you before you open your mouth to speak. Play nice with color, as it will double-talk you right out of a job. For this reason, understanding the hidden meaning behind color is crucial in avoiding mixed signals. The following describes the hidden messages behind some of your favorite and not-so-favorite colors:

▪ Black is not technically a color. In fact, it's the absence of color. Considered cool in more ways than one, black is *the* most popular color used for interview attire. Black commands authority and knowledge. (Think of the legendary Bruce Lee's black belt or Judge Judy's robe.) Because of the stigma attached to black, it is best to stay away from it during the first round of interviews. You want to come across as knowledgeable on a first interview, but not overpowering. Save your black power suit for the final interview when you're meeting the head honcho of the company and you are looking to seal the deal.

▪ White is the cool color on the opposite side of the spectrum to black. Unlike black, it is the presence of all colors. It is pure, angelic, and simplistic. However, unless you are up for an audition for John Travolta's role in

Saturday Night Fever, a white suit gets a booming "Are you off your rocker?" from me. While I'm on the topic, white shoes on an interview are reserved for nurses.

- Navy is your safety color, as it belongs to all of the seasonal categories. You really can't go wrong with a navy suit. It is the most enterprising color. I'm partial to navy. Spice it up with its complementary color, orange, or analogous blue-green.

- Red is a warm, action color. It is fiery, sexual, and bold. Red lips, red nails, and red stilettos are "off-color" unless you are interviewing for a position at Hooters. Red skirt suits are for those whose fashion icon is Nancy Reagan. Red ties and scarves are also too aggressive for a first interview, or even a second. The only time I would override this is if you are going for a position in sales, where you need to show your killer instinct right away. Even in such a circumstance, a burnt or muted red would be a better choice than a pure red.

- Brown is a warm, earthy color. It projects honesty, integrity, and loyalty. A brown suit can team up with any color on the color wheel, since mixing any color with its complementary color creates brown. A brown suit is a safe alternative for a first or second interview, as it is nonthreatening, reliable, and stable.

- Green is the color of balance and poise. It's the "G" in ROY G. BIV, sandwiched between red's longest wavelength and violet's shortest. Green is clean. These days, it's the signature color for the eco-chic movement. A dark-valued, forest-green suit is very acceptable to wear on an interview. This too could be a safe first- or second-interview suit color. As an autumn, I love wearing green, especially with rich creams and metallic gold jewelry.

- Orange is an energy magnet. It represents good health and an appetite for living. While an orange suit is too loud for an interview, an orange tie or scarf makes an awesome addition to its complementary blue or its monochromatic-turned brown.

▪ Yellow is a cheerful, youthful, and warm hue. A pale-yellow shirt looks great under a brown, navy, or dark-green suit. A yellow tie or scarf is a bit country club-ish; though if you are interviewing for a job at a hedge fund, a yellow tie works. In the suit category, a yellow suit will make you look like a life-size banana.

▪ Purple is identified as a noble and majestic color. Even in its darkest value, it looks too dramatic to be worn as an interview suit. In its lightest value or as a pastel, it makes a perfectly acceptable summer shirt under a dark tan suit. A purple tie or scarf on an autumn candidate adds a stately touch to an interview wardrobe.

▪ Pink is too fragile of a color to be worn on an interview. It's the color of romance. It's classified as a feminine color, though more and more men are inspired to wear it in a shirt-and-tie combination, which looks nice for social events. For interviewing, it's a no-go. On women, pink comes across as too much of a girly-girl color.

To live life without color is to ignore one of life's open pleasures. There's no premium attached to buying garments, accessories, or cosmetics that are in your ideal color scheme. Now that I've opened your senses to this world of possibilities, start taking advantage of this added value. As you gather your ammunition to conquer the fierce task of interviewing for a job, include color on your checklist of do's. It will lift up your emotional and mental psyche. Appropriate colors will help you absorb their energy and see yourself in a more positive light.

All this time you wanted Botox and all you needed was a simple color adjustment. Who knew?

Suit Yourself
Handpicking the Perfect Interview Suit

Dressing is a way of life. —*Yves Saint Laurent (French fashion designer)*

THROUGHOUT MY YEARS in the recruiting industry, casual Fridays gradually evolved into casual workweeks and casual workweeks somehow developed into casual interview attire. Says who? I don't know who gave the green light for it to get so out of control, but it's time to clarify this interviewing enigma. The interview suit is not dated and it's not over the top; it is *required* in order to present the most professional image you can. To this I will add that the suit and all the other accoutrements that help finish the look should be of the best quality you can afford, because skimping can be a costly mistake. Honestly, if you don't own the appropriate clothes and you're not ready to invest in them, then it's best for you to put your search on hold.

You wouldn't undertake a bike race without the proper helmet or the right bike if you were there to win. So why would you think you can get away with not dressing appropriately for an interview? You must go out there looking like a winner. If you do, you will be perceived as such. For those of you who are anti-suit or who feel like you break into hives whenever you even look at a suit (let alone wear one), this chapter is especially dedicated to you. You will realize that the reason you've been against dressing professionally is because you're in the dark about how to do it right. It's one thing that is assumed in life: You should be born with the ability to dress yourself—well. Unfortunately, many people aren't equipped with this natural instinct, and while trial and error may be your dressing technique as far as casual wear, dressing for an interview should be nothing short of an exact science.

Excuses, Excuses!

I've never heard more excuses than those given by candidates trying to dodge wearing an interview suit. They say, "I work in a casual environment and if I wear a suit my boss or my staff will definitely know I'm looking to leave." To that, I say, "Pull the Superman trick and change inside a phone booth." The response is, "Well, I hardly ever leave the office, and if I take extra time to change into a suit, those around me will start wondering what took me so long." I answer, "Take a day off and interview at your leisure." There's a slight pause, interrupted by, "Well, I would, but my brother's wedding is next month and I need to save my vacation days." All right! I know where this is heading and it's not a good place. Save your excuses and use some of the comp time you've been sitting on. Join me in the shopping experience that is meant to change the way you lay eyes on a suit. Some of you may choose to shop in a retail store or boutique, while others may find that undiscovered treasures exist right within their closets. My goal is to rid you of the suit phobia by teaching you the fundamental components of how to choose interviewing garb that will exude maximum self-assurance.

First Things First

Before we start our virtual shopping experience (whether in your existing closet or in a store) there are just a few things you need to do in order to prepare yourself. My preference is to shop in the morning when I'm well rested and on weekdays when the stores are as vacant as if they had been opened especially for my private shopping trip. Eat well and "take care of business" before you leave in order to avoid unnecessary stops during precious shopping time. Also, please wear comfortable shoes because I don't want to hear you griping about your achy feet. Before the big shopping day, examine your closet. Record your findings using the old reliable paper-and-pen duo or the memo pad feature of an electronic device. (I took my BlackBerry with me into the delivery room while in labor, so naturally that is what I use to take such notes, since I know they'll always be at my fingertips.) Take inventory before you go shopping, since doing it on the same day may make you too tired to shop.

I can't stress how important this pre-shopping exercise is, and the majority of people skip it only to pay greatly for doing so. Pre-shopping your closet saves you hours of shopping time and loads of cash. Imagine going grocery shopping without a shopping list or without a clue about what's in your refrigerator and pantry shelves. You may decide to make lasagna simply because you already have the noodles, cheese, and sauce, so all you need to buy are a few additional ingredients. Well, the same holds true with shopping for your interview wardrobe. Auditing your closet and drawers is the first step toward smart interview-apparel shopping. Don't equate your closet with a deep dark cave where moths hang out. (Speaking of moths, if they do live in your closet, you must remove them ASAP with cedar chips doused with cedar spray in order to protect your investment. Cedar hangers and shoe trees are ideal though quite costly, while a full cedar closet is a luxury high on my wish list.)

Don't be intimidated by your closet. Remember, you are just concentrating on your corporate attire for the purpose of creating the perfect interview collection. However, you may inspire yourself to continue the exercise along with the rest of your wardrobe. If you do, that's great, but don't lose sight of your main objective. Purging your closet and drawers is a great way to start your new career with a clean slate.

Perfectly Fit

Since suits are an equalizer of men and women in business, I will discuss fit in general and in androgynous terms. Developing the perfect fit involves going back to your individual silhouette (see Chapter 1), as you will be wise to details that contribute to a perfect fit. Other clues, such as your personal pattern, color, texture, scale, and proportion, will also be helpful. As you rummage through your closet, pay close attention to the following guidelines on fit. They will make your decision of whether you want to keep, alter, or liberate yourself of a garment crystal clear. You don't need any wardrobe shockers on the day of your interview. Look for these details:

▪ **Uncool stand-up collars:** Collars should sit close to the back of the neck with no gaps. Higher-quality suits are made with felt attached to the collar's underside to ensure it properly hugs your neck. Avoid looking like you borrowed your interview attire from someone who is two sizes too big.

▪ **Head and shoulders:** Make sure there is no bubble or bunching in the back. There should be ample fabric from the shoulder to the sleeve. In custom and made-to-measure suits, the buttonholes are not pierced into your jacket until you achieve a nice clean line in the front and back.

▪ **Let it roll off your back:** Don't let your pride stand in the way of achieving great fit. When purchasing ready-to-wear suits, you may need to go one size up just to make sure you have enough fabric crosswise and frontwise to prevent lapels from spreading apart and to facilitate shoulder and arm movement.

▪ **Have closure:** Be sure your suit jacket closes even if you intend to leave it open (especially when you sit down). Once it's closed, pay attention to how it closes. Does it look like if you take one deep breath, the button will pop out and shoot across the interview table? Also, look for vents and pleats that sit correctly around your hips.

▪ **Half-inch rule of thumb:** Pair these together so you remember: About one-half inch of your shirt/blouse collar should be seen if looking at yourself from behind and about one-half inch of your shirt/blouse cuff should show below the jacket cuff.

▪ **Reading between the hemlines:** Perhaps the trickiest to pin down or up are hemlines (no pun intended), as they are the most subjective. Do not associate hemlines with trends when it comes to interviewing attire. The goal is to be timeless, polished, and appropriate. Find your waist, and then place the trouser waistband right on it. By doing this, you will spare the pleats and pockets of your trousers the wear and tear of having your hip bone dig into them. Allow the trouser to cascade down your leg.

Suit trouser legs fall into one of three categories, and the hem is impacted by its fullness or narrowness:

– **Straight:** The front points down at the shoe while the back is slightly shorter to show the back of the shoe. This is the most traditional hem for corporate suits and the most universally flattering to different body types.

– **Full with or without cuffs:** The bottom of this hem almost reaches the floor, with a little dimple on the top of the shoe. The fullness of this leg creates a strongly defined horizontal line. Therefore, it should be reserved for very tall candidates. Cuffs create a more casual style and should therefore be forfeited on interview pantsuits.

– **Tapered:** This is narrow and short and above the shoe. This is a very contemporary look better suited for pantsuits that are not used for interviewing.

For women, skirt hemlines should fall within three leg points, depending on how you want to accentuate or camouflage:

– Above the kneecap for a taller appearance

– Below the kneecap to camouflage tallness

– Below the widest part of your calf to camouflage "molded" legs

Add Fiber to Your Wardrobe

It's a known fact: The "interviewing willies" can make you perspire like a pig. That is why choosing the right fabric begins with being smart about clothing's fiber content. Much like our primal ancestors wore their environment, we continue this tradition in our dress. The fabric we wear daily is composed of filaments that originate from natural sources such as fauna, flora, and minerals (natural) or synthetic fibers formed from chemicals. Choosing fabrics whose properties are the most "performance-desirable" based on their fiber content is the best way to ensure that good appearance, absorbency, comfort, and durability are present when you select your skin's protective barrier. Each of these properties brings added value to the fabric and ultimately the finished garment. As we make our way toward our first shopping stop, I will fill you in on some little-known details you should remember before choosing your "suit of armor" during the most important part of your job search—the interview.

- **Appearance:** The length of the fibers dictates how radiant and wrinkle- and pill-resistant a fabric will be. Natural fibers such as cotton, flax, silk, and domestic worsted wools (from goat and sheep) are chosen for their fine and luxurious qualities. For instance, a dress shirt made of Pima cotton has fibers that are extra-long staple (ELS) and would appear much more upscale than shirts made of regular upland cotton.[1] Woolen fibers are derived from thicker, shorter fibers that are fuzzy to the touch.[2] They are not as refined and should be reserved for everyday work attire, such as tweed blazers and sport coats worn during cold winter months, rather than for the interview suit.

- **Absorbency:** A higher level of absorbency within a fiber contributes to the comfort and durability of fabric, since it absorbs perspiration and humidity. This type of protection is important, particularly if you tend to perspire. Absorbent fibers are anti-static and are easier to launder or dry clean. Silk has very good absorbency and is therefore a choice for suit and coat linings, socks, and underwear. Cotton is another natural fiber that has super-absorbency qualities and is therefore a popular fiber for shirts.

Synthetic fibers such as sateen, nylon, and polyester, which are not as absorbent as silk but retain their shape better, are often used in place of silk for cost-effectiveness. Rayon and acetate are the only exceptions in the synthetic fiber group that have good absorbency qualities, as they are manufactured from wood or cotton pulp.

 • **Comfort:** Fiber blends increase comfort, strength, and versatility, as in adding spandex to any natural or synthetic fiber. Blends allow fibers to contribute properties that make for a multifunctional garment, as in the case of a cotton and cashmere wool blend with a hint of spandex. In such a fabric, you have the shared properties of cotton's breathability with the warmth and drapability of cashmere and the stretchability of spandex.

 • **Durability:** How fibers are intertwined to produce the fabric contributes to the look and strength of the garment and is called durability. Twisted and double-ply fibers have more resilience than straight fibers. When it comes to career wear, particularly interview wear, you want your investment to last, so look for these details. Plain or flat weaves are the firmest and most basic of textile weaves. They are created much like a basket weave with an over-under effect and they are smooth to the touch. A wool crepe suit is a fine example of a plain weave option with highly twisted fibers that is both durable yet luxurious enough to be used for suit making. Satin weaves are lustrous and silky, with a great deal of flexibility. Twill weaves have medium texture and weight, with a diagonal rib. This weave is also very resilient and durable, as in a wool gabardine suit. Dobby weaves are luxurious and delicate weaves, such as brocade fabrics, that have patterns and heavily textured designs embedded in the fabric. Such weaves are often found in high-quality ties or scarves. Wearing a tie or scarf with a brocade design is better left for evening events than for interviewing. Knit weaves are formed by interlocking loops. They provide extreme comfort due to their stretchability and suppleness. A jersey knit top under a women's suit would be a good example of combining comfort with practicality, even if it is too casual an option for completing an interview outfit (see Chapter 4).

Yes, No, Maybe So

Make three piles that you label "Yes," "No," and "Maybe." Pieces you love and feel great in belong in the "Yes" pile. "Yes" items are ideal items that consistently look great on their own. They are your cornerstone pieces with which you should build mini-collections or wardrobe capsules. Such wardrobe capsules contain five to ten pieces that work together to create different looks. Items you've kept with tags on that have been tucked away forever go in the "No" pile and should either be donated or sold on consignment or eBay. Also, corporate apparel that puts a damper on your flair (Chapter 1) and conveys the wrong message or is blatantly unflattering based on color (Chapter 2) is a sure contender for the "No" pile. Members of the "Maybe" pile need to show some sign of a redeeming quality. Such items may just need slight alterations or accessories to make them functional.

By the way, the most accurate way to qualify garment pieces into one of these three categories is to actually try each piece on. I know it's time-consuming, but I promise you *will* thank me for it. You'll need to layer over the appropriate socks, hosiery, and undergarments and wear the right shoes in order to properly evaluate yourself in front of a full-length mirror within a room bathed in natural lighting. Once you complete this laborious task of trying everything on and recording what you need in order to fill in the gaps, you are finally ready to join me on a virtual shopping trip. If you get lazy and decide to forfeit this step, you will end up with a reprise of the same unworn clothes that reside in your closet, so you're really not doing yourself any favors.

Road Trip

For the purpose of our shopping expedition, I've singled out a store that is widely known and is one of my personal favorites—Saks Fifth Avenue in Manhattan. Saks is a hop, skip, and a jump away from my office. I commonly refer to it as my "other" office. Maybe that's why sales associates who ring me up often ask me for my employee code. Having all of the goods we need to build your interview wardrobe under one roof is extremely convenient and time saving. Besides, my familiarity with all of the departments and my long-standing relationships with many of the store's employees make for a productive, error-free shopping experience.

Don't get me wrong, plenty of other large department stores like Nordstrom, Bloomingdale's, Lord & Taylor, Macy's, Neiman Marcus, and Bergdorf Goodman offer a multitude of brands and services for your shopping convenience, such as coat and package check, package delivery, and restaurants (so you don't pass out while you shop). They also have wardrobe-consulting services. I endorse the use of such services when you are on your own but only *after* you know what to ask for, so that *you* are in control.

If you lack fluency in shopping lingo, you are in jeopardy of being putty in the hands of a quota-driven sales associate with purchase authorization and your credit card in hand, resulting in lots of extra zeros on your final bill. Also, whenever you walk into a store sans a shopping appointment with a knowledgeable associate, you can well end up with the rookie just learning the ropes. That said, I am impartial to having you shop within one large department store, a mall of stores, individual specialty stores, or a private trunk show. The point is that if you know what you need, the choice is yours. Even catalog and online shopping for interview attire is a possibility, though it should be reserved for those of you who know your size is a close match to one of your chosen brand's standard sizes. Otherwise, the alteration costs will be astronomical, and you may still end up with a butchered suit—piling bad money on top of bad money.

Oh, and speaking of money, don't be intimidated by price. While Saks and other department stores try to appeal only to a "high-rolling" clientele and you may think you don't fit that category (yet or ever), one thing the current recession has done is bring prices down to an unusually affordable place. Recession or no recession, even the fanciest stores periodically mark down their merchandise. However, don't fall victim to buying an interview suit solely because it is on sale. If you're still unsettled by Saks' prices or its fashion-y allure, use your time there as an educational shopping retreat and apply your knowledge at a store that is within your comfort zone.

We Have Arrived

It's hard to believe, because I am a native New Yorker, that it wasn't until the age of 25 that I first entered a department store more luxurious than Sears or Alexander's on Fordham Road in the Bronx. I was so taken by all of the amenities, especially the doorman and taxi service. I still own and wear my very first purchase of that day—a Paloma Picasso silk print scarf. In fact, it is my lucky scarf. As we tour each section of this shopping haven, be sure to enjoy the fascinating ambiance and the aromatic scents. Yet don't lose focus of what we're here to accomplish: hand-picking the perfect interview garb.

Warning: Under Construction—Buyer Beware!

"Look out!" I say as we make our way through the store in pursuit of the best suit for you (on the sixth floor for men, and the fourth and second floor for women). "Keep your eyes wide open for construction." I don't mean the kind of construction this flagship store has undergone to create a shoe department that warrants its own ZIP code (10022-SHOE). I'm referring to the assortment of suits available for you to invest in. If you've ever heard of a garment mentioned in terms of "ready-to-wear," "made to measure," or "custom" but never bothered to find out the difference in terms, you've done yourself a disservice. There are lots of subtle details that separate the three categories of suits, and many of them go unrecognized. This can lead to spending the same or more money for a lesser-quality suit with a more identifiable name brand simply because you are unaware of what makes a suit a true power suit.

Hot Off the Hanger

In the world of men's ready-to-wear suits, we find ourselves surrounded by familiar labels like Ralph Lauren, Hickey Freeman, Giorgio Canali, Ermenegildo Zegna, and Brioni to name a few. They manufacture suits that are exactly that—ready to be worn with little or no alterations, constructed according to their particular *standard size* pattern and with details that have been specifically chosen by the company's in-house designer. As I navigate you through the racks of ready-to-wear suits, I point out the details that are obvious when a garment is mechanically constructed in high-volume quantities—hems, collars, buttonholes, and so on. The mass production of this genre of suits is precisely what makes them the most affordable option. They are also the most attainable for you if you are budget conscious or just starting a suit collection.

There is a caveat in purchasing ready-to-wear suits: Unless you happen to have the proportions of the fit model that was used to create the pattern for your *standard size,* then you *will* need alterations. Decent-to-good alterations are pricey, and in the end, the suit will still not look like it was made for you—because it wasn't. There goes your bargain! The secret to looking good in a ready-to-wear suit is finding a maker who carries suits made from a pattern very close to your proportions. When you do find your ready-to-wear designer, follow the line and patronize it even if it's not on sale, because you will ultimately save money by not having to make as many alterations.

In the men's department, we notice ready-to-wear suits are packaged as a complete suit, whereas women's brands, such as Piazza Sempione, Armani Collezione, Max Mara, Valentino Roma, and Ralph Lauren, sell suits as separates (tops and bottoms are sold individually). In women's ready-to-wear, I encourage you to purchase all of the pieces you are interested in at once, as dye lots will vary. Owning the coordinating slacks and skirt to a jacket is a smart way to add versatility to your look. Discreet patterns, such as sharkskin, pin dot, or bird's-eye, and solids camouflage any flaws found in seams sewn by machines. Now that I've educated you on fabric, you will be amazed by the multitude of synthetic blend fibers used in this category of suit. Sure, they look good, but the suit will not stand the test of time when compared to a suit made of natural fibers.

I know you need the suit yesterday and for you this is not a lifetime investment, but we just can't find one that fits properly, and that is crucial. I will not allow you to go on an interview looking like a chorizo (i.e.,

Spanish sausage). It may take some time, and we'll possibly need to look elsewhere, but I will do my best to have you choose your suit today. You may need to pay a little extra to speed up the alterations, but it beats going on an interview in jeans and a T-shirt. Ready-to-wear suits' retail prices generally start around $800. However, you can find them as reasonable as in the low hundreds, since ready-to-wear goods are marked down at the end of the season to make room for new merchandise. I can't stress this enough: If it doesn't look good on you and you're not going to wear it, it's not a bargain.

Made-to-Measure—A Middle Ground

For my fellow woman executives who scream about inequality in the job market, here's another little something to get you going: You are pretty much disregarded in the world of made-to-measure suits. It is hard to believe that we lack access to this middle-ground option, but when we roamed the second, third, and fourth floors and even the sixth floor (men's), the answer was clear: It doesn't exist.

For the men on this shopping expedition, made-to-measure provides a more personalized way of having a garment constructed to meet your proportions, though it's still *not* custom. This is a great solution for my extra-tall or extra-short interviewees who fall in love with an existing ready-to-wear suit's silhouette. You don't fit one of the standard sizes or don't want to risk a local custom tailor ruining expensive fabric *or* you may just not be up for creating a suit from scratch. As we admire the hundreds of beautifully made ready-to-wear suits that didn't quite fit you, I suggest you consider the Burberry two-button, chocolate brown, tone-on-tone striped one that caught your attention. As luck would have it, this sample is available with modifications as a made-to-measure suit.

I ask one of my favorite sales associates to assist us in locating one of their most experienced tailors. Within a half-hour, your measurements are taken and your order is written up with your size specifications. It is then sent to the company to be matched to a base pattern that best corresponds to your body dimensions. This is important for you to understand: The manufacturer will be using one of its existing patterns and modifying it to best match your proportions. A combination of hand-sewn and machine-sewn techniques will be used in order to complete your made-to-measure suit within four to six weeks. Some manufacturers will laser cut fabric, while others will hand cut to achieve a higher level of precision. You will need to factor in two or three rounds of fittings before you get to take your "baby" home, so be sure the commute to the store is not a difficult one. Also, keep the lead time in mind so that you plan your job search accordingly.

Congratulations! You managed to stick to your budget by not adding too many bells and whistles—generally starting at around $3,000 for this category of suit.

Custom-Made—The Upper Echelon of Garment Construction

What do Obama, Oprah, and most powerful and successful "O"s, as in CEOs, CAOs, CIOs, and CTOs, wear to make their mark? Why, a custom-made suit, of course. But you shouldn't feel as if you're not worthy of custom just because you're not yet interviewing for an "O" position. A well-designed custom suit is for anyone who wants to portray an image of supreme elegance, sophistication, and prestige. Custom-made men's apparel is the ultimate in true, one-of-a-kind workmanship. It is undoubtedly the most personalized indulgence in garment construction.

Meet Domenico "Mimmo" Spano (coincidently, his first and last name, as well as his nickname, end in "O"). He enters to greet us as soon as his assistant informs him we have arrived for our 10:30 appointment. His warm smile and genuine handshake, together with his impeccable attire (accented with his signature gold owl cuff links and bow tie), are all indicative of his brilliance and creativity as a master designer of custom power suits. There are no airs about him or the tastefully decorated boutique discreetly positioned in the back of Saks' men's department. He

The Custom Made Suit

single breast jacket

fitted collar

notch collar

double breast jacket

peak lapel

felt lined collar and lapel

adjusted shoulders and arm holes

contrasting sleeve lining

hand stitching

fulcrum button

horn buttons

hand sewn button holes

waist darts

anti-roll waistband

sleeve vents with kissing buttons

besom pockets

double side vents

premium fabric

inner canvas between outer fabric and lining

flap pockets

cotton Silesia lined pockets and fly

knee length pencil skirt

wastes no time, as I have briefed him on your background prior to our appointment. Therefore, he begins his work with that which clearly sets custom apart from ready-to-wear and made-to-measure contenders: He personally takes your measurements. By doing this, Mimmo assures himself that the finished product will conform perfectly to your silhouette. His choices are endless, narrowed by your physical characteristics, personal preferences, goals, and—let's not forget—your budget. Essentially, he is Michelangelo and you are his "David."

In this scenario, there is no standard pattern to compare *you* to because you are the pattern. After you are done being measured, the thinking begins. Details such as jacket, trouser, and skirt style are considered. A library of swatch books sits perfectly aligned on the shelves. Every pleat, dart, seam, stitch, pocket, button, and lapel is designed with a purpose in mind, which is to empower you. In addition, these details are handcrafted, and the fabric is hand cut. As a custom-made consumer, expect to commit yourself to several additional fittings. This will include the second fitting, where a shell of the baste stitch suit is marked and sculpted to your body. It is then re-marked, taken apart, and re-cut to guarantee exactness. The jacket's interfacing or inner canvas piece located between the outer cloth and the fabric lining is used to shape the garment to your body. An expert presser is then called to the scene to make certain this process is executed perfectly.

Each fitting (around three to five) within an eight-to-ten-week process will be used to ensure that the middle button of the jacket (the fulcrum) is positioned exactly at the natural waist; collars hug the nape of the neck just right; shoulders and armholes are properly adjusted to avoid the "straight-jacket" look; and anti-roll waistbands on trousers and skirts are accurately affixed to avert unappealing spillage of love handles. In addition, sturdy woven cotton Silesia is used throughout the entire trousers' zipper, lining, and pockets for durability. You'll find tasteful details such as a contrasting striped lining inside the arm sleeves (a signature of custom suits), "kissing" buttons on open sleeve vents, and double-side vents on the jacket, which help prevent wrinkling when sitting down.

Wow, how time flies! Is it lunchtime already? We've been so engaged in choosing all of the details while sipping our complimentary Perrier water, it's hardly felt like work (and it has been). Time to wrap up; you're losing focus—a sure sign of hunger. As we bid Mimmo "Ciao, for now," we joke about keeping lunch light so as not to distort the measurements he has meticulously taken. He is confident about his workmanship and assures us enough fabric will be incorporated to allow for a ten- to thirty-pound weight gain. Phew! Isn't that a relief? With this type of time and financial investment, it's good to know there's insurance to cover it.

The vicuña and silk fabric, along with horn buttons, are sure to make the double-breasted, peaked collar suit a real showstopper. You are up for the position of a lifetime! You're worth it. Custom is truly the ultimate approach for accentuating, balancing, and camouflaging your interview image. Suits in this category are generally priced around $4,000, depending on fabric and details. "See you in three weeks, Mimmo." We program the appointment into the BlackBerry and then it's off to the eighth-floor café. I recommend the warm goat cheese salad. Go easy on the breadbasket, or at least choose whole grain bread (see Chapter 8), as there's still more shopping to be done.

Elevator Thoughts

We've shopped for one interview suit (as determined by a matching pant/skirt and jacket, not coordinating separates) or a mini wardrobe of interview suits (ready-to-wear, made-to-measure, or custom). Each purchase is an investment piece meant to show that you are a capable person with intelligence, integrity, good judgment, and, yes, good taste. I was happy to guide you this time, but when you're on your own, remember what you've learned today and keep the following conventions in mind in order to save yourself time, money, and lots of headaches when it comes time to choosing the *perfect* interview suit(s):

- **The three "Ws":** Why do I love it? When will I wear it? What else lives in my closet that will coexist with this suit?

- **The price-per-wear formula:** Price divided by number of wear = price per wear (e.g.: $800 suit ÷ 8 interviews = $100 per wear)

- **The penny-wise and dollar-foolish syndrome:** Avoid shopping with only one criterion in mind . . . price.

- **The denial:** Shop for the weight you are at the time of your purchase and rationalize with yourself by acknowledging that if a ready-to-wear suit doesn't fit properly, your body is not to blame. Blame it on the fit model used to make the suit.

- **The dress rehearsal:** Bring the appropriate undergarment and shoes. Pretend it's your debut.

- **The procrastinator:** Avoid waiting until the last minute, since the pressure will only drive you to make rushed decisions and costly mistakes.

- **The rules:** Ask about return and exchange and guarantee policies on your wardrobe investment.

- **The interruptions:** Shop by yourself or with a trained professional.

- **The *perfect* fit:** Make sure to try on and factor tailoring needs, alteration costs, and lead time for made-to-measure and custom suits.

4

The Shirt Off Your Back

Many years ago, I concluded that a few hair shirts were part of the mental wardrobe of every man. The president differs from other men in that he has a more extensive wardrobe. —Herbert Hoover (president of the United States, 1929–1933)

IF YOU WERE a picture, your suit would be your frame and your shirt would be the matting. A well-chosen shirt will provide a great outline to help showcase you and your suit. It is yet another barrier of protection against embarrassing bodily secretions and hair peeking out of unforeseen places. Your face, being a major focal point, is outlined by this garment's most critical feature—the collar. Notice I say "collar," not "neckline," as the collar is the extra little piece of fabric that makes the shirt the appropriate option for interviewing. It baffles me to see candidates throw away an opportunity to attract attention to their most captivating physical feature by wearing ill-fitting shirts with collars that are chokingly tight or exceptionally loose—or loose around the arms, shoulders, backs, and torsos. A business shirt is tailored, in comparison to the "blousy" options worn by women in casual situations.

In order to choose the perfect interview shirt, you must first analyze your face as a means of finding which collars are in complete harmony with your appearance. Identify your face with one of the seven gender-neutral face shapes that follow.

- **Oval:** The oval face is the most balanced of all faces. It is longer than it is wide and has a rounded jawline.

- **Round:** Characterized by its wide cheekbones and its short neck, the round face is curvy, with no angles, including at the jawline.

- **Square:** The length and width of this face are equal, with straight side views. Its jaw is either straight or diagonally angular.

- **Oblong:** The oblong face resembles a rectangle, as its sides are straight and noticeably longer than its width. Its jaw is also angular with a pronounced forehead.

- **Diamond:** The diamond-shaped face consists of a narrow forehead and chin, with its cheeks and eyes as the widest area.

- **Heart:** The heart-shaped face is also referred to as an inverted triangle, with its widest point at the forehead and eyes, paired with a narrow, pointed chin.

- **Triangle:** The triangular-shaped face is characterized by its narrow forehead and wide jaw.

A Collar for You

The shape and fit of the collar are important details to consider when presenting an image that is professional and trustworthy. Women have more leeway, since collars may be worn unbuttoned. However, that may present other issues, such as collars that are so freely undone that they are the cause of embarrassing and awkward situations, perhaps not for the oblivious wearer but for the observant interviewer. Necklines sans collars are not recommended for similar reasons, as well as for their casual intention.

round

oblong

square

oval

heart

triangle

diamond

Button-down as well as hidden button-down collars also fall under the umbrella of "too informal" for an interview, not to mention too informal to be worn with a tie at all.

Contrasting-color collars (white collars) were popular when I first started in the placement industry in the mid-1990s. Today, men who have the flair to wear it with distinction carry the look. Designers of women's career ready-to-wear offer this look quite sparingly, so if you like it, be sure to include it as a detail in your made-to-measure or custom French-cuffed shirt order. Depending on your coloring, and the color of your suit, a bright white contrast collar can appear too stark around your neck (as if it's wearing you). However, if you have the coloring of a winter, then wearing a white contrast collar with a dark-valued suit would be in complete harmony with your coloring and would create a striking image.

Men require the fit of the collar to be a lot more exact, since all buttons are to be fastened at all times. Collar points should not curl up at the ends, and stays (even the plastic kind) should be inserted to ensure the collar doesn't curl on a humid day just as you approach your interview destination. Also, the clearance on the neck should be no larger or smaller than the thickness of two of your fingers slipped in flat. This is one prerequisite that is consistent whenever choosing a dress shirt. Once your suit jacket's collar accentuates your shirt collar, only about a half-inch should be seen from underneath.

If you can't find the fit of a ready-to-wear shirt's collar that complies with these specifications, then you should consider a made-to-measure or custom alternative. Having a seamstress take in a collar without reconstructing the entire thing and expecting it to look right is highly unrealistic. It's not only time-consuming and expensive, but just not worth the attempt, given that more customized options are at your disposal, with reasonable prices of about $120 per shirt or higher (depending on fabric and extra details).

Collars on a fine dress shirt should be hand turned, taut, and wrinkle- and spot-free. Accordingly, be careful not to shamefully stain your untainted collar with blood from harried shaving or ketchup from hurried eating.

COLLARS FOR EVERY CANDIDATE

Not all collars are created equal, and the length, width, and height are all determined by the shape of your face; for men, the thickness of the tie's knot is also a consideration.

▪ **Turndown point collar:** This is the most common collar among male and female candidates. Classified by its medium points, which sit not too high and not too low on the neck, it can be easily worn by you if you have an oval face, while it will effectively elongate round and square faces. It will accentuate diamond- and heart-shaped faces while balancing a triangular face. An oblong face could use a shirt collar with slightly rounded tips to balance the slight squareness of the jaw. For men, a four-in-hand tie knot or half-Windsor knot works well with this classic collar.

▪ **Spread collar:** The spread collar balances the slight contour of the oval face's cheekbones and the length of an oblong face. It will accentuate the shortness of a square and round face and the wideness of a triangular face's jaw, while camouflaging the narrow chins of a diamond- or heart-shaped face. The spread collar's wide space between front points accommodates a thick Windsor knot well.

▪ **Tab and pin collar:** The tab and pin collars both sit high on the neck and each has its points fastened together using tabs (as in the tab collar) or with eyelets through which a tie pin is inserted to keep them close together. A round face's short neck is enhanced by a high-sitting collar, making the face look like it's resting on the shoulders without a neck. The tab and pin collars will camouflage the full and angular jawlines of the square-, oblong-, and triangular-shaped faces. The tapered neck collar produced by the fastened tabs or tie pins highlights heart- and diamond-shaped faces' pointed chins. This type of collar balances an oval face. Narrow ties with a four-in-hand knot or half-Windsor will protrude out of the small opening left between the collar points.

▪ **Convertible collar (females):** The convertible collar is a classic and functional collar that will adapt favorably to all face shapes based on how you choose to button it. Worn open it resembles a notch collar with small lapels. The openness, which forms a "V" shape, will elongate a round- or square-shaped face and highlight a diamond- or heart-shaped one. It will also balance the narrow forehead of a triangle. Worn fastened, a convertible collar will camouflage an oblong face's length by shortening it. If you happen to have an oval-shaped face, you are fortunate enough to have a convertible collar flatter you either opened or closed.

A Wardrobe Staple

As the dress shirt is a wardrobe staple, the length or the "staple" of the cotton used is also an important consideration when choosing what to purchase. Inexpensive and mass-produced shirts are typically made of upland cotton, which lacks strength and durability because of the nature of its short staple. Durability is also determined by how many fiber filaments are twisted together to produce a yarn: one-ply or two-ply, with two-ply being the stronger.

While Pima cotton (a classification designated to generic, extra-long-staple cotton imported from any country) makes for a more desirable dress shirt based on the better quality of its fiber, a "Pima Supima cotton" dress shirt refers to its cotton content by a brand name. Pima Supima cotton is basically American-grown cotton that is recommended by Supima, a group that administers and markets the distribution of American cotton. Avoid overspending by recognizing marketing tactics for what they are. For instance, if you are paying a premium for what you think is Pima cotton, make sure the label designates it as *100 percent Pima cotton.* Otherwise, you may be buying a lesser-quality shirt that is created from a blend of Pima and upland cotton.

The same holds true for "Egyptian cotton," which you might expect to be the smooth and comfortable long-staple cotton grown in the Nile River Valley. In actuality, *all* cotton (long or short staple) grown in Egypt *can* be called Egyptian cotton based on technicality; that is, all of it comes from Egypt, even if it's not specifically from the Nile River Valley. Don't be fooled.

Likewise, "Sea Island cotton" is expected to be the extra-long and fine staple imported from the West Indies. Instead, "Sea Island cotton" has become a too-often-used term that simply describes a fine shirt fiber in general terms.

For fast-traveling business executives, there are wrinkle-resistant cotton and poly blend shirts, which look crisp and neat but are less breathable than full-cotton alternatives.

Fit Is "It"

Whether choosing ever popular broadcloth for its delicately ribbed, ultra-soft, breathable weave, pinpoint oxford for its smooth durability, or royal oxford for its lush texture and luster, it is all the other details related to fit that make for a quality dress shirt. You shouldn't feel like you are wearing a straitjacket, so there should be ample fabric around the shoulders, chest, and torso to allow for movement. Too much fabric, especially around the waist, will add unflattering pounds and shorten your silhouette. So if you are a ready-to-wear interviewee who is ectomorphic (see Chapter 1), opting for a tapered or *slim fit* rather than a standard or *classic fit* is best. Split yokes on a shirt's upper backside in combination with side pleats and waist darts that conform to your silhouette are solutions to an otherwise sloppy untailored look. The shirt's length as measured from your shoulder should be long enough (about six inches down from the waist) that the shirttails don't fly out of your pants or skirt.

Sleeve lengths are usually another area where candidates bury themselves. You should be able to shake hands and take notes without having to fix yourself every five seconds. At the bottom of your sleeve, your cuff should fit snugly around your wrist and not ride up and down when you wear your jacket; only about a half-inch of the cuff's edge is to be seen while your suit jacket is on.

The question of whether to wear French cuffs over button cuffs pops up over and over again. While I'm partial to the formal look of French cuffs, it's best to stay away from the style if you have short arms. In fact, if you really want to purposely shorten your arms, you should opt for a French cuff in a contrasting color. The strong horizontal line of the cuff will optically take inches off your arm length. Button cuffs with two to three buttons are a perfectly acceptable option if French cuffs are not a flattering option for you, though not in a contrasting color. No matter what the cuff style, let it be a cuff that is free of soil. Insist on a functioning button, sometimes referred to as a "gauntlet button," on the sleeve's placket for an enhanced fit around your forearm.

Breast pockets are a feature that should be reserved for button-down collars, a look that is too casual for interviewing. Substitute the breast pocket's fabric for use on the bottom of the shirt's gusset to reinforce endurance throughout the test of time and laundering.

Little Extras

Since it's fairly uncommon for candidates to carry a sewing kit along on interviews to remedy button malfunctions, it's best to make sure buttons are sewn well from the start. A solid cross-locked stitch is best at keeping buttons well attached at all times. Not only should buttons be sewn on firmly, but they should be reliable, dependable, and aesthetically pleasing, such as mother-of-pearl buttons. Hand-sewn buttonholes, hand stitching around the collar and cuffs, as well as single-needle seams show additional superior craftsmanship in a dress shirt and the wearer's impeccable taste. A placket or raised piece of fabric sewn along the front of the shirt, over its buttonholes, is a detail that looks best on a casual shirt, such as a button-down collared shirt with a breast pocket that is worn *without* a tie. Instead, a flat-front placket made of the shirt's own fabric shows a higher level of finesse and craftsmanship.

Monograms are a personal choice and, added tastefully to the edge of a button cuff, can add a hint of flair to your interview shirt. The key to

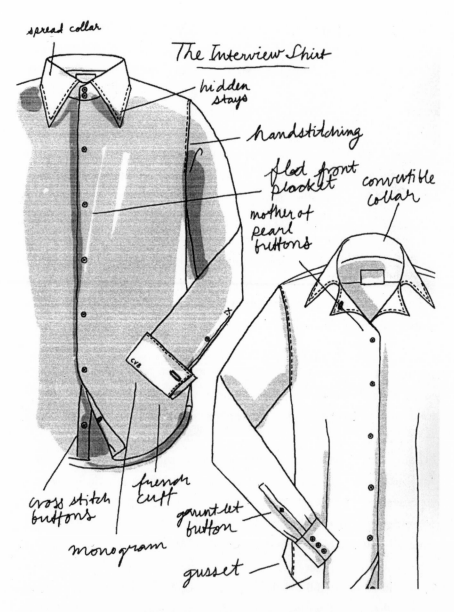

The Interview Shirt

spread collar

hidden stays

handstitching

flat front placket

convertible collar

mother of pearl buttons

cross stitch buttons

french cuff

gauntlet button

monogram

gusset

exuding elegance by sporting your initials on your shirt is to keep the font simple (preferably a block style), discreet in size (about a quarter inch), and in a color that doesn't scream your initials out loud. A monogram on a shirt is one of those details that should be chosen for your personal satisfaction, much like a beautiful brassiere. The whole world doesn't need to see it: It's your little secret that gives you that extra bit of confidence while you're in the "hot seat" interviewing for the job of your life.

Choose your interview shirt with the same discerning eye you use to choose your perfect interview suit. Once considered underwear (thus monogramming enabled identification in laundering), the dress shirt holds a more coveted role today. Whether solid or patterned in a multitude of plaids, stripes, and checks, the essential dress shirt functions as more than an accessory. Therefore, it is worthy of its own chapter.

5

Maximize...Harmonize ...Accessorize
Wardrobe Extenders

It is the unseen, unforgettable, ultimate accessory of fashion that heralds your arrival and prolongs your departure. —Coco Chanel (French fashion designer)

ACCESSORIES ARE THE absolute best wardrobe extenders. The versatility they provide can transform an otherwise nondescript interview outfit into a well-coordinated and balanced work of genius in the blink of an eye. Accessories can deliberately become the focal point of an outfit or unexpectedly add a splash of pizzazz. Best of all, they expand and contract along with weight fluctuation. On the other hand, accessories should not hijack an outfit and should be used cautiously and sparingly, particularly on a job interview. Used incorrectly, they will surely become the "can't put my finger on it" reason why you are turned down for a job. Typically, I will give candidates my notorious onceover right before I wrap up an interview. My recommendations usually entail keeping accessories at fewer than 14 items, depending on the industry; any more than that and you will look kitschy. And, yes, a pair of earrings counts as just that . . . *a pair* . . . meaning two.

Evaluating the aesthetics and appropriateness of accessories using the same principles discussed in Chapters 1 and 2 is fundamental. When choosing accessories to enhance your look, you should continue to adhere to the following principles: proportion, shape, line, pattern, texture, scale, and color. Accentuate, balance, and camouflage wherever you deem necessary. Additionally, your preferences, personality, job rank, and professional industry will have a direct impact on the accessories you choose and how you decide to place them.

Integrating accessories as part of your interview look requires a closer assessment of one of your most important physical attributes, the one I and all other interviewers focus directly on—your face.

Your face is a canvas of emotion and expression. Therefore, it is to your advantage to frame your face with the least amount of distractions so that your message is not distorted. The right accessories should enhance your body *and* face. In cases where your budget restricts a suit upgrade, a high-quality accessory can take on the role of advancing your look from moderate to fabulous.

Headwear: Hair Clips, Barrettes, Headbands, and Hats

If I had my druthers, I'd have everyone ditch the hideous hair clamp clips that look more like the ones at the end of a clipboard than something that should go on anyone's head—especially during an interview. The decorative versions usually have rhinestones and all kinds of other jazz that make them even less tolerable. As I always say, "Lose the clip." Combs and barrettes can be equally as offensive if the size is not monitored. Headbands look the neatest if kept simple, holding hair from covering the all-important eyes. If you *must* wear a hair accessory, make it one that blends with your hair color and tuck it away where it's not a glaring and distracting accessory, or worse yet, cutesy.

Winter hats, fashion hats such as berets, and sports caps are deadly if kept on when your interviewer comes out to greet you. Bicycle and motorcycle helmets are especially ridiculous to keep on even if you are interviewing for a position as a messenger. Oh, and for you fashionistas out there, a kerchief on your head or a turban is not cool, even if it was featured on the cover of Vogue and you are interviewing for a position as a fashion editor. Show your sense of style in some other way. If for religious reasons or because of hair loss from medical treatments you must wear a hat or the like, that is an entirely different story. However, if you do choose to wear a wig for aesthetics, secure it well enough for it not to slide off your head. I've witnessed such a mishap and, believe me, it threw me for a loop. Come to think of it, it was a toupee—talk about most embarrassing moments ever!

Eyewear: Sunglasses and Eyeglasses

Neither sunglasses nor eyeglasses should ever be worn on the top of your head when speaking to a recruiter. You are not dining al fresco with your bud on a veranda sipping a delectable drink. Eyeglasses should be placed on your face and they should be in a style that suits your face shape and facial particulars. For instance, if you have a diamond-shaped face with the widest part of your face being through your eyes, then bold, plastic-frame glasses will only maximize the width. Choose eyeglasses with decorative details at the temples if you have close-set eyes. This creates an optical illusion of eyes that are extended outward. Alternatively, eyeglasses with a decorative contrast at the bridge of the nose create an optical illusion of eyes that are more balanced if you have wide-set eyes. By the way, if you're wondering how to figure out whether you have close-set eyes or wide-set eyes, place yourself in front of a mirror and examine your eye area. If you can fit an imaginary eye (the same length as your real eyes) in between your two eyes, you possess well-balanced eyes. If you can't fit one imaginary eye in between your eyes, then you have close-set eyes and if you can fit more than one eye, you have wide-set eyes. Wire-rim glasses work best on heart-shaped or inverted-triangle faces to balance the broad forehead. To camouflage a hooked or protruding nose, the nose pads should be adjusted so that your glasses sit lower on the bridge of your nose. Sunglasses are to be kept inside their case and out of the recruiter's sight.

Be conscious of not taking your eyeglasses on and off during conversation and chewing on the end pieces. Refrain from wearing your eyeglasses on an eyeglass chain around your neck. Even the most beautiful one is an unnecessary accessory in the interview room due to the temptation to play with it as your nerves creep up. I've also seen eyeglasses clank and clatter against the table, and it too makes for an unwanted distraction.

Remember the following tips when you go shopping for eyewear:

- **Avoid repetition:** Choose shapes that contrast with your face shape.

- **Harmonize:** Choose a color that blends well with your eye, skin, and hair color.

- **Avoid "super sizing":** Choose size in relation to your face and body scale.

Jewelry: Earrings, Nose Rings, Rings, Necklaces, Bracelets, Watches, Cuff Links, Belt Buckles, and Ankle Bracelets

Beware of costume jewelry that looks costume-y from a mile away. Dangling earrings draw my eye to the ear and distract me from listening to your story. Play it safe: If you have more than one piercing per ear, stick to one earring per ear. If you are a man with an earring or two, consider leaving them at home. They may look fashionable with your leisure wear, but they don't carry the same cachet on an interview. Employers often reproach nose rings, no matter how miniscule in size. Eyebrow, lip, and tongue rings are offensive and distracting. Don't fight me on this—just trust me.

Be mindful of not overloading on stackable rings for an interview. Also, be cautious as far as which fingers you decide to arrange them on. Thumb and forefinger rings are very artsy and can sometimes be read as provocative. Pinky rings, especially diamond-encrusted ones on men, remind me of something worn by a character on *The Sopranos*. Engagement rings and wedding bands are a sentimental sign of commitment for you. To a potential employer, a fresh sparkling solitaire diamond engagement ring screams time off for a honeymoon. Sporting a huge rock around your family and friends is a sign of a successful fiancé; a potential employer may view it as ostentatious. A wedding band worn around your neck or on the ring finger of your right hand will raise questions about your sexual orientation. While you wouldn't want to work in a place that had a "hidden" issue against you being gay in the first place, questions regarding marital status are illegal (Chapter 19), so why volunteer such information regardless of whether you are straight or gay.

Another type of jewelry that gives unnecessary information to a potential employer are religious pieces. Again, the law protects your privacy regarding this information, so flaunting it may divulge unnecessary information that may put your candidacy in danger. Some candidates will challenge me on this and that's fine. I'm the one on the receiving end of the phone call in which employers ask how many religious holidays you expect to take during the year, to which I politely reply, "Don't know and can't ask." I'm all for being truthful; if you override what I tell you, that is fine with me. But isn't that the point of this book? It's meant to give you the scoop on *every* detail that can cost you the job. If you choose to do otherwise, I'm merely making you aware of the consequences that *may* transpire based on your choices.

For men, necklaces are hidden by a buttoned-collared shirt (hopefully). Women are more vulnerable in this area, as open-collared shirts leave the neck exposed. If you have a short, thick neck, it is best to drop the necklace altogether, as the horizontal line it forms shortens your neck even more. For women with average to long necks, one necklace is fine. If you choose to wear the "quintessential" pearl necklace, be sure the pearls are close in color to your teeth. They will only upstage your teeth if their color is much lighter and brighter. Nameplate necklaces might help the recruiter remember your name during conversation, but they are entirely too trendy to wear on an interview.

I had never given tie bars a second thought, as they seemed to be an accessory that came and went with fashion. Recently, I've noticed men using a simple tie bar and I happen to like the look, if for no other reason than its practicality—it holds the tie in place. Be sure the tie bar coordinates with any other metal jewelry or accessory (in your seasonal color)—especially a belt buckle. Other tie jewelry, such as tie tacks and tie chains, are either cumbersome or better suited for evening wear than business wear. A tie clip fastened horizontally across the tie knot to make it protrude is another accessory that is better left away from the interview room. It is better suited for social, dressy occasions.

Metal stays used inside the collar of a dress shirt to prevent the collar from curling up are another functional accessory worth investing in rather than settling for the plastic kind often included in shirts. Metal stays are a "hidden" accessory, so they don't really apply to the "fewer than 14 items" accessory rule.

Bangle bracelets are completely inappropriate during an interview even if you are up for a fashion or creative job. The jingly noise makes them a distraction during conversation. Unless you plan to have your hand bolted to your lap, they will jangle. A link bracelet is a quieter option, so if you absolutely feel the urge to wear one, that's the way to go. Ankle bracelets are better left for identifying livestock than for humans on an interview.

A leather band wristwatch is definitely an acceptable accessory for an interview. A metal band would be fine too, but be sure it is in your seasonal metallic color. Otherwise, it will outshine you. One of my pet peeves is to see a well-dressed candidate with a sports watch on his wrist. It looks bulky, out of place, and just plain tacky.

Cuff links on a French cuff shirt are a nice touch. However, stay away from ones that have diamonds or any other type of glitzy stones. Cuff links are an accessory that can be used to accentuate your overall silhouette, as they typically come in a variety of sizes and shapes—choose them wisely.

Belt buckles should not be excessive in size or decoration. Think functional when it comes to wearing one during this type of official meeting. If you have a short and/or thick waist, you should do without a belt or buckle altogether. Instead, choose pants or a skirt without belt loops or wear suspenders.

Neckwear: Neckties, Bow Ties, and Scarves

▪ **Men's neckties:** Neckties and bow ties are a hugely dominant accessory, as they will literally "tie" your interview look with color, pattern, texture, and flair. Considering the importance of the tie, it's astounding how little attention men pay to it being just right. Investing in a quality tie made from fabric (usually silk) that is cut on the bias is the first step in achieving a look that is complete with a necktie that falls flat and straight down. The method by which a tie is constructed also affects its ability to look its best. A necktie that is handcrafted by folding its fabric seven times and is left unlined is a superior and rare alternative to one that is made from three pieces of sewn fabric inlayed with wool, silk, or cotton.

While I'm on the subject of neckties falling perfectly vertical, they shouldn't fall down to your crotch area. Your goal should be to have the tip's widest part align with the top of your belt. Typically, standard-sized neckties are 52" to 58" long. Do yourself a favor and purchase a custom one if you are extra tall so you avoid looking like you borrowed one from a child.

Your necktie's knot should be stretched tightly to indicate you are pulled together and ready to talk business. A loose one shows signs of someone who is either hot or not serious about his interview. Tying a knot takes skill and lots of practice. The majority of men sport a four-in-hand knot because it is the easiest and quickest one to assemble. This popular knot is small, long, and slightly asymmetrical, which camouflages short, wide necks. Pair this knot with a diagonal stripe or pattern in a smooth silk fabric and it further elongates a stocky or athletic neck. The Windsor and half-Windsor knots are wider knots that camouflage long, thin necks. Couple these knots with a curvy paisley, large plaid, or any other broad-scale motifs in a textured fabric to disguise a pencil-thin neck. Regardless of the tie, be sure to tuck the tie's narrower blade inside the wider blade's self-loop to keep both blades from looking like bat wings. In mastering one or all three knot types, the result is one and the same: to produce the necktie's most coveted characteristic—the dimple.

tie dimple

The dimple is synonymous with savvy, confidence, and aptitude, all traits that are high in demand as you are considered for hire.

- **Men's bow ties:** It wasn't until I left the Bronx and moved to Connecticut (Wesleyan) that I saw men (students and professors) walking around campus in bow ties. Prior to that, I thought bow ties were for prom dates and grooms. Well, when I moved back to the Bronx after college while commuting back and forth to work in the city, I kept my eyes open for bow ties. There was not one in sight. (As you may have already guessed, I'm partial to bow ties. Most likely it's because they conjure fond memories of happy times during my late teens and early 20s.)

Bow ties are such an underused accessory that worn correctly they can send a message of individuality, confidence, and authority. Don't be intimidated by the bow tie; just make sure that you don't spill over your shirt's collar and that the ends are parallel with the outer corners of your eyes.[1] Experiment with wearing them in a variety of colors, textures, and sizes (keeping your physical characteristics in mind) combined with double- or single-breasted suits. The horizontal positioning of bow ties balances long and narrow faces and close-set eyes. Just don't let your interview be the first time you decide to wear one. If it turns out that you are completely uncomfortable wearing one, you don't want to find that out while you're sitting across from a recruiter or hiring manager.

- **Women's scarves:** Scarves are the equivalent to men's neckties and bow ties, except that for women this is an optional accessory when it comes to interviewing. I find that women are either scarf lovers or scarf haters. A scarf hater feels overly accessorized or views the scarf as something her mother wore "back in the day." I declare myself a scarf lover. (I've already shared my lucky scarf story with you in Chapter 3.)

Scarves come in all fabrics, prints, colors, sizes, and shapes. Silk scarves cut on the bias (diagonally instead of straight) will drape better than polyester ones cut straight across. Fabric-blended scarves are a lot tauter and will hold a crisper knot. Since scarves sit so close to your face, the color should resonate with your skin, eye, and hair color (see Chapter 2) and the print should harmonize with the scale of your face and facial features (see Chapter 4). The size of the scarf should resonate with your face and body's scale. Therefore, if you have a short, ectomorphic body, a gargantuan oblong scarf will look like it's about to swallow you. You don't want to be wrapped up like a mummy for any occasion, but especially not for an interview. Conversely, a tall, endomorphic woman would look like she ran out of fabric with a small kerchief that disappears when worn around her neck.

An oblong or square scarf arranged in a classic ascot style is a neat and professional option if you want to fill an empty neckline and/or add a splash of color to liven up your look. However, if you have a short neck, a better option is to tie an oblong scarf into a loose necktie, arranged neatly under the collar of your blouse, similar to a men's tie. The vertical lines of the hanging tails of the scarf add length to a short, stout neck. If you really want to stay away from a scarf altogether, then arranging a small, square kerchief inside the breast pocket of your jacket looks professional and adds style to your look. Adding visual interest to one side of your jacket also creates an invisible diagonal line for the eye to follow. This is a great trick to use in order to appear slimmer and taller. Large square scarves draped around your shoulders and knotted on one side with tails hanging on either side of one shoulder blade broaden a long thin neck and/or face while balancing narrow shoulders.

Leather Goods: Gloves, Belts, Suspenders, Portfolios, Briefcases, Totes, and Handbags

Calfskin leather and other exotic skins are costly, but as I mentioned earlier in this chapter, you can really upgrade your look by investing in pieces that can outlast you. If you live in a region where the cold warrants wearing gloves and you need to wear them to an interview, more than likely they'll be off your hands before your interviewer greets you. However, if the recruiter comes out sooner than expected and your gloves are still on, you should remove your right glove before shaking his hand (more on etiquette in Chapter 11).

Belts for men and women range between 1" and 1 ½" wide, and skinny belts for skirts are about ½"; your width selection should be based on the length of your torso. Long torsos can accommodate a wider belt, while short torsos look better with a thinner belt. A belt in a contrasting color to your trousers breaks the continuity of your waistline, making you look shorter and wider. It also projects a much more casual image, while a belt similar in value to your suit and shoes achieves the opposite effect.

Suspenders, or "braces" as they are often called, are made of elastic fabric or leather. While men can look quite dapper wearing them on an interview, as a woman you would look ridiculous sporting them. I can't say I've ever personally tried fastening suspenders to my slacks, but some men are literally hooked by their incredible comfort and functionality. Suspenders are a practical alternative to wearing a belt, especially for the "O"-shaped man. You may think what I'm about to say is common sense, but since I've witnessed it, I need to address it: Wearing a belt *and* suspenders at the same time is a major faux pas.

Portfolios should be used to neatly store your writing instruments, writing pad, and résumés. A note about anything that is stored in your portfolio that will be visible to an interviewer: Your writing pad should have fresh paper, résumés should be clean and unwrinkled, and writing instruments should be of higher quality than your everyday, half-chewed, plastic kind. Ideally, you should purchase a portfolio of quality leather. This is a lifelong investment, as you will use it not only on interviews but just about anytime you have a meeting once you get the job. "Pleather," or faux leather, ones can serve the purpose if you're just starting out, and you can always replace it with a higher-quality one later in your career. Regardless of the material, a textured portfolio helps camouflage its wear and tear. In the interest of traveling light on an interview and being free of too many accessories, a portfolio and wallet may be all you need. If you are someone who needs to bring samples of your work to the interview, an oversized portfolio is appropriate when paired with a backpack to free up your hands. In general, backpacks are very casual, especially when made out of canvas, but if you are an artist, it is an acceptable option.

For those of you who need to lug your laptops, lunch (for tips on eating in between interviews or on your way back to your present job, see Chapter 8), and any other belongings, then a briefcase or tote may be necessary. Slim, hard-case ones with sharp lines have a much more tailored look than the expandable nonconstructed kind. If you choose the latter type, try to choose one without too many zippers, exterior pockets, and hardware. Instead, opt for extra pockets on the inside of the bag so it looks more professional. Also, if there is a convertible strap, tuck it inside the bag so it looks neat when you place the bag against your body.

For women, a tote bag is a contemporary and practical option. Otherwise, a briefcase or shoulder bag is acceptable. The size should correspond to your scale, and the strap should be adjusted so that the bag falls right at the top of your hip, especially if you are an "A"-shaped silhouette, where width on the bottom half of your body would be unflattering. A shoulder bag that hangs lower than your hipbone adds pounds to your hips, which is not altogether bad if you're tall and are "V"-shaped. Smaller envelope and pochette-style bags can easily be merged inside your briefcase, so if you like to separate keys, cell phones, mirrors, lipstick, and other small doodads, then this is the way for you. A satchel bag is another acceptable style for business if you prefer to carry your bag on your forearm or by hand. Many satchels come with removable shoulder straps, so if you interchange how you carry your bag, this is a smart choice for commuting. However, once you arrive at your interview, you should remove long straps, as they can become cumbersome or cause you to trip. Hobo bags for women are spacious but too casual an option for interviewing.

Portfolios, briefcases, and handbags need not match the color or material of your shoes. Metallic colors are rather flashy for interviewing. Designer logos and hardware should be discreet since they can be interpreted as either garish or ostentatious.

Footwear

Ever hear of the expression "Dressed to the nines from head to toe"? It's a great adage because it really sums up how your head and your toes serve as bookends that sustain volumes of information communicated by everything in between. As such, in order to create a harmonious professional image, the value of your shoe color should correlate with the color value of your hair. In other words, if you are a person with hair that is dark in value, then choosing a shoe of similar value will tie your look together. If you have light golden locks, then black shoes will overpower your look. You are better off choosing a shoe in a lighter value, such as a natural tan hide. Before I discuss gender-specific footwear suggestions, I'll share a few more general rules about interview footwear.

Custom shoes are chosen for orthopedic reasons or if your foot is a hard-to-find size rather than for lack of finding superior workmanship. If you don't fall into either of those two categories, save your pennies and put them toward upgrading your suit. If you do have orthopedic issues but you have trouble finding an attractive custom shoe, remedy the problem by finding one that can accommodate comfortable innersoles, which can be purchased separately. Aim for comfort and flair but don't sacrifice comfort *for* flair. Your pain will be transparent and it's not worth it. Don't interpret comfort as sneakers or other types of active wear shoes meant for the gym.

If you must wear "commuter" shoes, change into your interview shoes before you enter the building, not in the reception area. Sandals, flip-flops, and other styles of toe-flaunting shoes are completely improper for either gender even in 95-degree weather. Dress boots are an acceptable option for either gender during inclement weather. Woven or braided leather shoes are too informal for an interview, and logo-embossed shoes make you look like a walking advertisement for the manufacturer. Shoes should be cleaned regularly and heel tips replaced (for safety and aesthetics) and placed inside shoe trees when not in use in order to preserve their professional appearance.

Men's Shoes

There are many fancy names used to describe men's dress shoes that are meant to be worn with a suit. To keep it simple, I've narrowed the interview finishing touch into three options: the plain/decorated/perforated oxford lace-up, the buckled monk-strap, and the dress slip-on (with buckle or tassels).

An oxford lace-up is the classic and traditional shoe for the interviewee whose goal is to look sleek and sophisticated. Choose a round cap-toe one to shorten an oversized foot or to camouflage an angular silhouette. A point-toe shoe will elongate a short foot and camouflage a rounder silhouette.

A buckled monk-strap shoe is for when you desire a wider fit, because it has a larger tongue. The wideness of the shoe relegates it to a less formal shoe than the oxford lace-up, though a perfectly acceptable option, especially if your foot is wide and comfort is your top criterion.

The dress slip-on shoe is the most casual of the shoes, though an option that is more fashionable than classic. After all, a dressy slip-on shoe is really a disguised moccasin with a more solid construction. Dress slip-on shoes portray a more contemporary and youthful flair. Slip-on shoes remind me of a time when I was interviewing a junior salesperson for a position at one of my client firms. Five minutes into the interview I noticed a foul smell. It was so powerful a smell I got up to crack a window and apologized to the candidate for the stench. As I reached my seat to proceed with the interview, I caught a glimpse of what was underneath the table. There I noticed his slip-on shoes, casually off his feet as if he were home watching television.

Note: Slip-on shoes are not to slip off your feet during an interview or any other type of business meeting.

Oxford

monk strap

dress slip-on

Women's Shoes

As a shoe fanatic, I own just about every style of shoe out there: everything from flats, wedges, espadrilles, mules, boots, clogs, and sandals to loafers, slingbacks, moccasins, and pumps. However, my preferred choice of inter-view footwear when advising a female candidate is without a doubt the pump shoe. "Pump" is a universal term that describes an enclosed shoe without ribbons, straps, or laces.[2] Pumps are distinguished by the height of their heel: flat, kitten, chunky, stacked, French, or stiletto. A Mary Jane shoe, a shoe that bears a strap in a T-bar shape across the top and has an encased toe, does not get my vote, as it is neither sleek nor flattering to the foot. D'Orsay pumps, characterized by their encircled vamps (the part of the shoe that protects your toes) and cut-away sides, are also not fitting, as they show too much arch and skin (too much sex appeal).

The size of the heel depends on your height, the image you are trying to project, and the overall condition of your foot. Choose a broad flat heel (around ½") if you are an extremely tall woman who does not want to tower over her interviewer. Ballet flats and, more specifically, the latest scrunch ballet flats with rounded toes, semiconstructed soles, and signature bowties in the front, are extremely casual for an interview, no matter how much you've spent on them. Other flats with a pointed or square toe, a more sub-stantial sole, and a geometrically shaped heel are more acceptable.

Kitten heels are a narrow and thin (1" to 1½" high) option for you if you want a manageable stylish height. You choose this heel if you suffer from chronic arch problems or heel spurs. Because of their thinness, they do take some getting used to. Until I mastered walking in them, my foot constantly turned inward. That is both dangerous and clumsy looking on an interview. If you like the height of a kitten heel, but feel too wobbly wearing that type of heel, a good alternative is the chunky heel (also 1" to 1½"). The chunky heel provides a look similar to the kitten heel with considerable steadiness, and a more traditional flair. A stacked heel (about 2" to 2¾") is a comfortable option for an interview in anything from a round, pointed, or square toe. This heel balances a molded leg. It elongates the body with professional diplomacy. A French heel (also 2" to

chunky heel

flat heel

stacked heel

kitten heel

stiletto heel

french heel

2 ¾") is a thinner, slightly curved heel that is also an acceptable option and balances a more slender leg.

Stiletto or spike heels (3" to 6") are ridiculously impractical and inappropriate for interviewing or business in general. How could you possibly be productive when you're walking around on stilts? Thick platform shoes are also inappropriate and carry a similar connotation of inefficiency. Even if you're interviewing for a "desk" job, you will be pegged as a Barbie or Bratz doll, so don't expect to be taken seriously.

Personal/Intimate Apparel: Undershirts, Briefs/Boxers, Socks, Brassieres, Shape Wear, Camisoles, Panties, Socks, and Hosiery

If you think your personal/intimate apparel is not visible to anyone but you, you are very much mistaken. Recruiters and the entire world can see when you are uncomfortable or falling out of your foundations. I cannot stress enough the importance of well-fitting undergarments made of breathable fibers. Cotton and silk are your best friends in this category.

Men

T-shirts provide you with the extra layer of protection you may need, especially when the sweat glands are gushing. Their short sleeves are particularly shielding during cold weather and can provide a barrier to avoid giving you embarrassing underarm spots. They have higher necklines that should never be seen peering out of your shirt collar.

"A" shirts are tank tops that are a cooler option and, in some cases, considered more slimming underneath a shirt. No matter how high the quality of your shirt, you should never skimp on an undershirt when dressing for an interview, even if you have a bare chest.

Boxers vs. briefs: It's your choice. Just be sure everything is kept in its place below your waistline.

Socks should be long enough to cover not only your ankles but the lower bottom half of your calf as well—enough so you don't show skin if you happen to cross your leg. Choose a color analogous to your trousers and shoes to give your leg continuity; contrast the color of your shoes and trousers if you have long legs. Patterns are acceptable and should ideally repeat a pattern found within the tie to better integrate the top and bottom halves of your body. For instance, if you are wearing a tie with a diamond-shape motif, then wearing socks in a subtle argyle pattern would be a smart pattern choice; a striped tie would work well with a vertical rib sock. Be sure to get rid of socks that have lost their elasticity because you will spend the entire interview pulling them up (not a pretty sight).

Women

Brassieres: I'm all for expressing femininity, but during an interview, anything frilly is not appropriate. In order to stay in the game, you need not be held back by your bosom. So in order to prevent back and front spillage, a form-fitting brassiere is exactly what you need. Granny-thick shoulder straps are not the answer, as a whopping 90 percent of the bra's support is gained from its waistband, as described in a popular article on bra violations (*New York Times,* July 25, 2005) by bra fitting expert Susan Nethero.[3] The right bra will favorably contour your body and improve your posture so that the clothing you've spent so much time choosing for the occasion fits well even when it's not custom tailored. A nude-color camisole with a touch of spandex worn over the bra is an awesome solution for those unexpected moments when things just decide to pop out of your shirt. The last thing you need is to be fussing with yourself when you should be focused on more important matters.

Shape wear that provides comfortable support around the bust, midriff, hips, and thighs will prevent buttons from popping open, seams from tearing, and pleats and vents from coming apart.

Panties come in all styles, ranging from hipster, high-cut briefs to boy pant, bikini, and thong. Again, don't have your protruding abdomen or jiggly derriere show through your clothes during an interview. While some women bark at my suggestion to wear a panty with fuller coverage because of the hideous panty lines that show through, given the lesser of two evils, I'd choose panty lines over the cottage-cheese look a thong never eliminates.

Hosiery possibilities are beyond endless, making it tempting to choose heavily textured tights and ornate fishnet patterns. Don't give in! Also, footless hosiery, even if nude and sheer, is in bad taste. Thigh-highs are a comfortable alternative for women with molded thighs, and knee-highs are to be used only with slacks. Many schools of thought argue that the color of women's hosiery should match the skirt's hemline or the color of her shoe. I'll keep it simple: Nude color is best for interviewing. The hosiery finish (sheer, semi-opaque, or opaque) should be determined by your region's climate, your leg's scale, and the fabric finish and textures of your apparel and shoes.

Last, here are two pieces of advice you should remember. First of all, even in warm climates, or if you have perfectly tanned legs, resist the temptation of going on an interview bare-legged. It's not only unprofessional; it is blatantly risqué. Second, no matter how expensive, always buy and bring an extra pair of pantyhose for insurance. It never fails—just when you are about to set foot inside the elevator, you look down and there is a huge run along the front of your pantyhose. It's better to be safe than sorry. Think back to your penny-wise and dollar-foolish rule of shopping (Chapter 3).

Outerwear: Coats, Raincoats, Capes, and Wraps

In regions where the climate gets frigid, it's impossible to get away with not wearing outerwear to an interview. Although your overcoat or raincoat will most likely be off and in a guest closet in the reception area, I still need to address certain specifications regarding these garments. A dressy overcoat made of natural fibers such as wool, cashmere, mohair, angora, or a combination of any of these is a staple in the smart interviewee's wardrobe. Be sure to wear your suit jacket underneath when trying on the coat you'll be wearing on the interview. A coat that is too tight around the shoulders and waist will surely wrinkle your suit and undo all the effort you've put into looking your best. You should be able to glide your arms through the sleeves while wearing your suit jacket, and the hem on the sleeve of your coat should be about a quarter to a half of an inch longer than your suit jacket.

Raincoats or trench coats are the most practical and versatile, so if you invest in only one piece of outerwear, choose this type. Trench coats are not only an obvious option when it is drizzling or pouring but also practical during cool days when a heavier coat would be cumbersome. Choose ones that have removable linings to give you added flexibility in breathable cottons or lightweight wool gabardines. You may also waterproof the fabric with a waterproofing solvent. Overcoats and raincoats for men and women should fall just below the knees, covering the length of the suit jacket, and for women, the length of the skirt.

Fur coats are beyond inappropriate for an interview. They are not only pretentious, but if the recruiter you are about to meet is an animal rights activist (e.g., a member of PETA), your chances of getting the job might be impacted. Fur-lined collars and cuffs are also uncool for interviewing. You're there to get the job, not stir up controversy. Women may also choose a cape or a wrap during mild weather when they just need that extra bit of coverage without a full coat. Be sure to treat capes and shawls as outerwear. They should be removed before you enter the interview, no matter how tempting it is to snuggle up in one. Remember that an interview is about being proactive.

Trims and Things

Trims such as decorative buttons, elaborate bows, zippers, ruffles, and flap pockets add visual interest that, in many cases, qualifies them as accessories. Women are especially prone to wearing suit jackets with enameled, metallic, and logo-embossed buttons. Those are equal to jewelry and should be counted as such. Flap pockets on a jacket add bulk to an ectomorphic body, while besom pockets create less attention.

Umbrellas are a functional accessory that can easily shift the tone of your interview garb. Be mindful of not choosing umbrellas with company logos or sayings that can stir up controversy.

Pocket squares or handkerchiefs may be worn inside your suit jacket's breast pocket. Embrace this accessory; it sets apart your flair. A simple white handkerchief is enough to fulfill your purpose. If a more ornate one is chosen, have it contrast with the color and pattern of your tie. If you match your kerchief with your tie, it will lessen the stylish impact you are trying achieve. How you tuck the kerchief into your breast pocket is up to you. There are hundreds of ways to fold a kerchief, including straight, puff, or corners-up style. There is no right or wrong way to insert a kerchief, so you are free to explore different styles, and stick to the one that makes you most comfortable. My only suggestion is to refrain from showing more than ¾" of fabric on an interview.

Human Groomin'
Flawless Finish

Cleanliness is indeed next to godliness. —*John Wesley (founder of the Methodist Church)*

THE CONDITION OF your teeth, hair, hands, nails, and skin can be used to forecast the meticulousness of your work ethic. After all, if you don't have the pride to present yourself at your absolute best, then how can you be expected to care about the aesthetics of your work?

Your genetic makeup determines the texture of your hair, but you have complete control of how to style and present it to the rest of the world. You are also responsible for not allowing it to grow like weeds in parts of your body where it will come across as offensive (e.g., top of ears, nose, brows, and lip).

So what keeps you from having well-groomed nails, smooth hands, and combed hair? Is it lack of time, money, or concern? Well, whatever your reason, it may be the thing that is holding you back from getting to the next level in your career. I know you all have busy lives and scheduling the time for a haircut is time-consuming, but if you don't wait so long to get a haircut, all you will need is a trim (which will take half the time). Grooming yourself regularly is not superfluous at all, especially if you incorporate it into your everyday regimen. Only then will grooming yourself become as natural as eating, because you do it every day, several times a day. Grooming is not about unnecessary pampering; it's about fine-tuning the mechanics of all of the pieces that make up the person you want to present on an interview. It's understood that you are intelligent, experienced, and perfectly capable of performing the duties of a particular job—and so is everyone else. However, no one else is you. No one has your exact skin, your exact coloring, or your exact anything. Why not optimize what you're made of in order to feel better about yourself and, in the process, gain the competitive edge that propels your career to the next level?

Skin Care

Your skin's appearance portrays an unedited version of your lifestyle. If you've smoked since you were a teenager, 30 years later, your skin may look so dehydrated and tired that it can be assumed that you lack prolonged stamina. If you party hard every weekend and you've shown up to two of your Monday morning interviews with your "after-party face," your skin may divulge a sense of irresponsibility and unreliability. Skin that has been abused and excessively exposed to either natural sun or salon tanning methods is surely at risk of developing premature lines and wrinkles. Environmental pollutants and contaminations are also to blame for lifeless and dehydrated skin, making it your responsibility to combat these early threats by taking on preventative measures.

Stress, lack of sleep, and hormonal changes will also contribute to your skin's daily challenges, so it's up to you to bring your skin one step closer to looking like it belongs to a healthy, viable candidate. It's not about unrealistically striving to look 20 years younger. It's about maintaining skin that looks healthy, lustrous, and hydrated. Many candidates fear being rejected for a job because of age discrimination (which is illegal; see Chapter 19).

But let's not kid ourselves into thinking that just because it is illegal, it doesn't happen. Yet nothing is more indicative of your age than your skin.

The following are some helpful steps for developing an action plan toward achieving skin that is clean, bright, hydrated, smooth, and protected. It's true that sometimes your skin possesses a mind of its own because of hormonal imbalances and the like; therefore, you may need to change things up a bit to accommodate such inconsistencies. Here is a regular regimen to be followed assuming there are no chronic skin diseases that should be addressed with the help of a board-certified dermatologist, who can be accessed through the American Academy of Dermatology Association:

▪ **Cleanse:** Washing away impurities in your skin will leave you with a fresh canvas. Choose a gentle, nonstripping cleanser regardless of your skin type. If you have oily skin, don't fall prey to a strong, abrasive cleanser that will deplete your skin of its natural oils. I'm partial to wash-off cleansers instead of the tissue-off type because I like to replenish my face with water. Toners then become a redundant product. In addition, toners and astringents may contain alcohol will contribute to drying your skin rather than balancing it. Women should invest in an eye makeup remover strong enough to remove eye shadow, eyeliner, and mascara, yet gentle enough not to irritate the eye area.

▪ **Brighten:** Dull, uneven skin may be due to lack of exfoliation. Men inadvertently exfoliate on a daily basis through shaving. However, the majority of you disregard evening out the top layer of your skin's texture by exfoliating it with either a manual granular scrub or a chemical brightener that contains alpha hydroxy acids (AHAs). By not exfoliating, you create a barrier that prevents skin from gaining active restoration. Products that contain AHAs help skin renewal with the presence of natural acids. Be careful not to layer on too many products that contain AHAs, as you don't want to overload.

▪ **Hydrate:** Quench your skin's thirst with lots of H_2O (at least eight glasses a day; see Chapter 8). Water is what our bodies are predominantly made of, and because our bodies don't have the ability to store water the same way we retain fat (too bad), it is our responsibility to replenish our skin by drinking lots of water. Do whatever it takes to make yourself drink the water: Flavor it with lemon or orange slices if you have to, but just make sure to drink some.

Keep your environment well hydrated by using a humidifier and infuse your skin with moisture with Evian mineral spray. Keep 1.7-ounce spray cans everywhere: home, office, car, handbags, briefcases, and so on. (I can't seem to stock enough of the spray. It's not that it's necessarily a product with an earth-shattering ingredient—it's really just water—but there's something about the convenience of the small can and the way the water evenly spritzes your face that makes you feel like you took an instant shower.) Topical moisturizers applied generously over your face and neck, under the eye, and on the lips and body also replenish your skin's natural glow and prevent it from cracking, itching, and blotching during an interview.

Everyone should aim to have great skin—men and women alike. Restore the appearance of your skin through proper hydration and plenty of rest and you will remain "fresh as a cucumber" even on your worst day of interviewing.

■ **Smoothen:** Clay masks and soothing masks are important for improving and redefining the texture of your skin. Clay masks used to deep-clean pores primarily help the appearance of oily skin types, while soothing masks are particularly relaxing and calming for dry skin types. Women may access pore-minimizing primers that fill in enlarged pores to create a silkier skin surface in preparation for makeup application. Beware of overpriced, well-marketed products that promise to smoothen and firm lines and wrinkles, making you appear decades younger. Many of those products involve gimmicks, so be careful not to fall prey to their bogus promises.

■ **Protect:** Lather up with sun protection using a minimum of SPF 15 on your face. Leathery, sun-damaged skin is not only unattractive but it also unveils an unhealthy mystery about you. Potential employers will wonder how they'll be able to keep you in the office on sunny days. At the first sign of a sunny day, they think, you will be out of the office catching some rays. This is an instant strike against you. Protect your skin to maintain a healthy external appearance in addition to saving your image of being a sun worshiper.

Makeup Application

Makeup should be kept simple and professional. Applying makeup for a job interview is about maintaining a certain level of transparency to show that you are not hiding the truth about yourself behind a mask. Eye shadow, blush, and lipstick should not have a frosted or iridescent finish, as they will make you look like you're going on a date instead of an interview. A note about makeup protocol is also in order right about now: Under no circumstances should you whip out a tube of lipstick, lip gloss, lip liner, or the like for the purpose of applying or refreshing during an interview, professional networking event, business dinner, and so on. This is poor business etiquette.

▪ **Camouflage:** Choosing the right concealer and foundation combination is the first step toward camouflaging excessive skin patterning (dark circles and other "imperfections" that may affect your self-confidence during an interview).

– *Concealers* are meant to be gently patted throughout your undereye area and should be slightly lighter in value than your natural skin color. Choose a creamy consistency to ensure that you don't wind up with dry, cracked ridges encrusted within the fine lines around your eye area. Choose lighter consistencies if you prefer lighter coverage and/or have oilier skin. Liquid, cream, mousse, and powder-to-cream foundation colors should match the color of your skin exactly. Ignore this guideline and you will end up with a dreadful demarcation along your jawline. Otherwise, you'll need to apply foundation on your neck, chest, hands, and so on just to look uniform. Where does it end? That's why finding the right color to match your skin and applying it evenly throughout your entire face (excluding your eye area) will create a flawless canvas for the rest of the products that will highlight and contour your facial features.

– *Loose powder* or *compact powder* is the finishing touch that seals the foundation. Be sure to choose one that is transparent. Powder is not meant to alter the color of your skin, so be careful not to choose one that will make you look like a powdered donut.

▪ **Eye shadows, blushes,** and **lipsticks** used to create the ideal interview face should be selected with the following in mind:

– Cream consistencies glide well on lines and wrinkles and provide maximum coverage.

– Liquid consistencies glide well and provide medium to sheer coverage.

– Powder consistencies cling to lines and accentuate wrinkles.

– Iridescent and glossy finishes highlight lines and imperfections and have sheer coverage.

– Matte finishes camouflage oily skin and provide maximum coverage.

– Translucent finishes have clear coverage.

– Colors should not be matched to your outfit; they should be harmonious with the color of your skin, hair, and eyes (see Chapter 2).

– Cool, light, and bright colors highlight.

– Warm, dark, and muted colors contour.

▪ **Accentuate:** Take a moment to examine your face. What is the feature you should accentuate for the purpose of interviewing? I hope you've chosen your eyes because that's where you'll want to direct attention during business. Refrain from doing so by applying harsh liquid eyeliner and gobs of lengthening mascara. By the way, exaggerated cat eyes and mascara applied to your bottom lashes are also not appropriate for interviewing. Instead, choose an eye shadow palette that suits your natural coloring and season (see Chapter 2). Apply mascara to your top lashes, with an extra little emphasis on your outer lashes, to give your eyes a slight upward tilt that makes them look cheerful and attentive. Eyeliner should be used to fill in missing eyelashes rather than to create a smoky effect or a harshly defined line. Find exactly where to apply your blush by smiling; highlight the "apples" of your cheeks and accentuate the "hollow" area located directly underneath the fleshy part of each cheek.

▪ **Balance:** One of the great advantages of wearing makeup is that it can magically balance facial characteristics that may be in disproportion with the rest of your face and make you feel uncomfortable during face-to-face situations like interviewing. Here, you will find easy application modifications to balance your features:

– *Eyes too close:* Apply eye shadow that is a darker value to the outer corners of your eyes and apply lighter-value eye shadow on the inner corners.

– *Eyes too far apart:* Apply eye shadow that is a darker value to the inner corners of your eyes and apply lighter-value eye shadow on the outer corners of your eyes.

– *Protruding eyelids:* These eyelids show a lot more surface than the "standard" eye and may sometimes appear to be bulging out. Use a darker-value shadow across your entire lid and use lighter colors moving toward the brow bone. In addition, slightly thicker eyeliner applied to the upper lid would also balance this eye; go light on the mascara.

– *Deep-set eyes:* Lighter-value eye shadows will help these eyes project. Eyeliner will only outline the depth of the eye, so use mascara as a way to add dimension.

– *Prominent foreheads:* Sweep your blush brush along your entire hairline in order to bring the contour forward. Use dark, matte colors to minimize this type of forehead.

– *Narrow foreheads:* As with triangular and diamond-shaped faces, extend the sides of the forehead by using a blush or bronzer one or two values lighter than the one used on your cheeks.

– *Narrow chins:* Apply a blush or bronzer one or two values lighter than the one you use on your cheeks around your jawline to create an illusion of a more balanced chin.

– *Wide nose:* Apply blush or bronzer one or two shades higher in value than that applied on your cheeks around and under the nostrils.

– *Flat nose:* Apply blush or bronzer one or two shades higher in value than that applied on your cheeks down the bridge of your nose to create the illusion of cartilage.

– *Thin lips:* Use a lip liner to create definition around the lips and apply it just (and I mean *just*) above the natural lip line. Choose high-intensity lipsticks and pair them with clear gloss that will give the lips just a bit more shine (avoid goopy-looking ones). The added shine will give your lips an expanded illusion.

– *Plump lips:* Apply lip liner to the inner part of your natural lip line. Choose sheer lipstick colors that are matte in texture. Avoid wearing additional gloss.

Hairstyles

What to do with your hair on an interview? Shall I wear it up, down? Should I get a haircut? Oh, how I wish more candidates would be agreeable to getting a haircut. I never realized what a security blanket hair can be for some people. Your hair's texture, together with your face shape, should dictate how your hair should be styled to make you look and feel confident. Keep your height in mind. Long hair will make you appear shorter than hair that is short in length. If you are 5'5" or shorter, you should consider hair that is no longer than shoulder length. Also, long necks can carry longer hair, while short necks benefit from shorter hairstyles.

From an interviewing perspective, you should keep in mind that long hair that is left untied can tempt you to toss and twirl it during an interview. Consider tying your hair back if you're dead set against cutting the length to ensure your face and, most important, your eyes are fully visible during your interview. There's nothing more annoying than interviewing someone who has only one eye showing because of a hair style that covers the other eye. If you're someone who prefers bangs, realize that the horizontal line they create will cut the length of your face aesthetically. For practical interview purposes, bangs should be cut in a manner that doesn't hide your eyes. Faces with unbalanced features look best with off-center parts or asymmetrical hairstyles that don't hide the face. Men with receding hairlines or baldness should keep the remaining strands of hair short rather than long and stringy. Regardless of gender or face shape, hair should be freshly trimmed and rid of split ends, knots, or long-overdue-to-be-dyed roots.

Here are more specific suggestions based on face shapes:

- **Oval face:** Since oval faces are the most balanced, you are fortunate to be able to sport your hair in a variety of styles. Length can be short (men and women), midlength, or long; hair can be curly or straight. You can also pull it back or wear it loose, and you are able to part down the middle or to either side. Bangs can be kept long, cut straight across, or cut asymmetrically.

- **Round face:** A round face can use hairstyling techniques that elongate it. You can use some height at the crown of your head. Choose a style that is tapered at the sides and has body or curls at the top. Parting your hair down the middle will reinforce its roundness. Instead, opt for parting your hair to one side. Bangs and a Caesar or buzz cuts for men also emphasize the circular curves of the face's silhouette. The sharp lines of a blunt-cut "bob" on a woman will detract from the circular forehead, cheeks, and chin.

- **Square face:** For men, the best hairstyles are ones that elongate the crown of the head to camouflage the boxy-ness of the shape. Men can also choose a hairstyle that softens the temples. Women have the option of softening the squareness of the forehead with side-swept layered bangs or layers around the jawline to soften the sharp edges of the jaw. Hair should not be severely brushed or gelled back for either gender, as it only reiterates that the forehead, jawline, and cheeks are the same width. Curls will soften the edges found on the corners of the forehead and jaw.

▪ **Oblong face:** Bangs are the perfect way to balance the high, prominent forehead of this face. Either gender can use fullness on the sides rather than at the top of the head to detract the eye from the longness of the face. Women with this face shape can carry longer hair that frames the face. Parting hair down the middle is another method of shortening this face's length.

▪ **Triangular face:** The narrow foreheads of this face need to be left uncovered—no bangs here. The objective should be to add width throughout the crown and temples to balance the wide jawline. Curly hair will soften the wide, angular jawline.

▪ **Inverted-triangle face:** In order to balance the narrow, pointed chin, hair should be kept short around the crown and cheeks for men. Women too can opt for cropped hairstyles or simply add volume below the cheeks to balance the width of the forehead.

▪ **Diamond face:** Keep hair close or cropped at the crown with added volume around the temples. You may also want to add volume around the jawline to extend its width.

Facial and Body Hair (Women)

Facial hair on women can look truly unattractive, particularly when it's dark and coarse in texture. I can really sympathize with you here, as I've spent thousands of dollars throughout the years trying to get rid of facial hair. After years of waxing, threading, and plucking, it was electrolysis that finally zapped those unwanted roots. This is especially problematic for my fellow Latina, African American, and Caribbean "sisters." What can I tell you? We're blessed with beautiful skin but we're hairy beasts! I'm not referring to light peach fuzz; I'm talking about dark, thick, prickly types.

Those are the kind that, if left untreated, will put you in the category of either "She doesn't have eyes to see the dark whiskers" or "She doesn't care enough about herself to have them removed." The first category implies lack of attention to detail, and the second implies a sense of aloofness; neither one is a positive connotation when looking for a job.

Using a magnifying mirror to check areas of the upper lip, chin, neck, sideburns, and brows can give you a better perspective. Then wax, tweeze, thread, laser, or zap (through electrolysis) the heck out of those unwanted follicles. If you plan on wearing a skirt, consider shaving your legs. (Wesleyan girlfriends may balk at hearing such advice, as it is against their feminist mantra, though I couldn't help but notice during our last alumni reunion that most of you had succumbed to my ways—and you looked great!) I'll leave underarm hair to your discretion. Just think about the impact it will make on your hygiene.

The significance of well-groomed eyebrows should not be overlooked, as they frame the expression of your eyes. I'd sooner go without a stitch of makeup if I were short on time than have eyebrows that weren't perfectly brushed, trimmed, and filled in. Be cautious about shaping eyebrows into pencil-thin lines; it will make the rest of your features appear as if they are floating around your face without a barrier. Thick, straight, bushy eyebrows will not only make you look like Groucho Marx, but they will also give you a severe and angry grimace. Well-groomed eyebrows can be achieved through the following:

- **Daily care:** This is the best way to find those eyebrows that are long, wiry, and unruly. When they pop out, trim them with manicure scissors. Investing in good quality tweezers with a slanted tip and a magnified mirror and using the tweezers near a window with lots of natural light are key for routine maintenance.

- **Cleanup:** Follow the natural line of the brow and remove the area above the bridge of your nose and under your brow arch. If you can see fine hair on the top of your brow, remove it just for the purposes of cleaning up, not for shaping.

■ **Shaping up:** Sculpting and shaping should be performed from the bottom portion along your natural arch. Contouring your brows from the top will make you look weepy, wilted, and tired. Overplucking eyebrows from the bottom will leave you with an expression of permanent surprise.

■ **Filling in:** Overzealous plucking will result in having missing patches of hair along your eyebrows. Fill in those areas with an eyebrow pencil (using short strokes, not a line) and then soften and set using an angled brush and brow powder similar in hue to the pencil. Extend short eyebrows so that they cover the length of the eye.

■ **Balance:** Eyebrows should balance your face shape and facial particulars. As such, the horizontal lines of straight eyebrows shorten a long face, while the arches of ones that are curved lengthen the face.

Facial and Body Hair (Men)

While men are expected to have more facial and body hair because of their higher levels of progesterone, it is best to keep any exposed locks neatly trimmed for an interview. Isolated strands at the nape of the neck and in and around ears, eyebrows, and nostrils show signs of a sloppy disposition. Electric trimmers take just a few minutes to remove unwarranted hair. As for eyebrows, they should be brushed and naturally groomed, without any exaggerated arches or defined tails. A clean-shaven man looks the most groomed. Nonetheless, well-groomed mustaches, beards, and sideburns are also acceptable. Like women's makeup, if worn correctly, mustaches, beards, or sideburns can independently or collaboratively balance your face shape and complement your individual facial characteristics. One thing I don't advocate is a five o'clock shadow. It's a dingy, messy, "neither here nor there" look that serves no purpose.

Here are some balancing tricks for those of you who choose to harmonize your face and features through facial hair:

■ **Mustache:** A well-groomed mustache can work wonders to widen a small, narrow mouth or shorten the space between the bottom of your nose and lips. It can also aid in balancing a pronounced nose, elongating a round or square face, and shortening an oblong one. If you have a receding or lost hairline, you may choose a mustache as a creative method of camouflaging baldness. Thick, handlebar, and paintbrush mustaches should be avoided, even if they are tempting camouflage for large, bubble lips.

- **Sideburns:** Sideburns derive from facial hair, not scalp hair, for those of you who think otherwise. Worn longer, they will balance the length of an oblong face and the narrowness of a diamond or an inverted triangle's chin. Longer sideburns will also strengthen a chin that is disproportionately small, whereas thicker ones camouflage rounder faces or ample cheeks. As usual, oval faces look balanced with sideburns of varying lengths and widths. Bushy sideburns look completely inappropriate in an overly conservative environment, even if the goal is to widen a narrow face.

- **Beards:** Today, beards are more popular than mustaches. Goatees worn without integrating a mustache or sideburns are a favorite, though they will highly emphasize the pointed chin of a diamond or inverted triangle face. They also project evilness to your character that is not favorable when looking to establish trust on an interview. A small patch of hair sculpted directly under your lower lip looks like you either forgot to wipe some dirt off your face or you're looking for a job as a bouncer or bodyguard. A well-groomed door knocker beard,[1] which connects the mustache to the beard, forming a circle, is an acceptable option for camouflaging a double chin or weak chin, in addition to extending a round face. A full beard that connects your mustache and sideburns or a long beard is not often approved of on a conservative job interview. Otherwise, it does camouflage a triangular face's wide jaw and is a great shield against cold, windy weather.

Hands and Fingernails

Monitor the condition of your hands and fingernails. When you are interviewed, your hands and nails are second to your face as the most visible parts of your body. Before you even sit down, the only point of physical contact when you meet your interviewer is the handshake. Dry, scaly hands are a sign of negligence. Regardless of your gender, nails should be manicured. This means that messy hangnails should be clipped. Cuticles should be pushed back, with all 10 nails approximately even in length. All ridges can be smoothened by buffing and filing into a shape that follows your nails' natural shape.

Nail polish is optional for women, but if you do choose to wear it, keep it the least distracting color you can: Keep the color clear or light in value without frost. Dark values show every little chip, so if you don't have time to manicure your nails right before the interview, you will look careless with "chippy" nails. Ornate designs, or even simple ones for that matter, with glue-on stones and beads are not meant for the workplace and especially not the interview. Reserve your budget for upgrading your interview wardrobe rather than for heavily decorated talons.

Tattoos

Blame it on my Bronx upbringing, but if you point out that you have a cute tattoo on the outside of your ankle, I will tell you that "cute" and "tattoo" don't belong in the same sentence. Countless times, candidates have tried to justify tattoos as creative marks of self-expression. Where I come from, people with tattoos were not to be messed with. After all, if you willingly put yourself in the position of withstanding unwarranted pain (no matter what the degree), you must want to portray an image of being a real tough guy or gal. Employers want to hire candidates who will not be controversial or difficult to manage. Tattoos don't exactly send a ringing endorsement about you in this department. So if you're contemplating getting one, be mindful of how it can impact your odds of getting a job. If you absolutely must get one or a collage of tattoos, choose a discreet part of your body that can be easily hidden during an interview.

The subject of tattoos also applies to tattooed eyebrows, eyeliner, and lip liner. Consider their permanency in making your expression appear rigid and harsh. Whenever possible, strategically camouflaging tattoos through your attire or accessory choices is a good way to discreetly handle this potentially job-hindering obstacle. Specialized tattoo-concealing kits and skin peels performed by doctors are other options for hiding your inked skin. Often, attempts to camouflage tattoos are unsuccessful, in which case you just have to live with your decision and accept the consequences graciously.

Fragrance-Free Interviewing

Really, don't chance being the interview candidate who triggers a huge migraine, allergy, or asthma attack. You'll surely be remembered—though not in a good way. It's just one of those thoughtless actions that I am particularly sensitive to, resulting in extreme migraines, allergies, and other distorting symptoms that put an end to my workday. It's not as if I don't enjoy wearing my own fragrance. I just don't need your overpowering one layered on top of mine.

To be on the safe side, significantly reduce or completely lay off fragrance altogether, as you never know whom you'll offend or make sick. Strong fragrances will linger long after you're gone and are not a pleasant memento to leave behind. Remember, fragrances are not only found in perfumes and colognes; you should also be mindful of powerful scents in hairsprays, body gels, soaps, lotions, shaving creams, aftershave balms, and deodorants. So think of the effects before piling on too many fragranced products while grooming yourself for the interview.

Cosmetic Dentistry

Don't put yourself in a situation where you are afraid to show an open-mouth smile during your interview because of an overbite, underbite, or crooked, missing, or stained teeth. Consider your teeth your inborn strand of pearls. Treat them as a precious commodity. Visit your dentist's office for custom bleach plates or lasering to restore the whiteness of your teeth if you feel self-conscious about your smile. If such procedures are out of your budget, try rinsing with a hydrogen peroxide mixture for several consecutive days to see a noticeable difference in brightness. Consider visiting an orthodontist who can advise you on the types of understated braces options available. An oral surgeon can replace your gap-toothed smile with an implant that fits in beautifully with the rest of your teeth.

Dental enhancements are expensive and time-consuming, but you should think of them as lifetime investments that aesthetically augment your appearance and pragmatically impact the quality of your articulation (see Chapter 18). Find qualified professionals in your area through the American Dental Association (www.ada.org), the American Association of Oral and Maxillofacial Surgeons (www.aaoms.org), and the American Association of Orthodontists (www.braces.org).

Wardrobe and Shoe Grooming

Whether the suit, shirt, or shoes you are wearing are brand new or not, if you take care of your investments, your efforts will be rewarded with an appearance that is notches above plain old acceptable. It's really such a shame when a candidate takes the time to get dressed for an interview only to have a wrinkled shirt or scuffed shoes. Exercise one or all of my top maintenance tips for your interview apparel, accessories, and shoes to stay in tip-top shape for one or twenty interviews later:

▪ Use sturdy cedar hangers for hanging your interview suit and shirt in your closet. Be socially responsible and take wire hangers back to the dry cleaners for reuse. Using sturdy hangers will help garments retain their shape when they are not on your body.

▪ Avoid sandwiching your interview clothes so close to one another when storing. Hang your interview attire in an area of your closet that allows the fabric to breathe. Doing this will help minimize wrinkling while it's not in use.

▪ Invest in a tie rack, which may also be used for storing scarves and/or belts.

▪ Steam wrinkles off garments whenever possible. A hot iron presses the fibers down, thereby imposing on their natural beauty. Wear garments free of poorly ironed creases around shirt collars and cuffs.

▪ Check for loose or missing buttons and loose fabric thread on your suit jacket, trousers, skirts, shirts, ties, and scarves. Do not wear garments that need obvious repairs. You will not only look sloppy, but in the case of missing buttons, you will risk showing a lot more than your résumé. Carry a mini sewing kit as long as you know how to use it.

▪ Make sure your suit, shirt, and tie (men) or scarf (women) are free of stains (oil, food, ink, and the like). Choose organic dry cleaners that use natural cleaning solutions for your natural fibers. Remove garments from dry-cleaning plastic as soon as you get home as another means of letting the fabric breathe. Carry a spot-removing pen for spur-of-the-moment spots that happen seconds before your interview.

▪ Be sure to wear shoes that are free of scuffs and marks. This is an area where men are less guilty than women, as men get shoeshines as often as women get manicures. Ensure that your shoes are clean and rid of chewed-up soles and heels. Replace laces as needed, and waterproof shoes to prevent them from being ruined in the rain.

▪ Keep shoe trees inside your shoes to stop the tips from curling up and looking like a circus clown's shoes.

▪ Make sure socks, hosiery, and underwear are not thrown in a dryer, as the elastic will fall apart, causing you to lose support under your fine-tailored, well-cared-for clothing.

▪ Always carry a lint brush to get rid of the visible fuzzies or hair (yours or your pet's).

Low-Rise Hygiene
B.O., V.O., and Other Delicate Acronyms

Man does not live by soap alone; and even hygiene, or even health, is not much good unless you can take a healthy view of it—or, better still, feel a healthy indifference to it.
—Gilbert K. Chesterton (English writer and critic)

YOU MAY CONSIDER it awkward to discuss, but hygiene is nothing to keep under wraps. When it comes to interviewing, it is the impediment you'll never know as being the actual cause behind losing out on a job. Potential employers need not get into the situation of addressing the problem once you're on their payroll. So at the slightest stale whiff, the easiest thing for them to do is to nip your candidacy right in the bud. Leave it to me to be the one to break it to you.

I promise my intentions are sincere. I've just been held captive behind closed doors without so much as an open window to rescue me from offensive body odors, bad breath, and other foul stenches far too many times to keep it a taboo subject any longer. Hey, I understand; we're all human and we're not perfect, right? Well, due to negligence or ignorance, some people seem to forget that good hygiene is appreciated by all who are near (and sometimes far), especially those of us who interview candidates in an enclosed room. I assure you, it's really quite straightforward. All it takes is getting into the ritual of abolishing bacteria through a simple concept—cleansing. Miraculously, all sorts of opportunities will appear at your feet . . . so be sure to keep them spanking fresh.

Body Odor, Known as B.O.

It all makes perfect sense: As your body temperature rises, your sweat glands come to the rescue by secreting fluid, known as perspiration, to cool you down. It's our built-in sprinkler system. But don't blame perspiration for not smelling fresh, because the clear secretion produced by our glands is actually odorless.[1] It's only when the bacteria found in our skin and hair takes over the secretion that odor is emitted. I often wonder how people can endure being trapped within their own wretched scent, but, like everything else, it takes awareness to engage in a proactive solution. Taking a preventive approach is a safe route, as you never know where or when odors will kick in. Here are some helpful reminders that can dramatically improve your grooming scorecard:

- **Body odor:** The first time I heard someone say it was "bath day" I almost fainted. What do you mean "bath day"? I've never known life as anything but bath day being every day. A bath invigorates you in the morning and relaxes you at night. It's not as if I'm advocating for you to go through the "trouble" of bathing twice a day, but I do urge you to consider doing so on the morning of your interview.

Bathing on a daily basis with an antibacterial soap and really scouring the areas that matter most—your scalp, neck, underarms, groin, feet, toes, and just about every place where there is a crease or skin fold where bacteria can linger—is highly recommended. Finish off by drying yourself well in order to avoid trapping moisture, which will quickly intermingle with bacteria to cause "smelly syndrome." Don't forget to dry your belly button and in between your tootsies. While you're at it, trim and shave body hair that will only serve as a haven for bacteria and perspiration to convene. Wear freshly laundered and/or dry-cleaned garments made of natural fibers that allow your body to breathe. What's more, explicitly tight clothing not only looks inappropriate, but it also impairs your body's ability to obtain air, therefore causing it to perspire.

Trust me on this one—how you smell is a big part of how you're perceived. You are not fooling anyone by masking it with perfume or cologne. It only disguises the smell, which ends up being a pungent and strange concoction of B.O.

■ **Vaginal odor (V.O.):** For women, vaginal odors are most challenging to keep in check, as it is an area that is continually secreting fluid. Menstrual odor due to excessive bleeding and other toxic smells derived from yeast infections or constipation need immediate attention. Vaginal odors need more focused and frequent attention. As annoying as it can be, this may require changing all sanitary dressings as often as every half hour depending on rate of flow. Carry an extra pair of underwear and flushable wipes for quick, easy changes on the go. As uncomfortable and troublesome as it is to interview while menstruating or dealing with other female-related hygiene issues, you must not let it stop you from challenging your male competition.

■ **Underarms:** Roll it, pump it, or spray it! The choice is yours. Should you go for deodorant or antiperspirant? Deodorants control the growth of bacteria on the skin and contain certain types of fragrances that defuse the armpit stench; antiperspirants diminish the total sweat released.[2] If you find that there isn't an over-the-counter product that can save you, try some of my favorite remedies. One remedy entails mixing a few teaspoons of lemon juice, witch hazel, or alcohol along with baking soda or cornstarch. Keep the consistency powdery so it can effectively absorb the moisture under your arms. I've also found that using peppermint soaps makes a considerable difference in having a fresh feeling and invigorated underarms. Disposable underarm shields add yet another barrier of protection. Change them regularly to keep moisture from building up, which ultimately increases smells.

Dandruff

Dandruff is aesthetically embarrassing as well as an uncomfortable toxic condition, and high-stress situations, such as interviewing, can aggravate it even more. Poor food choices, lack of sleep, bowel dysfunction, and excessive use of hair products may also be responsible for aggravating dandruff. Unfortunately, certain dandruff shampoos can further dry the scalp, though a clean scalp is a good first step to dislodging the dead cells. Maintaining a balanced diet and choosing high-fiber foods that help cleanse your system (see Chapter 8) is a healthy solution. Try home remedies, such as adding cider vinegar to your shampoo regimen for cell removal or massaging mineral oil onto the scalp before shampooing to help restore moisture. Brushing the scalp regularly also helps stimulate it and removes the flakes. It's a combination of shampooing, conditioning, and eating right that can alleviate this ever-frustrating challenge.

Halitosis, aka Bad Breath (Oral Hygiene)

You speak—I faint! You rushed out of your office to see me without eating a thing, and I smell your empty stomach from the moment you greet me. You smoked a cigarette on the way to my office to calm your nerves and the nicotine smell lingers on your breath. Worse yet, you had a moment to gulp down a broccoli-and-cheese-stuffed baked potato before seeing me, and I not only smell it on your breath but I have the visual to support it. You may even be getting over a cold or sinus infection and the "sick breath" is still persistent. For all of the previously mentioned reasons, in addition to poor oral hygiene (e.g., not flossing, brushing, and rinsing, or playing hooky from seeing a dentist), you could be cursed with bad breath and rotten teeth. Such negligence is sure to keep potential employers more than an arm's length away from you.

Floss and brush after every meal. Examine food choices that may be the cause of gastric issues that permeate through your breath. Gum or measly little breath mints are only temporary fixes in masking odor because they don't remove the particles of food that are often the cause of bad breath. A tasty and practical solution if you are rushing between interviews is to pack an apple or pear for the road. Both act as natural flossing agents and dislodge particles of food from your teeth. Gum chewing is not an acceptable solution during an interview. The last thing you want is to project yourself as a gum-cracking slouch.

Eye Crud

Call them "yuckies," "sleepies," "slimies," "eye gunk," or "goop." Sometimes they're soft and milky or sticky and yellowish-green. Other times, they are grainy deposits at the corners of your eyes. One thing's for sure, no matter what their color or consistency, they are a turnoff to the interviewer who has to endure looking at them. Rinse out your eyes with tepid water or with a refreshing eyewash. Eye drops will also help clear your eyes. Inspect your eyes using a small hand mirror right before an interview to make sure all debris is removed. Refrain from playing with your eyes and removing particles in front of your interviewer. While excusing yourself will interrupt the flow of the interview, it beats the distraction of you playing with your eyes to fish the crud out. If you must remove something from your eye during the interview, be considerate and use your left hand so that your handshake hand remains free of bacteria.

Cerumen, aka Earwax

This is a tricky one since I still remember my own pediatrician telling me not to ever put anything in my ear to clean the wax. The wax acts as a repellent against debris so it needs to stay in your ear in order to do its job. I don't want to be held responsible for any perforated ear drums, but I will say one thing, at least remove visible earwax buildup that sits outside of your ear with a wet washcloth, especially if your hairstyle exposes your ears.

Mucus

Consider your nose your very own vacuum cleaner. It sucks up environmental gunk, with the tiny hairs inside acting as brushes that sweep everything up. Once the particles dry up inside your nose, they suddenly become a recreational toy for many candidates. It's an involuntary act, but it is nonetheless disgusting to pick your nose in public—much more so during an interview—but people do it. Saline drops or sprays will dampen these hardened waste particles. However, if you're sensitive to the additives in the saline solutions, warm water is sure to loosen those suckers up. Bring tissues and graciously excuse yourself while you empty out your schnozz. Use your left hand so that your right hand is clean for handshaking.

Clean Hands

Keep hands as clean as you possibly can. I'm talking about removing not just germs but food and aftershave smells as well. As much as you may like the scent of your grooming products, recruiters may not necessarily want to walk around the whole day with a hand that reeks of it. I live for hand sanitizer. Call me a germophobe, but with as many hands as I shake in one day (not knowing if you've taken the necessary precaution to keep your hands clean), I need all of the protection I can get. Hand sanitizers shouldn't replace a nice scrubbing, but they beat not cleaning at all. My infant's baby nurse shared a special tip with my eight-year-old daughter to ensure she thoroughly cleaned her hands: She had her sing two verses of the "Happy Birthday" song before it was time to stop scrubbing.

Gassiness

Gas has got to come out somehow, but belching and passing of intestinal gases are best kept outside of the interview room. Still, involuntary functions do happen, and an occasional burp or the like may slip out of your mouth and other places. Bacteria that reside in your intestines, precisely the colon, bring on flatulence.[3] Add fiber to your diet to avoid bowel dysfunction but don't load up with fiber-rich food, such as legumes, brussel sprouts, and cauliflower, as your stomach may not be able to handle it (see Chapter 8). Relieve yourself before going on the interview just to be on the safe side. If you still feel like you will "erupt" during your interview, asking for a moment to use the restroom is better than killing the recruiter with your gas. Practice consuming smaller meals that are eaten more frequently and avoid eating quickly, even if you are late for an interview.

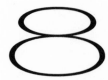

Food for Thought
Eating Well to Endure
the Interview Marathon

To eat is a necessity, but to eat intelligently is an art. —*François de La Rochefoucauld* *(French author)*

EMBRACING THE mentally and physically demanding task of interviewing for a job can seem like competing in an Ironman competition. Juggling every-day professional and personal responsibilities around interviews is exhausting and draining. Your objective is to get through the process and find employment. Caught in this frenzy, you can often forget about fuel-ing your body and mind through healthy eating choices and moderate to vigorous physical activity, causing you to wind up even more tired and stressed. As important as it is for you to reach your objectives, it is equally vital to maintain yourself in order to complete the interviewing process and carry out the duties and responsibilities you'll be assigned once you do land a job. As an added bonus, you will radiate confidence and fortitude.

I know, there are times when you may feel like all of the odds are against you and you just don't have the strength or the time to think about what you're eating. This is precisely when nourishing yourself well will help you battle feelings of defeat. Like many busy people these days, you may wake up in the morning and find you're not really hungry, so a cup of coffee becomes your "complete" breakfast. You arrive at your interview on an empty stomach and when I engage you in conversation, the growling noises of your stomach compete to answer on your behalf. In the midst of gastric rumbles, you hold your stomach with embarrassment and try to gain composure. It's too late; your concentration is broken and your only salvation is the glass of water I've offered you just before we settled down to talk. You've gotten yourself off to a shaky start, during a time when all of your resources should be used to your advantage.

Ignoring the need to replenish yourself properly is a colossal mistake, one you should by no means replicate given the abundance of choices. Read on and take note of smart and healthy consumption choices bound to physically and emotionally stimulate you enough so you can sail through the gateways of gainful employment.

A Rainbow of Possibilities

The Center for Nutrition Policy and Promotion, a U.S. Department of Agriculture organization formed to endorse dietary knowledge, uses the MyPyramid Food Guidance System (www.mypyramid.gov) to classify the five food groups, as well as oils, discretionary calories (leisure foods), and physical activity. Through this system, colors are designated to each food group, encouraging you to "eat from the rainbow."

- Orange → Grains

- Green → Vegetables

- Red → Fruits

- Yellow → Oils

- Blue → Milk

- Purple → Meat and Beans

The recommended daily intake of each depends on your age, gender, and level of physical activity, and I encourage you to find a qualified nutritionist through the American Dietetic Association (www.eatright.org) if you need assistance with customizing a diet that focuses on weight loss and general health. For the purpose of this chapter, I write about general recommendations for the specific purpose of improving your interviewing stamina. Therefore, the following information is not intended to constitute an authoritative statement under Food and Drug Administration rules and regulations.

You're Not a "Loser"

In my quest to research valuable information to guide you through your pursuit, I contacted someone whose expertise is turning everyday people into "losers." Cheryl Forberg, RD, is the award-winning chef and nutritionist for NBC's *The Biggest Loser* and has cowritten the eating plan for the show. She is a *New York Times* best-selling author, having contributed to eleven books, including *The Biggest Loser: The Weight Loss Program* (Rodale, 2005); *The Biggest Loser Complete Calorie Counter* (Rodale, 2006); *The Biggest Loser 30-Day Jump Start* (Rodale, 2009); and *Positively Ageless: A 28-Day Plan for a Younger, Slimmer, Sexier You* (Rodale, 2008). Cheryl's recommendations for preparing for an interview are practical and simple to remember.

On the eve of your interview, you should:

- Refrain from alcohol consumption to ensure restful sleep.

- Avoid anything that would interfere with your sleep pattern, such as eating too late.

- Drink water to maintain optimal hydration (at least eight glasses daily, as recommended by the Food and Nutrition Board).

- Avoid beans and legumes that can cause gassiness (especially if they're not a part of your regular diet).

On the morning of the interview, you should:

- Eat to preserve even blood sugar levels, which aid in increasing energy and staying alert.

- Avoid or significantly reduce your caffeine intake to minimize interview jitters.

- Work out to release anxieties (a minimum of 30 minutes daily of moderate to vigorous activity as per MyPyramid).

Expert Advice

Fellow mom, strategic partner, and nutrition consultant Deborah L. Rosenberg, MS, RD, CDE, CDN, offers ten ways to jump-start your interview day:

- Wake up and maintain concentration by combining a protein (eggs, egg whites, or peanut butter) that keeps you satiated with a whole grain carbohydrate (whole wheat flour, cracked wheat, brown rice) to kick up your metabolism.

- Nourish your mind with high-fiber foods such as bananas, pears, apples, nuts, and whole grain oats.

- Maintain regular bowel functions with insoluble fiber found in vegetables, fresh fruits, nuts, and seeds. Insoluble fiber requires adequate fluid intake, so stay well hydrated.

- Improve your memory by consuming foods with high levels of Omega 3 (salmon, trout, herring) or adding it as a dietary supplement (1,000 milligrams per day).

- Include zinc (fish, beef, and poultry) in your diet, which may increase your immune system and minimize mood swings.

- Purge your system through antioxidants found in fruits and vegetables (beta carotene keeps skin healthy, magnesium relaxes muscles and clears fatigue, and selenium contributes to a healthy immune system).

- Build strength (bones, teeth, and bone mass) by drinking low-fat (1%) or fat-free milk, which is rich in calcium and vitamin D, yet low in saturated fat.

- Avoid wasting your discretionary calories on simple carbohydrates (e.g., donuts, white bread, and white rice), which are absorbed in the bloodstream too quickly, causing over-response and a "fast dive."

- Calm your nerves by including fatty acids found in fish.

- Add a daily multivitamin.

Take It to Go

So the next time you're preparing to go on an interview, remember to prepare yourself before, during, and after the interview. Anticipate delays and prepare for them by being in a good physical and mental state of mind. Keep the aforementioned advice vivid in your mind and include it as part of your interview checklist. You should also plan to pack a survival kit of travel-sized emergency snacks that can be consumed during a quick trip to the restroom. Believe me; you will be enlivened during unexpected callbacks or digressions.

LIZANDRA'S SURVIVAL KIT

- Bottled H_2O

- Whole grain cereal bar

- Nuts

- Dried fruit

- Reduced-fat string cheese

- Peanut butter on grain crackers

PART TWO

BEHAVIOR

Have 'Em at Hello
Attitude, Gait, Eye Contact, Introduction, and Handshakes

You can't shake hands with a clenched fist. —Indira Gandhi (prime minister of India, 1966–1977, 1980–1984)

BELIEVE IT OR not, whether officially or unofficially, the interview begins the minute you walk into the lobby of the potential employer's building. Bad news travels fast, so just because you may think a security guard has zero input on your interview, he or she could very well be dating the assistant who reports to the recruiter who is about to interview you. The elevator ride up may also be a very telling experience about you. As a quick reminder, many buildings have cameras for security reasons, so watch your behavior while inside an elevator, because the evidence will be used against you.

Along the same lines, you should be in full interview mode from the moment the elevator doors open on your desired floor because the person who is about to interview you can coincidentally be within earshot as you announce yourself when greeted by the receptionist. Therefore, the manner in which you behave, walk, gaze, and introduce yourself will be evaluated as part of your overall professional image far before you reach your interview seat. It takes seconds for people to form their first impression about you, and if it's not a good one, you may not have a chance to make a second one. Display confidence, poise, and panache. Keep them wanting more of you—have 'em at hello.

Attitude

Regardless of any discord that may be going on in your life, when you're at an interview, all of your preoccupations are to be left outside of the building. I know it's difficult, because life has a funny way of getting to you, but you must show your professionalism early on, and that means leaving your 'tude in a place other than on your sleeve. Remember, how you behave on your first interview will be the only information the interviewer who is just meeting you has to go by. Be pleasant to all those you encounter along the way: the doorman, the maintenance engineer, and, most especially, the receptionist. Make the receptionist your ally, as he or she can have some input on the final decision. So many times I will hear that a candidate I interviewed and liked was a total monster to my receptionist, making me completely rethink his or her candidacy.

During the interview, your attitude should be positive, calm, and amenable even in situations where the interviewer's attitude is questionable. Think of it this way: If you really want the job, your goal is to get past this person. If you realize the moment you get to the interview that the place is a loony bin, use the interview as practice and get out graciously. It is important to exercise the following whether your goal is to nail the job or just to save face. You have a long career and anything you do or have done in the past will without a doubt come back to haunt you.

▪ **Be positive:** You may not even realize it, but before you know it, within five minutes of sitting down, your interview has turned into a gripe session. Leave negative emotions about your boss, your coworkers, and your company's style and structure out of the interview room. Avoid showing your bitterness. It may feel good to unload your frustrations, but not at the expense of losing out on a great career opportunity. Instead, find other measures, such as exercising, meditating, or even finding a good psychiatrist, to help diffuse your pent-up negativity. Attitude is contagious, and the last thing a potential recruiter wants to do is bring in a bad seed who will contaminate the rest.

Be positive about yourself: your talents, your education, your skill set, and your appearance. You may feel destitute, beaten, angry, or panicked, but in the eyes of the recruiter, you must appear optimistic and emotionally ready to take on a new challenge. A positive disposition should not be confused with arrogance, because inflated egos can be as detrimental as lack of confidence. Actually, I view arrogance as a way of masking the absence of self-belief. Being positive during an interview tells me you are able to do well in a team environment where you can thrive in a position of leadership—if not immediately, then sometime in the not-so-distant future. It also tells me that you are open and flexible to unexpected situations, such as working late to finish a project or entertaining a client at a moment's notice. Most of all, a positive attitude assures me that your body, mind, and soul are all sound and in good standing. The best way to convey a positive attitude is by smiling, since a happy expression is reflective of a positive inner self.

• **Remain calm:** My late friend and mentor, Sharon, was famous for advising candidates to remain calm. It was her universal remedy for just about anything that could go wrong during an interview. She used it as her solution for all interview mishaps, and it must have worked because she was an extremely talented and successful recruiter. You could have missed your train or your flight to your interview or forgotten your name at the interview and Sharon's reaction was always, "Were you calm?" Having started my staffing career in my mid-20s, I didn't understand or value the importance of remaining calm during stressful situations. However, throughout the years, I've learned how staying calm is a powerful means for diverting fear, anxiety, and stress.

Remaining calm is essential for showing your aptitude for handling interpersonal conflicts, a stressful environment, or a demanding boss. In addition, it proves your talent for meeting tight deadlines without freaking out. Having total control of your thoughts and emotions helps you handle unexpected questions and circumstances like a pro. In the hurried lives we live, it seems like a waste to go to a spa for any type of therapeutic service in the hopes of finding inner relaxation. Nonetheless, if you can somehow take a piece of that experience or any other occurrence that puts your mind at ease and substitute it for one that makes you feel anxious or uncomfortable, your effort will be rewarded with not being prematurely dismissed during an interview, and possibly moving on to the next round.

"Gait" Keeper

It's one thing to have a hop to your step to show that you possess energy and passion for your work, but charging in like a bull in a china shop is not the way to show oomph. We all have a particular manner of moving our limbs during motion. Aside from an irregular gait due to ailments or disease, a distorted or exaggerated gait due to cockiness, "ghetto-ness," laziness, tightness of clothing, or unruliness of heels truly needs serious attention.

▪ **Cocky strut:** As I mentioned earlier in this chapter, cockiness is a mask for insecurity. Accompanied by the attitude, the cocky strut is the one I loathe most. A cocky strut is a hybrid of John Wayne meets Richard Gere in *American Gigolo*. This walk insinuates that the enlarged crotch area is too large to walk with legs apart normally. It's forced and wannabe domineering—and, all in all, overkill on an interview.

▪ **"Ghetto" strut:** Growing up with inner-city kids, I am no stranger to this strut, and after all these years, I am still highly critical of it. The gait on this one has a distinct sway of shoulders and arms along with steps that have an overstated skip to them. This style of walking is completely unappealing and unprofessional even if you're interviewing for a cashier spot at the local fast-food restaurant. Surprisingly, I've met candidates who live in the suburbs who have adopted this walk as being cool. Let me assure you—it's not!

▪ **Lazy strut:** If you're too tired to come to the interview, I'd rather you cancel than schlep in like you still have your morning slippers on. This walk bears shoulders rolled forward, chin down, and arms just hanging on either side without a purpose. Talk about coming across unproductive, uncreative, and unlikable—it's not to be believed! Regardless of what position you're interviewing for, the nature of work is to be agile, and that entails being quick on your feet.

▪ **"Cloth-bound" strut:** The "cloth-bound" strut is one that is easily fixed with properly fitted attire. This strut has short and constrained steps, with arms and shoulders that are as stiff as a storefront mannequin—not a good gait, my friend.

▪ **Unbalanced strut:** Stiletto heels are the main culprit of this strut. However, for the novice heel wearer (even as low as kitten heels) because "you're supposed to" on an interview, your wobbly gait is making you lose concentration on the matter at hand—your interview. Sacrifice fashion for practicality.

If your gait is off, you will be perceived as clumsy, and that will certainly not add points to your interview scorecard. Be aware of how you walk, and practice a natural and professional way to walk your way into the future of your career. Highlight your confidence by aligning your body from head to toe and camouflaging your inability to walk heel to toe every time you walk into an interview.

Keep It Real by Focusing Your Gaze

Maintaining eye contact is one of the most important things to do on an interview. Shifty eyes make me feel like you're hiding the truth or you have something up your sleeve. A lowered gaze tells me you're unassertive or pretending to be submissive, so even if I don't completely take a pass on you, I know you're better suited for a job with little to no people contact. A gaze that is fixed above my eyebrows makes me think you're either sizing me up or I have bird poop dripping down my forehead. If you are an eyeglass wearer, looking over your glasses comes across as condescending.

So where exactly are you supposed to look and for how long? Well, for the purpose of interviewing, the area where your gaze should be focused is restricted to the area across the brow bone, from the outer edges of the eyes and coming downward toward the tip of the nose, forming an imaginary inverted triangle.[1] Dropping eye contact any lower than the tip of the inter-

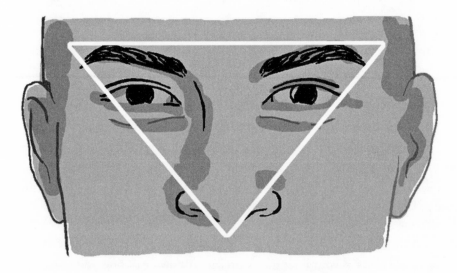

viewer's nose conveys nervousness or even intimacy as you fix your eyes on her lips for too long. Remember, the purpose of keeping eye contact is to show attention and participation in the conversation, not to make eyes at your recruiter. You may break your gaze by looking down to write notes regarding the interview, by blinking, smiling, or switching your eyes to another area within the inverted triangle. Avoid staring, which for me means keeping your eyes fixed on a person's feature for a prolonged period of time because of curiousness or nosiness. For instance, if the person interviewing you has some type of physical abnormality and you can't help but look at it, then you are staring. Avoid staring at anyone or anything around the room at all costs, since it will blatantly show your lack of interest.

Introductions

There are so many times that while making my way to the reception area, I cross my fingers in the hopes that you have the sense to say your first and last name when I go out to greet you. Sometimes it's an unusual name or other times it's a name that can be pronounced in different ways. Very often, the name on the résumé is the proper name, but you prefer to be called by a truncated version, as in the case of "Elizabeth" (you may be a "Liz," "Beth," "Betsy," or "Betty"). The introduction is the time to establish how you'd like to be addressed. Another thing to keep in mind is to allow the interviewer to introduce herself first before you say your name. Basically, the introduction should sound something like this:

Me: "Hi, I'm Lizandra Vega."

You: "Good morning, Ms. Vega. I'm Beth Clarke."

Me: "Nice to meet you, Beth. Please, call me Lizandra."

Notice how I set the tone of the interview with my casual "Hi," by calling you "Beth," and authorizing you to call me "Lizandra." Don't take any liberties of getting all too familiar and calling me "Liz" unless I specifically offer you the opportunity to be less formal. Doing so will guarantee your interview starts off on the wrong foot. Whether it's the beginning of a long business relationship or a brief professional encounter, the introduction is your moment to exude a warm, engaging, yet professional first impression by smiling and keeping your body in an open position while up on your feet. All this, coupled with eye contact, prepares you for the first of two physical contacts between us—the handshake.

Handshakes

Some cultures kiss, while others bow, but in America the proper business greeting is a handshake. You have two opportunities to leave your handprint on the recruiter's mind: at the introduction of your first encounter and at the conclusion of your conversation. Each time, your objective should be to seal the deal as far as your candidacy. Unfortunately, many botch this simple courtesy so terribly that there is very little room for impressing beyond it.

Throughout my years as an executive recruiter, I can honestly say I have experienced dozens of versions of the proper business handshake. I've been greeted with a drippy "gazpacho soup," which, just like the food, is cold and wet. There's also the "dead fish," classified by its cold, stiff, and scaly characteristics. The "dog's paw" grips only the tips of my fingers, while the "cat's paw" is limp and turned backward. Some candidates warm up to me by

engulfing my small hand between two hands at the end of a positive conversation. This is suffocating and much too familiar for business. Others will extend the palm faced downward, showing a glimpse of a domineering streak, whereas countless candidates extend their palm faced upward, similar to a vagrant waiting for a handout. I've even gotten a knuckle bump here and there. Besides the outrageous handshake styles, there have been more than enough bone-crushing grips and power-saw pumps that have soured me on candidates during our greeting or departure.

So once and for all let's all finally get on the same page. I addressed the condition of your hands in Chapter 6, but the proper interview handshake is an animal of a different sort.

Step 1: Stand up.

Step 2: Face right palm inward (toward your body).

Step 3: Extend arm (never across a desk or table).

Step 4: Approach.

Step 5: Clasp web to web.

Step 6: Grip (use moderate to firm pressure).

Step 7: Pump two or three times within five seconds (up and down, not back and forth).

Step 8: Release.

10

Silent but Deadly
Maintaining Space and
Pace and Body Language

Behavior is a mirror in which everyone displays his own image. —*Johann Wolfgang von Goethe (German playwright, poet, and novelist)*

INAPPROPRIATE NONVERBAL behavior can silently slay your career probabilities. Whether it's keeping your distance, monitoring your pace, or managing your body language, it's necessary for you to realize that such actions do speak louder than words. Old habits are hard to break, but when your bread and butter are compromised due to unspoken gaffes, it's time to start working on breaking such tendencies. Know your boundaries, adjust your tempo, and align your gestures. Doing so will support your professional image by reinforcing that your ethical and emotional characteristics are all in good standing.

Get Off My Tail

"Back off, sister" is what I really want to say to the candidate who feels the need to suck air from me by standing too close. You know the saying "Keep your friends close and your enemies closer"? Well, I'm neither, so I don't need to have a close-up of your molars to place you in a job. I realize that many times you don't even realize you're invading my space because you may have grown up in a culture that nurtures close proximity and touching. Sometimes, I'll even take some responsibility for making you feel so comfortable that you consider yourself closer to me by the end of the interview than you did when we first met. The bottom line is that physical closeness should be reserved for your nearest and most intimate relationships. Crossing the line with a prospective employer is a sure way to make her feel harassed and defensive.

To avoid embarrassing and uncomfortable encounters, I rely on the body space zones, or *proxemics*, identified by researcher E. T. Hall in the early 1960s. His theory separates dimensional space zones into four main groupings:

• **The intimate zone** (0" to 18") is meant for your significant other, spouse, children, parents (whom you like), or dear, dear friends. At 0", you may be kissing or hugging, and at 18", you may be holding hands.

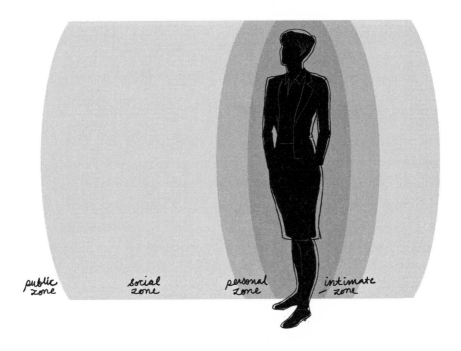

public zone   social zone   personal zone   intimate zone

- **The personal zone** (18" to 48"), at its closest range, is still meant for those individuals in our lives whom we know and love. As the distance widens, we begin to allow new encounters in, but they should remain on the periphery of your inner personal circle.

- **The social zone** (4' to 10') is the one most recommended between candidate and interviewer. This zone is wide, so where your distance falls exactly during an interview depends greatly on the size of the room in which the interview takes place. In addition, if one recruiter is interviewing you, you may remain within the closer distance of your social zone, whereas a group interview may require you to step back and open your social zone wider to include more people in conversation.

- **The public zone** (10' and over) is one used when dealing with complete strangers. Maintain this distance with a recruiter or company representative who is holding an informational meeting or an open house.

More on Space

There are times when I can easily read a candidate's level of confidence just by how much space he takes up. I'm not talking about the person's scale in this instance; I'm referring to ways potential hires will spread out to show their presence. This too can prove to be obnoxious if done to intimidate or somehow usurp office space. It often entails placing hands on hips with elbows out or sitting with legs spread out. One of my personal favorites is when a candidate places his hands behind his head with elbows pointed out at either side to support his neck. This bold stance is extremely arrogant and unprofessional. Spreading your portfolio, keys, phone, BlackBerry, or handbag all over the table and placing your outerwear, umbrella, and the like on several chairs is another rude way of commanding space. Beware not to be labeled a space hog; rein in your body parts and other belongings so you're not perceived as wanting to be the "Lord of the Land."

Pace Yourself to the Finish Line

One of the biggest challenges while on an interview is maintaining a comfortable pace while battling nerves. You don't gain points by being a chatterbox. Alternatively, candidates who take what feels like hours to answer one question come across as "slow-track" rather than top-choice contenders. Moving too fast makes me think you're on something that you shouldn't be taking, and moving too slowly leads me to believe you're tired or depressed. Adjust the rate of how you walk and talk to match your interviewer's. You will avoid stepping on the recruiter's words or having lags of time between questions, making the interview more conversational. Establish your pace by:

- Breathing for relaxation

- Thinking for anticipation

- Observing for education

Posture

Whether you are standing, walking, or sitting, good posture exudes confidence from a mile away. It supports breathing and voice control in addition to melting pounds and years away faster than Photoshop can. Challenged with scoliosis, this is something I am always super-conscious to maintain. Other factors, including obesity, stress, pregnancy, wearing high heels, or sitting in front of a computer too long, are also huge contributors to having poor posture.

The thing I find about poor posture is that if you ignore it, it gets progressively worse, to the point where it actually hurts when you try to correct it. So why bother to take care of it, right? We might as well stay looking like Quasimodo. Even though I suffer from chronic posture issues, I still cringe at the sight of candidates who are twisted and turned like a pretzel, because it reflects a negative and negligent image. Don't disregard poor posture; it will not only hinder your appearance, but it will also affect your health for the rest of your life. The following practices are

recommended by the American Chiropractic Association (www.acato
day.org) to combat poor posture:

STANDING

- Allocate weight to the balls of your feet

- Pull everything in: chin, shoulders, stomach, buttocks

- Maintain limber knees

- Keep shoulders back

- Drape arms naturally on either side

SITTING

- Avoid crossing legs

- Relax shoulders

- Support your lower and mid-back (use your bag instead of a pillow
  during an interview)

- Rotate your sitting position

- Maintain knees at or below hip height

Positioning

Positioning yourself in a manner that keeps sight lines open works well in
your favor; therefore, situate yourself in a position that disperses any type
of adversarial energy. If the interviewer chooses to sit behind a desk, then
create a diagonal line by simply turning your chair and your body. If you
are being interviewed in a conference room that has a table with lots of
chairs, wait to be directed to sit and choose a chair that is either at an angle
or diagonally across from the one the recruiter chooses. (*Note:* Avoid plop-
ping yourself into the interview seat like a ton of bricks.)

Ask if there is a preference on where you should sit and try to time it with when your recruiter sits down. This will help you steer clear of irritating a recruiter who may be protective of his territory (rightfully so). Suppose he has a preferred chair (as I do); he may not appreciate you occupying it. While on the subject of positioning, as difficult as it may be, please refrain from touching or repositioning anything in the surrounding areas. I always remember a candidate whom I will refer to as "Irene." All of my interview rooms and conference rooms were occupied, so I interviewed her in my office. It's a good thing I had my desk to separate us because she touched and arranged everything on my desk. Was she a neat freak, nervous, overbearing, or all of the above? In my record, she became a DNS: "DO NOT SEND." At any rate, whenever in doubt, mirror the interviewer. It will not only create an immediate bond, but it will also instantly demonstrate respect and cooperation. Position yourself to be valued and trusted enough to be hired.

Body Talk

You're impatient about a recruiter not seeing you on time, so you put your hands on your hips, which shows your annoyance. You're defensive about being asked why you were the only one terminated during a "major downsize," so you fold your arms or, even more protective of yourself, you fold your arms *and* cross your legs. Clenched fists tell me that you despise your present boss even though you vow your adoration for him, but you're looking for a new job because you want out of your present industry. A foot pointed toward an exit tells me you are dying to get going, whereas acknowledging what I'm saying with a closed-mouth smile lets me know you are just being polite and are not at all inspired by me.

Whether you realize it or not, gestures subliminally underscore your spoken words. This is where most messages become distorted. Align gestures as consistent clusters that send out one strong message as opposed to many mixed messages, which are often interpreted as fabricated and deceitful. What follows are some of the most common interviewing gestures I repeatedly see:

- **Sexual:** Pen chewing, hair tousling, ring fondling, winking, lip licking

- **Deceitful:** Mouth touching, nose scratching, pupil dilating, eyebrow raising

- **Negative:** Arm folding, fist clenching, leg crossing, closed-mouth smiling

- **Positive:** Palm resting (down), hand clasping (behind back), forward leaning, open-mouth smiling

11

Dial 911
Protocol Police

Good manners sometimes means simply putting up with other people's bad manners.
—*H. Jackson Brown, Jr. (American author of* Life's Little Instruction Book*)*

IT NEVER FAILS. I finally find the perfect candidate on paper for that oh-so-difficult job. When I greet her, she looks the part, and her handshake and eye contact rate a 9 on my scale of 1 to 10 (score!). We're past the introduction phase when all of a sudden I notice she is toting a venti-sized Starbucks coffee cup in her left hand. She doesn't ask for a coaster or place the napkin that's wrapped around her cup on the table. Before I move from our initial break-the-ice small talk, the super-sized cup (which I later find out is a venti skim, extra-hot, no-foam latte) tips over and spills on the newly shampooed carpet in the conference room. My assistant comes to the rescue to clean it up. Not only does the interview get off to a shaky start, but I don't even get a humble apology. Perhaps she was embarrassed, or maybe she was too stubborn to express regret. I finally come to the conclusion that she was completely oblivious to the fact that bringing the coffee cup into the interview (whether it spilled or not) showed poor protocol.

Protocol, etiquette, or just plain good manners are pivotal to conducting business with confidence and flair. Candidates, and people in general, are often embarrassed to be caught using proper protocol because they are afraid to be classified as stuffy or passé. I guess it's better to be considered tacky, sloppy, and wacky. As far as I'm concerned, exercising proper protocol is as effective as wearing the power suit. This chapter focuses on gaffes that have prevented candidates from displaying exemplary business protocol, thereby costing many jobs. Read on and identify yourself in scenarios where you now say to yourself, "Oh, so that's why they took a pass."

Interview etiquette is one of those things you don't need to spend extra money on, though you do need to spend extra time thinking about it. Keep the protocol police away by refraining from making some of the most common blunders I've witnessed throughout my interviewing years.

Keep It Light

Yourself, a briefcase, tote, and portfolio (with résumés and references) is about all you need for the interview room. Shopping bags full of purchases or other tchotchkes make you look like you ran out of closet space and need to carry your belongings wherever you go.

Food and drink are really thoughtless and inappropriate, especially if you're just bringing for yourself. Besides causing you to be extra careful not to spill them, food and drink come with their own set of smells that will linger long after you've left. That said, if you're offered a beverage (e.g., water, seltzer, or even coffee or tea) or a snack by the interviewer, you should accept it. Doing so shows openness to your recruiter's hospitality; in addition, it will guarantee that you will not be rushed out of the interview, as it gives you time to bond with the recruiter over a drink, even if it is only water. By the way, if a coaster is placed under your glass, be sure to place the glass on top of it after you've taken a sip or two. Be conscious of not ruining the furniture. The general rule here is to travel light so that you have room to acquire things that are given to you: drinks, snacks, brochures, and other types of company paraphernalia.

All That Is Wet

All outerwear, hats, umbrellas, and rain or snow boots should be left outside in the reception area. Carry dry shoes with you and change in the restroom. If you weren't aware it would rain and you have on regular dress shoes, be sure to clean them off before you go in, so as not to make a total mess of the floors. Again, you don't want to bring too much stuff into the interview room. In addition, excessively wet clothing, accessories, and footwear is apt to ruin upholstery and wood finishes. Be conscious of such soggy details.

Nervous Habits

Whether it's nail biting, nose picking, knuckle cracking, hair flipping, or crotch fondling, it's often about nerves. There is nothing more unsettling than interviewing a twitchy person. Some candidates become human instruments by anxiously whistling, restlessly finger snapping, or impatiently finger and foot tapping. Keep a pen in your dominant writing hand at all times (don't fondle it), with your second hand on top of the desk with palms down flat. Feet can be anchored by crossing your ankles or placing your bag between them without letting the bag hit the ground. Nervous habits are difficult to break, but at the very least work on keeping them in check by securing the parts of your body that are apt to play a faux pas symphony.

Timing Is Everything

While overstaying your welcome makes you look oblivious and self-indulgent, checking out the time either by looking at a wall clock or constantly catching glimpses of your watch makes you appear like you're not interested in the position. If you aren't interested and this is your passive-aggressive way of showing it, remember that such behavior is irreversible. I'll share a quick story of a candidate who did this and was thoroughly sorry she did.

I sent the candidate to one of my well-known jewelry clients and she consistently checked the time on her watch throughout her 30-minute interview with the human resources manager. The client's feedback was positive about her regarding all other fronts except on how rude she was to constantly break her eye contact to look at her watch. When I debriefed the candidate, she admitted to doing so while also confiding that she knew she had already clinched her first-choice interview and that they were already checking references. Somehow, her first choice never did make her an offer and it turned out that my jewelry client was her second choice. I tried to smooth out the mishap but no matter what I said, the client just couldn't get past her rude behavior.

Overstaying your welcome can be equally bad. Look for signals like the interviewer standing up and starting to walk toward the exit door. That should be a clear sign that she has ample information to reach a decision about you. Don't think that a short interview means that you've been dismissed as a candidate, because sometimes it's quite the opposite. Sometimes, it's the candidates I'm on the fence about that I keep longer because I need to pinpoint the exact reason for my apprehension before they walk out the door.

Cursing and Swearing

Cursing and swearing are not smart ways of emphasizing your feelings and emotions. "This job sounds *bleeping* awesome" may sound like you've really expressed your desire for the job—to you only. To me, it sounds like you are not to be left alone with a high-net-worth client. Who knows what else is likely to come out of your mouth? Swearing is vastly disrespectful. Interviews are not a place for bringing up body parts or their functions as a form of casual expression. In addition, racial and religious slurs are a glaring display of your bigotry and intolerance toward social diversity. Be aware that religious slurs can be as innocent as mentioning Jesus, Jesus Christ, or God in your everyday vocabulary.

Gum Chewing

A recent article in the *Los Angeles Times*[1] reports that "Studies have suggested that something about chewing gum reduces stress, improves alertness and relieves anxiety." That may be so, but as far as business protocol goes, chewing gum is ranked high in candidacy fatality rate. There's no way of hiding it under your tongue or on the side or roof of your mouth. If you need to keep your mouth moist, drink water. If you have bad breath, brush your teeth.

Mind Your Manners

Whenever my daughter is off on a playdate, the last words I whisper in her ear as I kiss her good-bye are "Mind your manners." I tell the same thing to my candidates, because manners are something many people seem to outgrow. You may believe that just because your interviewer is your contemporary as far as age, level of experience, salary range, and the like, you no longer have to use "please" and "thank you." Nothing could be further from the truth. Respect is something that everyone is worthy of getting. You'll be surprised at how quickly it will be reciprocated. Use the following guidelines to smoothen out your interview path:

- Say "please" when:

  1. You ask for a question to be repeated.

  2. You ask for clarification on the spelling of the interviewer's name and title.

  3. You ask for a business card.

- Say "thank you" when:

  1. You are offered a beverage, food, a business card, or company information.

  2. You are given constructive criticism of any sort. Be gracious!

  3. You reach the conclusion of your interview. Thank the recruiter for his or her time.

- Say "I'm sorry" when:

  1. You arrive late to the interview.

  2. You don't follow up as promptly as you should with additional information.

  3. You forget to bring a résumé or any other document that has been requested of you (driver's license, green card, Social Security card, academic transcript, diploma, etc.).

Equal Protocol

Courteous behavior should be exercised by all—regardless of gender or age. For all of you men out there, don't feel emasculated if I open and hold the door for you. It is my office and I am leading the meeting, so I am showing graciousness by opening the door. By the same token, women should not feel dominated by a male recruiter who is well mannered, but don't expect him to be that way just because he's a man. Also, don't expect the chivalrous act of having assistance with your coat unless your arm is broken.

As far as whether you should rise to your feet whenever someone you are about to meet or be introduced to walks in, the answer is, yes, you do rise to your feet. This should be done regardless of your gender and regardless of the gender of the interviewer who walks in. The main reason for this is that you always want to shake hands while standing up; therefore, standing up upon a recruiter's arrival or departure shows respect and gets you on your feet. In addition, your behavior toward an interviewer who is your junior or senior in age should not be affected in any way. Refrain from addressing me as "sweetheart," "honey," "darling," "Lizzy," or any other diminutive pet names just because I'm close to your daughter's age. The trick is to think of the business and specifically the interview playing field as an equal one. Don't have the expectations you would in a social arena, and be courteous to show good pedigree no matter what your socioeconomic status is or has been in the past.

12

Whining and Dining
Tipping the Scales with Appropriate Etiquette

Manners are a sensitive awareness of the feelings of others. If you have that aware-
ness, you have good manners, no matter what fork you use. —Emily Post (American
etiquette authority)

IT MAY NOT HAPPEN on the first round or even the second, but at some point
during a lengthy interview process, you will be invited to dine out. This
often happens when you're seeing multiple decision makers in one day or
when the 9–5 hours are too precious or impractical to spend on interviewing. When this happens, I let out a huge gasp, because it is precisely
the point when many leading candidates go down. Couple a relaxing
restaurant setting with a cocktail or two and all of a sudden you are an
open book, resulting in the dreaded TMI (too much information). There
are all sorts of inappropriate conversation choices, and they all seem to be
a topic of discussion during a dining interview. Out of the blue, you are on
the subject of your divorce and how you are every bit to blame for it.
There's alimony talk, then you reminisce about the old days, and finally the
tears start rolling down your face.

Then, there are seating and entrée choices along with how you handle your knife and fork. It's easy to descend into a bottomless pit of trouble when dining on someone else's expense account. But really, it doesn't have to be this way because this is an area you can easily master. I have seen miraculous transformations in this area. I'm speaking of myself, and it's made all the difference in the world for me. All it takes is a little practice and a lot of self-control. It's a lot to think about, I know, but good dining etiquette is one of those skills that, once learned, can be executed effortlessly. I equate it to being a good driver: There's plenty to maneuver but once you dominate the skill, you can simultaneously drive, eat, and speak. Distinguish yourself from the pack and do away with awkwardness that will label you as "unrefined." Stop *whining* about the challenge and shape up your dining habits by exhibiting good table manners while choosing appropriate conversation topics to combat these killer dining interviews.

Predining Prep

You've been given a date, a time, and the name and location of a restaurant as the venue for your final interview with the last and most influential of decision makers within the firm. As soon as you are privy to this information, it's homework time. Start by researching the restaurant: Access its Web site, read a review, call to find out what its cuisine is like, and do a trial run by visiting beforehand to time your commute. See with your own eyes what the space and lighting are like. You don't have the advantage of doing this when your interview venue is in an office, but in a restaurant you certainly can find out and, believe me, it will help take the edge off. You will be familiar with details and you won't have to think about them during your interview.

Choose a business suit that is authoritative in color and silhouette, as you will be meeting with the person who is to give the final stamp of approval. The last thing you need is to be embarrassed by the maître d' who insists you wear an ill-fitting loaner jacket to sit across from the person who holds your fate in her hands. That would be a huge mistake! Be sure to have at least three moderately priced entrée selections in mind that you feel comfortable managing. In addition, get food allergies out of the way when you scope out how dishes are prepared. You don't want to get into a whole song and dance about your allergies and health in front of the interviewer. Besides it being personal, it's time-consuming and you want the dining experience to go as smoothly as possible (at least from your end). I've recommended candidates do this, and they have been forthright with the hosts/hostesses about their reason for pre-examining the surroundings. They are often happy to help them acclimate to the environment as well as answer any questions. Be proactive and avoid surprises.

Food Choices

It's not about being a picky eater, but you hope the restaurant has options that are simple to eat. It's also not about indulging. Remember, you're not out celebrating with your family (hopefully, that will be the case after you get the job). It's about avoiding distractions that heavy sauces, splashy soups, and cumbersome bones, shells, and noodles often cause. Here you will find interview-friendly food selections as well as anti-interview choices to help you narrow down your food alternatives:

▪ **Interview-friendly food/beverages:** Boneless meats or fish, short pastas in white sauces or "al'olio" (ziti, bowties, fusilli), ravioli, grilled vegetables, rice, roasted potatoes, couscous, salads, bread, water, seltzer, cookies/biscuits, coffee, tea

▪ **Anti-interview food/beverages:** Cornish hens or any other bone-in meat, lobster, soup, long pastas in red sauces (spaghetti, linguini, angel hair), ribs (anything barbecued), French fries, carbonated soft drinks, alcoholic drinks, creamy dairy desserts

On the Day of the Meal

After several months of interviewing with what felt like everyone, including the building's maintenance engineer, you will finally be dining with "her"—the one everyone has described. She is *the one* who signs the paychecks. Arrive with about 15 minutes to check in, use the facilities, and basically get yourself settled. It's a good idea to nibble on something light before you get to the restaurant so that you are not ravenous when the food finally arrives and you end up eating like it's your last meal. If for some unforeseen reason you are running late, be sure to call the interviewer's assistant, the recruiter who arranged the interview, or, as a last resort, the restaurant host or hostess. Avoid being late at all costs.

If the interviewer is running late, you may be asked whether you'd like to be seated at your table to wait for her arrival or wait in a lounge area. Regardless of your preference, it is poor etiquette to start the meal early by ordering so much as an appetizer. Nonetheless, accepting or requesting water is acceptable. Remember, if you remain in the lounge area, you have the freedom to check e-mails and be productive while you wait. Once you sit down, you've pretty much lost your freedom to work on electronic equipment, so you're confined to people watching. Also, you are her guest, so the seat with the wall behind you that faces toward the view of the room is perfectly acceptable.

Oh good, this must be her now, cutting your people-watching time just before you get bored. She's being escorted toward your table. As she approaches, stand up, meet her gaze, and extend your arm for a "web to web" professional handshake. Allow her to introduce herself first (not based on gender but on rank) and say your full name for her to hear. After the five-second handshake, wait for her to make some type of gesture that guides you to sit. Ah, you're finally seated again, and while the official order of business is not to be discussed until after your entrée plates are cleared, the nonverbal part of your interview began with your gaze and will end with where you place your napkin when it's all over.

"Order" of Business

As soon as you sit down, place your napkin on your lap, folded once with the open side facing your body. This will allow you to wipe your greasy fingers under the fold to ensure that food stains don't end up on your suit.

The waiter appears and asks if he may present a wine list (awkward). You hold your breath, but her response is, "No, thank you. Perrier with lime is fine for me." Then she turns to you and you follow her lead: "I'll have the same, thank you." Off goes the waiter with the two wine glasses he has just removed from your table; the less clutter at the table, the less chance of making mistakes. Phew, that one was easy. Had she opted for wine, it would have been a bit more uncomfortable for you to decline one your-self, though perfectly acceptable. It would have been her faux pas to drink while meeting a potential employee. Thank goodness she had the sense to show some discretion.

The waiter returns now offering each of you a menu, which you will pretend to read (though you've already predetermined your choices). Politely, you listen to the specials but you stick to your premeditated selec-tions. You each keep it simple, limiting it to two courses before coffee and dessert: The tricolor chilled asparagus in a creamy dill dressing to start, fol-lowed by grilled salmon and vegetables with baby roasted potatoes as the main entrée, are safe, while she orders the Tuscan bean soup, the baked red snapper with fennel, and baby carrots on the side. Isn't she a brave one?

Small Talk

This is the part of the dining interview that worries me the most because you're not restricted to chatting about professional matters. This is where the bulk of candidates get into major trouble. How I wish I could insert a dime-size earpiece in your ear to tell you what to say. It's not that I don't trust that you can hold an intelligent conversation while handling your silverware, but you'd be surprised at how many bright candidates lack social graces and finesse at the table. So, just for today, I will be the voice inside your head.

Ah, there you are—and there she is. She's not a date, so don't comment on how lovely she looks. Where do you start to "peel the onion"? Okay, so she has a tan and she hadn't been available to see you until now . . . Perhaps you can start by making a comment on how rainy it's been and how it's a great time to be away on travel. "Turks and Caicos," she volunteers. "It really beats the weather we've been having here." Talk about industry books that are on the top of your reading list or this swine influenza . . . yada, yada, yada. Small talk is tricky when you are meeting someone for the first time who should clearly not be privy to intimate details of your life. Still, you want to come across as personable and engaging enough to bring that extra little something to your potential position. Be sensitive to your professional boundaries. Feel safe sticking to success topics and steer clear of washout subjects:

- **Success:** Noncontroversial books, plays, concerts, movies, television shows, or current events; travel; sports (if you can diplomatically divulge allegiance for your team); volunteer/community/board involvement

- **Washout:** Marital status and other personal information, religion, politics, racism, jokes/riddles, diet/weight, gossiping, divulging trade information, criticizing, sexual activities, age

A "Course" on Table Manners

Finally, the waiter returns with the bottle of Perrier and lime wedges. You're really holding your own with the small talk, and I believe this super executive thinks you have what it takes.

The waiter is back again, this time with her Tuscan bean soup in an individual tureen and your asparagus with dill. She reaches for her spoon, and the slurping you hear is not coming from the next table. The embarrassing sound is coming from your interviewer. You maintain composure by focusing on handling your asparagus with your fingers (as well you should). However, you don't want to lose eye contact for too long, and as you pick up your gaze you are further horrified by watching her cut her bread roll with her butter knife. She then proceeds to dunk the bite-size morsels inside her soup. By the way, you've earned kudos for breaking your bread with your hands and for not pointing out that that she stole the bread from your plate in the first place (solids on the left and liquids on the right). She tilts her soup bowl toward her body instead of properly tilting it away. The slurping sound intensifies. Will this course ever end? At least she knew enough to place her soupspoon on her service plate when she was done.

The main course is served, and I see you've remembered everything we've talked about: upright posture, feet on the ground, forearms leaning against the edge of the table instead of lazy elbows on top of the table, and you've even tasted the food before asking for salt (salt and pepper should be passed together, as they are a pair, even if only one is requested). I've hardly had to interject to make many corrections, though across the table, you are seeing quite the opposite in the way of table manners. Does she have to talk giving us a full view of the food in her mouth, and doesn't she know that the Perrier is not to be swooshed around her mouth? It's a drink, not mouthwash.

Continental, American, or Barbaric

Take your pick: continental, American, or barbaric. I'm referring to dining styles and, for its practicality, I'm partial to continental, though American is perfectly acceptable, too. Barbaric is neither for social nor business dining, though it is the one people gravitate to most. It usually entails stabbing your food with your fork and reslaughtering it with your knife.

With continental and American dining, being left-handed gives you permission to use your dominant hand for cutting. Even if it means holding the fork with your right hand, it's not so much about which hand you use to slice or pierce as it is about having good form by holding utensils properly (using your dominant hand to handle precision duties). Instead of rearranging the table setting to accommodate your left-handedness, it's best to assume an eating style that allows you to have a safer grip on your food. Subsequent to learning my dining style from a right-handed etiquette coach, I am an incognito lefty when I dine. You shouldn't have to fake it. Teaching yourself to eat righty if you're lefty is as old school as teaching yourself to write righty to ward off evil spirits.

Regardless, you have two dining styles to choose from. Choose one or the other, but whatever you choose, do not integrate them to create your own version. That is precisely where you run into trouble. Ah yes, and in case you're unsure, both styles involve using your utensils from the outside in toward your plate(s). Use your place setting as your navigation system en route to the dining choices that are available to you. Most of all, the most sacred rule of thumb is to never place a utensil that has been used back on the table.

▪ **Continental** dining is my preferred style of eating because it's smooth. There's no clinking or clanking. You simply hold the knife in your dominant hand and the fork in the opposite hand with your forefinger supporting the spine of each utensil as the blade and tines face downward. The knife will slice, dice, and push food into position to be speared by the fork, which will transport the food into your mouth with tines facing down and comfortably fitting onto the roof of your mouth. Meats are pierced, while veggies, mashed potatoes, and rice are given a piggyback on top of the fork. The fork is brought toward your mouth with the tines downward.

Notice the knife held by your dominant hand is never switched over, and only during resting mode are the utensils placed on the plate, forming an inverted "V" shape (8:20 on a clock) on the bottom portion of your plate with its blade facing inward and the fork tines facing downward. When you are finished with your meal, your nonverbal signal should involve placing the knife with its blade facing inward and the fork with tines downward in a diagonal (10:20 on a clock) position.

▪ **American** dining involves more of a song and a dance. It's not only cumbersome and noisy but I find it leaves a lot more room for blunders. Okay, so here I go. Place the knife in the dominant hand and the fork in the other hand in a fashion similar to continental style. Slice *one to three* bitesfull with your knife and then rest the knife on the top-hand portion of the plate of either the left or right hand (depending on which hand is your dominant one). While the knife is resting with its blade facing inward, you pull the "switcheroo" and place the fork in the now free dominant hand in

Continental dining

resting position

*closed position,
fork tines down*

a similar fashion to holding a pencil. (I hope you're following!) You then scoop the food with the tines of your fork facing upward, carrying the fork and food inside your mouth with the tines pricking the roof of your mouth. See, this is where you, along with a slew of candidates, run into trouble. If your pushing utensil is resting, then the only other natural pusher is your finger and that's, well, yuck.

Want to take a break from eating to chat? Then place your fork diagonally (tines facing upward) across the center of your plate, parallel to the knife that is already resting diagonally on the upper portion of your plate. Finally, when you want to let the waiter know that you're done, place your fork and knife at the 10:20 position as with the continental style, except your fork tines should be placed in an upward fashion.

How Sweet It Is

Congrats on your entrée choice and on managing to ingest it gracefully; you went for the safety choices. At least you didn't have to struggle with a bony fish or loose carrots that instigate poor form. As your plates are removed from the right-hand side, she searches for the lipstick tube buried in the bottom of her makeup case and she begins to apply it (gasp!). Now that's gauche! She then excuses herself to use the restroom (couldn't she have applied the lipstick in the bathroom?), and you stand up to acknowledge her departure. She leaves the napkin . . . in her chair! Wow, she finally did something right. I thought for sure she'd leave it on the table.

Upon her return to the table, you rise to your feet again, but don't pull her chair out. Leave that job to the waiter. He earns his gratuity and pulls out her chair. Coffee and dessert are ordered: You choose the cheesecake and she selects the crème fraîche. Finally, let the business talk begin after an hour and 20 minutes of poor dining etiquette and idle chatter. She may not be able to handle a fork like a pro but now that she's *talking trade,* you can certainly tell she knows her stuff. Once the coffee and dessert arrive, she shocks you for a second time by using her spoon for her creamy dessert. You in turn, chose a cheesecake with a crust, so the

American dining

resting position

*closed position
fork tines up*

fork will suffice. Had you added the ice cream I discouraged you from, you would need the fork and spoon (the spoon as your pusher). Aren't you glad I kept it simple for you?

By the time the coffee is served, you've succeeded in what you needed to accomplish: having her like you enough to give her stamp of approval. Stir your sugar in well, and then place the spoon on your saucer. You're almost done here; just about 20 minutes to go. See, I told you there was nothing to be nervous about. She was the one who needed the earpiece all along.

Wrapping It Up

The cheesecake was good and the coffee is gone. It's time to go. She makes eye contact with the waiter and asks for the check. Don't even think about reaching for your wallet! The meal is part of her hiring expenses. By the way, absolutely no doggy bags allowed, no matter how tempted you are to bring home leftovers you were too nervous to enjoy. You may, however, thank her for the meal and, of course, her time. You both stand up and leave the napkin on the left-hand side of your plate. This time, I think she took your lead.

You walk toward the coat check area, and she neglects to tip for your coat. She struggles with her raincoat and you ask if you may be of assistance, but just as you make your offer, she manages to slip into it. Okay, it's really the home stretch. Shake hands, reiterate your desire for the job, and once again thank her for her time. You are officially released from your interviewing duties. You did great.

You wonder, "How could *she* have gotten this far with such frightful etiquette?" Did you forget? It's a family-owned enterprise. Oh yes . . . that explains it. Who cares about how she got to the top? Worry about getting yourself there, too, so don't fall off the face of the earth after your dining interview. Be sure to treat it like any other interview and deliver your thank-you note within 24 hours.

13

Seal the Deal
Negotiating, Accepting, Extending, or Declining with Finesse

Let us never negotiate out of fear. But let us never fear to negotiate. —John Fitzgerald Kennedy *(president of the United States, 1961–1963)*

ALL OFFERS ARE not created equal and, more important, they're by no means written in stone. That means that there is room for discussion before you and your potential employer come to a meeting of the minds. I'm not advocating negotiations if your visceral response is to accept an offer on the first proposition, but very seldom is an offer so straightforward that there isn't even one question to be asked, let alone a quibble about it. You know what it takes to get to this point: You look, act, and sound the part; you have the experience, credentials, and education to support your candidacy; and the offer validates that you are the quintessential fit for a given role. Bravo! Job well done! However, if you think the job is in the bag, you are mistaken.

Finally, this is the moment you've either been waiting for, or dreading. Regardless of whether you actually decide to negotiate, you owe it to yourself to completely understand all of the specifics of what is being offered to you. This is not a fly-by-night decision. Therefore, the more you uncover and understand, the less likely you are to hastily accept or decline an offer. So much for thinking your task as a candidate is done. The fact is that all those who collaborated on making it happen will note how you handle this portion of your interview. Yes, the ball is in your court right now since you've succeeded in wooing a hiring proposal out of them. However, be very careful how you handle their vulnerable and seemingly generous gesture; if you behave in a disrespectful, ungracious, and poor manner, you will face consequences that are less than favorable.

A rescinded offer is the worst-case scenario of a poorly driven offer negotiation, while to a lesser degree, you stand the chance of starting your new job having left a bad taste in everyone's mouth (not exactly the best way to start a new job). So before you even think of negotiating an offer, the first thing you should do is acknowledge the offer either verbally or in writing. Your acknowledgment serves two purposes: (1) to thank the employer for offering you the opportunity for employment and (2) to confirm that you have some time to understand the details of the offer. You shouldn't need weeks to process a job offer. The groundwork for understanding/negotiating should have started as early as before you even submitted your résumé, by gathering information during the early preparation stage. Once you've completed the preparation stage, follow it up by exploring the offer, appraising the circumstances around the offer, devising a plan of action, and conquering the situation.

This five-step process will enable you to carve out the integral components you must weigh before making a decision to accept, decline, negotiate then accept, or negotiate then decline with professional decorum.

Step One: Prepare

Right from the moment you decide to put yourself on the market, your preparation process begins. You will examine yourself as a candidate and scrutinize your marketability within one or several industries if your experience allows you to cross over. You will then collect names of target companies with positions that are matches to your profile. All this takes hours, days, weeks, and months to compile, as the process unveils more information to be added to the list of considerations. However, once you have collected and input all of the information into your "prep guide," it will map out exactly what you are pursuing. So when the time comes for you to handle an offer, you can refer back to this list and determine how much of it has been fulfilled. Begin your preparation by researching answers to the following:

- **Know your worth**

  – What is your market value based on factors such as years of experience, education, title, industry, geographic region, and other defining criteria? (Use online sites such as Salary.com, Salaryexpert.com, Payscale.com, Careerjournal.com, and Jobnob.com for assistance.)

  – What unique or difficult-to-find skills do you offer that are pertinent to the job? For instance, if you are a CPA who is fluent in Swahili and the job requires heavy interaction with one of the locations in East Africa and you know your competition is narrowed down because of the language requirement, then you are worth *gold*.

  – What is the importance and impact this position has on the overall department/company performance?

  – What will others (past employers and character references) say about you?

- **Know your limits**

  – What are you willing to compromise?

  – What, if anything, is nonnegotiable?

  – What, if any, terms and/or conditions do you deem unacceptable?

  – Are you financially willing or able to take a lateral or reduced salary for the right situation?

– Are you unemployed or the sole breadwinner?

– Where do you fall short in achieving your goals? Do you lack a degree or special certification?

- **Know your preferences**

  – What type of environment will make you happy?

  – Do you prefer a small yet entrepreneurial start-up, mid- to large-size company, or a giant conglomerate?

  – Do you prefer a corporate, academic, nonprofit, or creative environment?

  – Is there anything you would value as much as or more than an increase in salary?

  – Do you prefer a more modest base salary with an aggressive incentive package or do you prefer the safety of a higher base pay with less significant incentives?

  – Do you prefer an inflated title with less pay or a higher compensation package with a less prestigious title?

- **Know the scoop**

  – Research data about each target company and delve into the profiles of company executives and employees who might be on a similar career track within a firm. (Try business research sites such as Hoovers.com, Insideview.com, Jigsaw.com, Zoominfo.com, InfoUsa.com, and Implu.com.)

  – Search your target company's Web site.

  – Use Google as a search engine to find out information on companies.

  – How does this company compare with your present company of employment? (Do not compare it to a position you're not currently in.)

– How many candidates have been extended an offer for the position?

– How many people have been in this position in the past, and are they still with the company?

– Is this a newly created position?

– Does the company have an inability to attract and retain talent?

– What are the expectations attached to the position?

- **Know your purpose**

  – Is this a money job *only?*

  – Is this a change-of-career job?

  – Is this your first paying job?

  – Is this a career opportunity of a lifetime?

  – Are you window-shopping for an offer just to improve your interviewing skills and test the waters?

Step Two: Explore

One thing I must make clear is that the offer is not composed of the base salary alone. As obvious as it may be to some, many lose interest in hearing or reading past the base salary, especially if it turns out to be considerably lower than expected, which is referred to as a lowball offer. Realize that each piece of the compensation or remuneration can critically impact the value of the offer. Thus, it is the individual parts that must be thoroughly scrutinized for any hidden rewards or disincentives. Remember to ask for an offer in writing if a verbal one has been extended. However, even with a written offer, much of the information you need to make a levelheaded decision will not be stipulated. Therefore, this is the point where you become a proactive explorer to find out all of the factors that may not have been appropriate to ask prior to an extended offer.

Appraise each portion of the offer by rating it on a scale of 1 to 5 (1: unacceptable, 2: satisfactory, 3: good, 4: very good, 5: excellent). If you are currently employed, rate your current job on the exact checklist so that you may compare the two lists against each other during Step Three ("Appraise").

- **Compensation**

  – Base salary

  – Bonuses (sign-on, merit, and group)

  – Performance reviews and increases within the first year

  – Benefits: medical/dental/vision (employer/employee contribution, deductibles)

  – 401(k) (employer matching program)

  – Profit sharing

  – Life insurance

  – Disability insurance

  – Vacation (accrual and waiting period)

  – Sick time (separate from vacation)

  – Paid company holidays

  – Flexible spending

  – Perks (gym membership, childcare/eldercare contribution, employee discounts, company car)

  – Relocation costs (move-in and closing costs, loans, assistance in selling present home)

- **Resources**

  – Tuition reimbursement (wait period and percentage of reimbursement)

  – Skills training (any exclusion)

- Technical support

- Administrative support

- Marketing and promotions

- Infrastructure

- **Quality of Life**

- Commute

- Business travel

- Overtime

- Flextime

- Telecommuting

- Job-share

- **Restrictions**

- Noncompete agreements

- Nonsolicitation agreements

- Nondisclosure agreements

- Intellectual property agreements

- Internet usage agreements

- Drug tests

- Background checks

Step Three: Appraise

Evaluate Step One and Step Two. Is all of the information you've input still accurate? Tally up the average score of each portion in Step Two in order to identify the areas that need serious consideration as far as being negotiated. The sections with the lowest average call for inner deliberation. Among the highest-ranking issues (the ones with the lowest average), you may choose to negotiate one to three items of contention with your potential employer, though more than three matters will make you appear like a difficult and ungracious candidate. That's exactly when your offer goes "bye-bye" if handled poorly. Re-evaluate the criteria you used to assign each ranking, just to be perfectly sure that they stand accurately. At this point, you may choose to accept or decline the offer without any negotiation.

Step Four: Devise

Now it is time to formulate a plan of action. Remember that how you behave during this part of the process will determine whether you have a successful outcome. Therefore, every decision must be carefully crafted to influence a positive response. Your strategy should include the following:

- Select a means of communication (phone, e-mail, in-person, snail mail, etc.).

- Figure out who would be most receptive to negotiation or find out who has the authority to make modifications on your offer.

- Develop and demonstrate concentration.

- Choose a time of day and place where you have privacy.

- Neutralize your emotions.

- Decide what you can be flexible on.

- Have a positive outlook.

- Think of ways during your conversation where you can exhibit graciousness.

- Develop your one to three areas of negotiation. Have your "prep guide" in front of you or know it well enough to cite it if you are about to negotiate in person.

- Start with the most important item on your list, as you may encounter a resistance toward entertaining any sort of negotiation (so you may have to cap your request to the single most important item on your agenda).

- Have income verification documents ready and at your fingertips in case you need to show proof of wages.

- Keep expectations in check. You will most likely not get results right away.

Step Five: Conquer

Your request to have offer particulars clarified is viewed as resourceful. However, the moment it is understood that your intentions are to have specific elements within your offer modified in order to suit your requirements, the perception may not be so positive. Maintaining a negotiation style that is equivalent to the interviewing style you've been using is important, as too often I see candidates turn into unrecognizable beings when it comes time to negotiate. Identify yourself within the profiles that best depict your personality as a negotiator. Each approach contains qualities that are detrimental and beneficial to countering your offer.

- **Nervous Nellie or Willie**

    – Characteristics: Timid, apprehensive, paranoid, dubious, and reverent

    – Detriment: Easily discouraged, can be short-changed, needs constant reinforcement and clarification

    – Benefit: Can graciously approach and embrace compromise

- **Conservative Ed or Edwina**

    – Characteristics: Traditional, logical, precise, stubborn, guarded, practical, prepared

    – Detriment: Difficult to convince, overanalyzes every bit of information, lacks creativity

    – Benefit: Meticulous and detail-oriented, exacting, professional demeanor

- **"All-in" Jim or Jean**

  – Characteristics: Daring, enterprising, impulsive, bold, aggressive, fearless, arrogant

  – Detriment: Unstructured, easily negotiates opportunities away, sometimes unrealistic

  – Benefit: Masks emotions well, reaps high-stake rewards

- **Curious George or Georgina**

  – Characteristics: Inquisitive, exploratory, tentative, flippant, impatient

  – Detriment: May lack commitment (i.e., is a window-shopper), may easily lose sight of details

  – Benefit: Amenable to change, is pressure-free when making decisions

Keep Your Eye on the Ball

Once you've expressed your concerns and brought forth the areas where you would like to see modification, you've put the duty of responsibility back in their hands. You've placed the ball back in their court, and it could be days before you see it again. Often, the person with whom you may have discussed the changes is purely the messenger. He or she now has to locate the decision maker or decision-making team to reassess your requests.

One piece of advice I'll offer you is that when the decision arrives, you should not receive it with an entirely new set of requests. This will only irritate and offend your potential employer, which is exactly how offers are rescinded. You may, however, ask for additional clarification or variation on your existing requests; in doing so, know your limits as to how many times you will harp on the same thing. Also, consider what you would be willing to give up for the thing(s) you are hoping will be granted. For instance, an additional vacation week can be negotiated by compromising to take it unpaid. You can also volunteer to make up the time by working during days when normal business hours are not in session. Just remember that with every request, you are passing the ball back, and they can decide not to give it back. Also, you run the risk of having the company lose interest in you, as sometimes potential employers will continue their candidate search until there is an official accepted offer. They may find someone who is more flexible or better qualified for the position, so don't get carried away by handing them control one too many times.

There are times when, assuming all discussions have gone smoothly, the client will conclude deliberations by letting you know that what you are about to hear is truly the final offer. That puts the ball back in your hands again. Finally, it's time to decide whether you will be accepting or declining your offer.

Acceptance

You've carefully weighed *all* of your options, including staying at your present position, and your findings, along with your instincts, tell you that this is indeed the right opportunity for you. You don't even need to finish the process at other pending companies. This is absolutely, positively it. If that's the case, then accept the job wholeheartedly. Call the company representative with whom you've been interacting and let her know the great news right away. Follow the acceptance phone call with a written acceptance.

Your next order of business is to contact other companies where you have been interviewing. Notifying prospective companies not only shows excellent protocol and consideration, but it also proves you are an ethical person who is worthy of being considered at any other point in your career. For some candidates, contacting companies to let them know they are off the market is uncomfortable, and they opt for the "missing in action" method of communicating instead. I highly discourage this practice, as it will mislead other companies into thinking you are still interested, which can get sticky, especially if you're presented with another tempting offer once you've accepted and/or started your new job.

Extension

There are times when, even after all of the due diligence and negotiation is completed, a candidate may still not be able to give a yes-or-no answer. In this case, an extension may be requested, both verbally and in writing. It is my belief that asking for an extension after all of the steps that it takes to make a decision communicates that you have your sights set on better prospects. You may request it in the most mannerly way, but in my book it is rude and self-righteous. This is exactly the time when you can end up shooting yourself in the foot by prolonging an offer you have for one that may never materialize. Companies are not naive to this tactic, and they will protect themselves by continuing the interview process or completely turning themselves off to you and rescinding the offer they've put on the table. After all, if you have so many reservations, you must have ulterior motives. On the other hand, if you decide to be forthright and let them know that you are waiting to hear the results of another offer, you are still gambling the extended offer, but at least you are letting the company know where you stand. Either way, you jeopardize your offer by asking for an extension, and for that reason, I would advise you to think twice before requesting one.

Declining

Declining an offer may be contingent upon consideration of the offer at face value or evaluation of the terms and conditions against multiple simultaneous offers. If your decision is to decline an offer, it is professionally courteous to do so verbally *and* in writing. Be sure to thank all those who took the time to interview you, as you are inconveniencing them with your decision. That's not to say that you are wrong for declining an offer, as you should accept the offer that best meets your professional goal and compensation requests. However, in this instance, you should be extra-sensitive to the fact that many hours spent on considering your candidacy have now gone in vain. Be gracious, even if you despised your interviewing experience because you never know where you can meet up with them again. You may define your reasons for declining the offer, as it might help them in their continued search. However, you are not obliged to do so. Remember that the world is too small to end business transactions on a sour note.

Regardless of what your answer is, how you deliver your final decision will speak volumes about you and your image. Your candidacy might even be revisited for another vacant position within the firm.

14

Leave Happily Ever After
Resign Graciously and Beware of Counteroffers

Every exit is an entry somewhere else. —Tom Stoppard (British playwright)

THERE ARE VERY few things more intimidating than making your way into your boss's office or a human resources office to share the news that you are moving on. It doesn't matter whether you have the opportunity of a lifetime waiting for you once you step out the door or whether you're taking this brave step in order to have the time to find your next opportunity. The fact is that you will conjure up all sorts of emotions as you prepare to make your exit out of this professional chapter once and for all. Perhaps it's your first job out of college where you debuted and matured as a professional, or maybe you're leaving colleagues and staff members behind who depend on your mentorship. The reasons are infinite, but in the end you must think of what is best for you (and your family if it applies), and there's absolutely nothing wrong with that.

In truth, the only thing wrong with resignations is how they are handled. There is just no telling how the resignation will be received, because as much as you think you know the players involved, or you've seen how they've reacted in the past when employees have resigned, you've never witnessed their reaction when *you've* resigned—and you may just be in for a shock. You could be asked to pack up and go as soon as you say, "I'm resigning." You might face a manager or an owner who becomes completely indignant about the timing of your departure (because there is never a good time) and chews you up and spits you out. Alternatively, your boss may ask you to stay longer than the standard two-week notice (even if it's not stipulated in your employment agreement) or, worse, beg you to stay indefinitely by offering you the sun, the moon, and the stars. No matter what, maintaining your professional demeanor will be appreciated and remembered long after you're gone. Handled poorly, your resignation may be the basis of burning a bridge forever.

Do As I Say . . . Not As I Do

I was a placement manager for eight years at another staffing company before joining Perennial Resources International (www.perennialresources.com) as a partner, The prospect of contributing my efforts and ideas to a start-up venture that offered financial equity rewards had always attracted me, and finally the opportunity for such an endeavor was available. The timing couldn't have been better, as many internal changes had been introduced at my current company due to new ownership. Among the changes were new nonsolicitation agreements and retention bonus agreements to be signed by each employee. Of course, I had complied with the rules and signed months before I learned of the opportunity that lay ahead. Both agreements seemed reasonable in what they stipulated: The nonsolicitation agreement precluded any employee from soliciting other employees to a new job opportunity, and the retention bonus specified a length of time wherein if my employment was terminated (by my own doing or the company's doing), the undisclosed amount was to be returned. I wasn't worried, as I had no intention of soliciting any coworkers, and the retention bonus could easily be returned.

My mind was made up to move on. While I'd coached candidates on resigning hundreds of times before, I never realized how difficult this would be until it was my turn to sever ties with the company I had grown up in. On the morning I had designated as the "deed day," I approached the manager who had hired, fostered, and promoted me throughout my tenure. She had grown to know me so well that she knew exactly what I was about to tell her from my stance. Let's just say it was much more emotional (for both of us) than I ever imagined it would be. I had prepared exactly what to say and do beforehand because I was aware that my industry's practice was to have you off the premises upon resignation. I had all company property and files ready to be relinquished; I complied with my exit interview and was neutral in my tone and demeanor.

All in all, it was a more than civilized exchange. I did everything right except . . . return the check with the retention bonus amount. It wasn't as if the sum had been life-changing, but I had been advised (by someone whose opinion I highly respected) to negotiate keeping two-thirds of it since I had fulfilled two-thirds of the time required to earn this bonus. Why I went along with it I'll never know, but it made sense to me at the time. It was clearly reiterated by the president of the company right before I set foot into the elevator, "Don't forget to return the retention bonus." All I can tell you is that when I walked out of the place I'd called home for so many years, I didn't quite have the winning feeling I thought I'd have. There was still time to return the entire amount, but the more I thought about it and consulted "reliable" sources, the more I convinced myself that I had earned it (or at least part of it).

A few weeks after my resignation, the attorney letters started to appear in my mailbox, and rather than reconsidering my decision, I turned into the impulsive "all-in" Jean I describe in Chapter 13. I went as far as hiring a legal team that also thought I stood a chance of winning, given the language used to draft the retention agreement. As the months progressed, the threatening letters turned into depositions and a full-blown lawsuit against me. By the time I recognized I had made a mistake, it was too late. The final judgment was not only in my former employer's favor to receive the entire retention bonus amount, but I was also ordered to pay a deficit that had been accumulated against my commissions (this had never been enforced with past employees).

What a disaster! Oh, and it gets worse; no sooner had I gotten the decision in the mail than my assets were frozen until I paid what I owed. I then had to deal with all sorts of returned checks on top of owing double the amount I would have paid had I not allowed my entitlement issues to stand in the way of a sound decision. At this point, my attorneys presented me with the option to appeal the decision, which meant continuing the battle. Who knows if I would have won the case or at least mitigated my losses. I finally came to my senses though and did what I should have done all along. It was time to move on with my career, and the fact that I've helped build a business that has thrived and survived the ups and downs of a tumultuous economy is proof of that. However, I could have saved myself a lot of aggravation and money had my resignation choices been less impulsive. All it would have taken was three more months to complete my retention stay or to return the check in full and I could've started in my new venture without a noose around my neck.

Interestingly, once everything was resolved, I ran into my former manager at a professional association meeting, and instead of avoiding me, as she had since my resignation, she approached me with amicable intentions. I reciprocated her greeting, and we shook hands as a peace offering. I have since visited my former company and have even established a working relationship with it. It hadn't been personal, and now that I see it from an owner's perspective, I understand it even more. We all have regrets in life, and this is mine. I share it with you to emphasize how a poorly executed resignation can erase years of loyal service. As you now know, it's happened to the best of us. Learn from my mistake and handle your resignation not as I've done but as I say.

Resignation Declaration

Be absolutely certain that resigning is the right action to take. You can't take back a resignation so quickly once you've declared it. Also, be sure that your offer has been authorized by all who need to validate it; that your background and credit check results have been cleared; and that you have a signed offer letter or employment agreement confirming *all* of the details of your offer—especially your start date. Be firm about your decision and avoid succumbing to spur-of-the-moment counteroffers (more on counteroffers later in this chapter).

Resignation Discretions

Exhibit a high level of diplomacy during your resignation and throughout your exit interview, and follow your discretion beyond your last hours at the job. It will go a long way. Be gracious for having been given the opportunity to earn a living even if you believe your former employer got the better end of the relationship. You're on your way out, so don't let bad feelings out now. Point out positive experiences or projects that have been particularly enjoyable or noteworthy. Avoid bashing your boss and other coworkers, though if you feel that you can describe a situation that can be rectified (and you can do so effectively), then feel free to bring it up. However, less is more in this category. Also, be clear that your decision to move on is not relevant to anything they haven't given you. Assure them that you have nothing against the company or its employees, and that you will not solicit or instigate anyone to follow in your footsteps. You will not be the cause of a mass exodus.

Resignation Altercations

I've been there. I know it's a tough pill to swallow, but resigning any other way than in person is lame. If you really anticipate that things will get ugly, the second alternative is communicating via phone. A "Dear John/Jane" letter sent via e-mail or U.S. Mail prior to a verbal discussion is evasive. Alternatively, if you fear that your immediate supervisor will be confrontational, you can request a human resources representative who can act as an intermediary to join the meeting. If no one is available to act as a buffer, you may reconsider the timing of your resignation. If you are hard-pressed to squeeze in your standard two-week notice, then bite the bullet and proceed with your plan of action. Remain calm and even-tempered and remind yourself that it's not personal. If you're unexpectedly asked to vacate the premises without as much as a detour to the restroom, avoid conflict at all cost and follow instructions. Request that your personal belongings be shipped to you. Maintain a neutral tone, stay in control of your emotions, and, most important, do not add fuel to the fire by mir-roring hostile behavior.

Resignation Obligations

Fulfill your obligations as an employee until the end. Act in accordance with your employment agreement and be productive during your notice period leading up to your last day. Coming and going as you please is not recom-mended. In some cases, when you don't have another job opportunity wait-ing for you or you have other reasons why you may be taking a hiatus from the job force, you might offer an extended notice. Otherwise, if you are bound to staying longer than the standard two-week notice (as per your employment agreement), be sure this is not a compromising factor with your new company's plans for you. If you are not bound to a notice period of longer than two weeks but you are asked to stay, be sure doing so doesn't jeopardize your new job offer. Offer to help with the replacement of your position or to train an internal candidate who is being transferred into your position. Tie up loose ends by cooperating with the completion of an exit interview and returning all company property (e.g., employee identifica-tion cards, entry access cards, corporate credit cards, laptops, cell phones, supplies). Write a letter of resignation for company compliance.

Resignation Ramifications

As tempting as it may be not to, leave proprietary information and com-pany commodities, especially human commodities, behind. Re-read employment agreements, employee handbooks, and all agreements and policies you have signed. Seek legal counsel before signing documents you are having trouble interpreting and don't assume you'll never have agreements enforced. It can save you money, aggravation, awkwardness, and general peace of mind. Own up to what you've agreed to. Otherwise, prepare for a lengthy, expensive, gratuitous feud.

Resignation Information

Don't be in such a hurry to leave that you forget to check on information regarding what is owed to you, causing you to leave money behind. I'm not talking about a paycheck per se, but about earned sick, holiday, and vacation pay. As far as earned commissions and merit- or incentive-based bonuses (excluding retention bonuses), you may want to time resigning until after they've been issued to you. It's not to say you won't get them, but they may just be delayed or held as collateral. Also, be well informed on how long medical benefits will be active, because as luck would have it, you or one of your dependents is bound to get sick just when your coverage ends. If you are not taking on another position immediately following your resignation, be sure to ask for details about continuing health coverage. Lastly, find out specifics on how to withdraw or roll over funds from pension plans or 401(k)s; your new employer should be able to assist you with carrying out these procedures.

Resignation Summation

As soon as you've cooperated with tying up all of the loose ends of a resignation, it is perfectly acceptable to ask for a reference in writing. Written references are gold because you can retain and reuse them as often as you change a job (which hopefully isn't too often). Request a written reference because, just as you are moving on, others who can vouch for you may also move on with their careers, and it will be much more difficult—and often impossible—to reach them. If a potential reference feels uncomfortable writing a reference letter, ask for an e-mail address, cell phone number, or any other contact number where he or she can be reached if you need a reference down the road. Don't be surprised if an employer is resistant to providing any type of reference these days, even if you are leaving in good standing, as the employer may be wary of defamation claims. Ease an employer's concern by offering to sign a liability waiver releasing your right to take legal action on the basis of the reference. Be absolutely certain that this person's evaluation of your professional work and conduct will be a positive one before relinquishing your legal rights.

Poisonous Bite

Accepting a counteroffer is synonymous with biting into a poisonous apple. The prospect of staying within the safe niche of your current job may appear sweet on the periphery, but once you delve into the motives behind why a counteroffer is proposed, you'll realize how deadly it would be to accept one. Sure, you'll feel flattered, or feelings of guilt may coerce you into considering the possibility of staying. You may even second-guess the elements of what makes your existing offer so appealing. However, once you open your mouth to announce your resignation, you had better be sure that it is definitely the path you want to take. Keep your decision to leave firm and independent from your company's reasons to keep you. I guarantee you that once you've given notice, the company's basis for keeping you will be much more short term than you might think. A resignation often takes the wind out of an employer. Therefore, enticing you to stay is a desperate and hasty response to your unsettling news. You can be sure that once the shock wears off, feelings of resentment and betrayal will start to fester. Don't fall prey to the counteroffer trap. It will come back to haunt you in more ways than one. Let me count the ways:

COUNT YOUR COUNTEROFFER CONSEQUENCES

- Money will be a temporary fix, and its novelty will wear off quickly.

- You will be faced with the original reason that made you look elsewhere in the first place.

- You will act as a bandage for your employer to bide time in replacing you.

- You will be overlooked for promotions, as you will be branded with the scarlet letter "T" for "traitor."

- You will accept a premature review and increase disguised as your counteroffer increase.

- You will be among the first to be downsized during times of recession or corporate restructuring.

- You will, in essence, be accepting a bribe called a counteroffer, which reinforces in the company's view the character flaw you showed by resigning in the first place.

PART THREE

COMMUNICATION

15

Network It
Weaving Your Human Web

Networking is an essential part of building wealth. —*Armstrong Williams (American political commentator)*

DO YOU EVER feel like it's not what you know but who you know? Such thoughts are roused as your counterpart accepts the promotion you had been eyeing, when in your mind it's clear that your performance and credentials far exceeded hers. What's her advantage?

You may choose to call her a brownnose, but actually the fact that she's been active on task forces and advisory boards within the company makes her a proactive employee who is about to reap the benefits of networking. She's not only created an opportunity to strengthen her ties with senior executives in a closely monitored setting without additional compensation, but she's also positioned herself in a forum where talents other than the ones she's been officially hired to perform will be showcased. All the while, a sense of trust and professional likability has been nurtured with your colleague's unfailing involvement in activities that have gone beyond the scope of her job description. Instead of begrudging her, learn from her ability to turn voluntary services into profitable opportunities as she reinforces the ties of her "human net" with those who have a favorable say in her future. Kudos to her for putting in her time, as the art of networking is not a quick fix, nor is it a one-hit wonder. It's also not synonymous with selling, though good networkers can be successful at self-promotion or advocating a product.

Networking is a genuine skill of building and maintaining human relationships that are mutually gainful. It's the "one-hand-washes-the-other" assumption, though to presume that you will immediately be the beneficiary can lead you to dire disappointment. While some of you may be born networkers no matter what the situation, others may be obliged to develop and enhance this ability if only for the purpose of enhancing your career visibility while increasing your hiring probabilities. This chapter is meant to help you if you feel isolated from everyone who can be instrumental in reaching your career objectives. Be sure not to underestimate the value that certain unexpected contacts bring to your job search. I've also intended this chapter for anyone who feels like they've reached their potential in fortifying and widening their net. While networking applies to all facets of life, applied well in your career search, it can substantially even out the playing field of hiring possibilities.

Safety Net

As you walk on a tightrope over endless job search pitfalls, you should rely on a safety net that can sustain the stream of disappointments. The strength and endurance of your safety net is composed of relationships that are neatly intertwined—some tighter than others. You are the architect of your social and professional network. Similar to a spider's web-spinning phenomenon, a primary thread is spun (an introduction) followed by series of radials (connections) created to seize their prey (information). Coincidently, both nets gain strength from the labors of recurring contact.

Parents, grandparents, siblings, spouses/life partners, children, and other close family and friends act as the nucleus of your net. Members of this primary structure provide you with unconditional support and counseling regardless of whether they can directly help you reach your professional goals. If they happen to be in a position to help you, don't be too proud to use it to your advantage. I've come across candidates whose primary family members have access to individuals and organizations that would be instrumental in achieving their goals; instead, they foolishly choose not to ask for help. Somehow they feel that asking for an introduction waters down the merit of achieving success on their own. Well, let me be the one to tell you that is neither progressive nor accurate thinking. Even when an introduction grants you an anticipated and even welcoming response, it's your doing that will nurture it beyond the introductory stage.

The secondary radial consists of friends, neighbors, teachers, colleagues, employees, recruiters, doctors, babysitters, housekeepers, and just about everyone you can directly access through your personal and/or professional encounters. No contact is insignificant. For instance, babysitters have an extensive network because of multiple-job juggling. Though your level of interaction and familiarity varies greatly among members of this group, the common link is that your success can still personally impact them. For instance, a recruiter who places you in a job receives payment, a professor who pulls strings to get you in the door of a prominent company gains personal satisfaction, and a neighbor who directs you toward a viable lead gets rid of hearing you complain about not finding a job. Each may have implicit expectations of how you can reciprocate: The recruiter might anticipate client referrals, the professor may await future alumni support, and your neighbor may look forward to your next barbecue. The emotional dependence is not as strong as it is with your primary structure, but these members are still within reach of reaping the benefits of your success.

Members of the tertiary radial are acquaintances, friends of friends, or extended relatives whom you see at weddings and funerals. Your primary or secondary contacts are often the threads (circular trails) that connect you to these constituents, though third-party organizations or associations can also be a vehicle for linkage. They may not be your closest ties but they do contribute to the size and range of your net, as there's no telling where or how far you'll fall. These bonds may also be solidified when there is an explicit purpose that links your paths (e.g., finding a job).

The last radial is the most difficult to construct, as its members' "unattainable" status is not accelerated or noticeably changed by adding you to their human net (at least not immediately). As scary as it may be to contact someone who is widely sought after, remind yourself that he or she is a mortal who may have had to overcome plenty of hurdles before achieving success. As long as your intent is properly defined and your delivery is sincere and respectful, you stand a chance of getting a response. Show persistence without coming across as a stalker, value your time as well as your effort, and know when to move on. Most of all, realize that even in your grimmest job-search days, you have a network to act as your sounding board as well as a practical source of information.

Tools for Weaving Your Web

Assembling a toolkit of tangible and intangible items is a practical way of integrating networking as part of your lifestyle. You will no longer feel like networking requires wearing a suit, paying an entrance fee, and working a room. Quite the opposite, as some of the best bonding takes place on the sidelines of your child's soccer game, at your local supermarket, on the golf course, or at the nail salon. Prepare for the unexpected, and view every interaction as a relationship-building opportunity. Keep a variety of tools at your fingertips and reach for specific ones based on the scenario. Remember the mutually benefiting principle of networking: "It's not all about you." Therefore, your tools should present value to you and your recipient.

■ **Business card:** A business card is your calling card, and offering one opens the lines of communication beyond your initial connection. Ending a one-on-one conversation with someone during an organized networking event without offering your business card communicates a lack of interest. That's not to say that you are obliged to give your card to someone who makes you feel completely uncomfortable; just know that if you don't offer it, your message is loud and clear. If you do exchange cards with someone and you choose to use your company business card, be careful it doesn't backfire. It is risky to receive job search–related phone calls or e-mails at work because:

– You don't know who is listening around you.

– You are using company-owned communication systems, and your employer has every right to be privy to your dealings.

I have often suggested that candidates create a business card for the express purpose of job-search networking. This card should contain your name (including any certifications or designations), private phone number(s), private e-mail(s), address (optional), and either your title or an interesting quote or tag line that can be a subject of conversation when it is read. Choose quality card stock and emboss your initials or some type of industry-related logo for distinction. The compact size of your business cards will make them highly transportable and easy to store in your wallet, pocket, or car. Handing a business card along with a résumé is redundant. Also, when you are offered a business card, it is polite to acknowledge it by reading it before putting it away. If you are attending a large networking event, choose a pocket or bag where you place winning business cards separate from the duds.

- **Résumé:** Résumé formats are discussed in Chapter 16. However, for the purpose of networking, résumés should be offered by invitation only. If during a conversation a connection offers to pass your résumé along to his company's hiring division, then it is appropriate to offer one. You may even want to include a cover letter along with it. Otherwise, handing an unsolicited résumé out is highly aggressive and sales-like. There is an exception to this protocol and that is while attending job fairs. In that scenario, it is appropriate to offer your résumé to a company representative, as that is the purpose of the event. In that case, you would be safe to bring along 20 to 50 hard copies of your résumé, depending on the number of participating companies. Under normal circumstances, have at least 10 hard copies of your résumé ready for distribution, given the right forum.

▪ **Stationery:** Quality stationery adds style and class to handwritten follow-up, thank-you, and "staying in touch" notes. Whenever you're composing this type of correspondence, be sure to include details of when and where you met. As much as you think you may have left a lasting impression on someone, you'd be surprised how quickly others can forget about you. This is where your meticulous notes will refresh your memory to compose an accurate and genuine message. Be sure to choose stationery that is not overly ornate or fragranced, as your intentions can be misinterpreted.

▪ **Resources:** Develop a genuine rapport by forwarding articles, newsletters, announcements, invitations, information on museum exhibits and debuts, and other useful materials you come across regarding a topic you have in common with a network member. If you've written or contributed to an article that you think would be of interest to a particular contact, be sure to forward it. Even if you haven't written something but you've read something or know about an event that is relevant to your contact's interest, it might be worth forwarding with an accompanying note. The note should be personalized so that it's clearly not part of a mass e-mail. If you have an address, mailing it will prevent it from getting lost in the mounds of daily e-mails. The main thing is to come across as genuine, thoughtful, and full of informational resources. Establishing yourself as a resource will add value to your connection. You can gather information through Web sources, internal Web sites, trade publications, business journals, directories, newspapers, and personal contacts.

▪ **Elevator pitch:** An elevator pitch is your 30-second commercial to introduce yourself. Formulating a 30-second commercial is helpful for many reasons. First of all, it forces you to really think about who you are and what you do. An elevator pitch may be used to communicate what you do to all of your contacts. It's easy to say, "I'm a lawyer," or "I'm a designer," but it's also not descriptive enough to have someone help you with your job-search objective. After all, there are so many types of specialties in law, and designers can design apparel, graphics, or theatrical sets. Practice your elevator pitch on family and friends, leaving out the first sentence, since they obviously know your name. You'll be surprised at how oblivious they are to what you actually do for a living. Create a more interesting introduction for yourself by answering the following five questions:

– Who am I?

– What do I do?

– How do I it?

– How am I different?

– What is my goal?

Sample elevator pitch:

Hi, I'm Lizandra Vega. I help people achieve their career objectives by improving upon their professional image. I've successfully guided thousands of job seekers of various levels in attaining and maintaining job security within a wide range of industries. Through my recently published book, I hope to further stimulate image awareness and inspire change for individuals who aspire to reach new heights in their career.

▪ **Tracking system:** The effort and energy you use to make connections every day would be wasted if you didn't gather your information in a reliable tracking system. What good would it do to have 100 new business cards if you didn't input them into a system that makes it easy for you to follow up and strengthen your connections? Alphabetically arranging business cards in a binder is the minimally responsible practice if you don't have access to electronic capabilities. However, using a system where you can generate mailing lists or merge e-mail addresses is a more time-effective solution. Add information about each of your entries as you learn more about him or her. Include information about birthdays, names of children or pets, graduations, and other bits of information that will give you a reason to touch base and be a source of conversation. A tracking system can also be a helpful reminder, letting you know that you haven't touched base in a while and maybe you ought to reach out if you want to keep the lines of communication open.

- **Information resources:** Keep your bag of current local and world events full. Know a little bit about as many things as possible, because you never know how far you'll have to reach to keep up in conversation. Also, improve your knowledge in your area of expertise, whether it's heart surgery or basket weaving. Become an authority in your field and you will be sought after by many, including potential employers. Be generous with your knowledge; it will be reciprocated when you least expect it.

- **Listening skills:** There are three types of listeners: competitive, passive, and active. Competitive listeners interrupt your every thought, which is rude and selfish. It's next to impossible to build a relationship with someone who finishes your sentences or doesn't even let you get a sentence out of your mouth. Passive listeners may be hearing what you're saying but not acknowledge what you're saying. That makes for a pretty boring, one-sided conversation. Active listeners are the most balanced listeners. They wait their turn to ask questions and will often confirm or rephrase what you said. This avoids misunderstandings. Practice your listening skills by smiling, nodding your head in agreement, and using positive body language to convey that you are absorbing your contact's message. You are apt to attract more contacts to your network by engaging in an equal conversation. It is the happy medium between being an overbearing or a dull listener.

Diversifying Your Network: Getting Out of Your Bubble

Not so long ago (it hardly seems like it) when I was a senior at John F. Kennedy High School in the Bronx, I had selected several universities where I would apply for admission. All of them were top schools, as my grades, extracurricular activities, and aspirations had always been grand. Some of them were local institutions, but my top choices were out of state. As the decisions arrived, I was flattered by acceptances but I was pretty sure I'd ultimately attend one of the universities close to home. I had never even gone to sleepaway camp, so the prospect of leaving home petrified me. Still, for some inexplicable reason, I sat on my decisions to accept or decline any of my offers. That is until one evening when I received a call from a student at one of my acceptance schools, Wesleyan University.

The caller congratulated me on getting in and then offered to host me at the annual "Pre-frosh Minority Weekend." I guessed that was our common ground, and while at first I was offended to be singled out for my "minority" status, she worked on me enough to convince me to go. That weekend was life-changing for me. Upon stepping out of the bus I rode with other accepted students from New York, I realized I had been living in a bubble. It was quite clear why the *Barron's Directory* had dubbed it "Diversity University." Everything about the weekend was refreshing: the trees, the campus, the seminars, the speakers, the professors, and especially the student body. Let's just say that the weekend merely scratched the surface of what I had in store during the next four years, for I earned a degree in life. I realized it was Wesleyan's mission to diversify its student population for the benefit of enrichment, and it became clear how I contributed to this endeavor.

My college experience enriched my networking capabilities greatly, as I explored relationships with students whose differences complemented my deficiencies. For that reason, I urge you to "think outside of the box" and engage in situations that are outside of your safety net. Therefore, if your lifestyle permits it, go out of your comfort zone and engage in educational, professional, social, and philanthropic opportunities that compel you to interact with individuals outside of your occupational, sociological, cultural, and generational comfort zones. Such connections will broaden, balance, and enhance your network in more ways than you can imagine.

So Many Networks, So Little Time . . .

Networking resources are available in a variety of circles. Choosing one that feels comfortable for you will depend greatly on your personality and style of making connections. Some avenues worth exploring are shown here, and specific resources are located in the Appendix.

• **Online networks can help** you expand your global networking capabilities. Through online sources such as job sites, social networking sites, podcasts, Webinars, blogs, chat rooms, and forums, you can instantly create your profile, download your résumé, access job postings, and join groups and forums to discuss questions or concerns related to your job search. This is a cost-effective way to benefit from millions of resources any time of the day, any day of the week, right from the comfort of your own home.

• **Professional trade associations** provide great opportunities to establish your profile and visibility with contacts who have skills, education, and practice similar to yours. The time commitment for this type is usually once a month if you are a "member at large." However, you may opt for a more active role as a committee or board member to heighten your involvement and networking possibilities. Trade associations offer industry-specific workshops, seminars, certification preparation, and conferences, as well as client referral services. You may also benefit from being included in professional directories, which can grant you recognition as well as stir up potential business.

• **Business associations** offer similar benefits to trade associations except the focus is on general business development. Business associations can provide you with a wider list of strategic partners who complement your professional course of action. These associations address a wider scope of topics through their conferences, speakers, workshops, and other career- and business-related events.

• **Service organizations** range from local, community, and school boards to volunteer involvement through city, state, national, and international nonprofit associations. These can include Big Brother, Big

Sister, and similar organizations where the focus is to make a humanitarian difference by contributing your unpaid talents and resources. Services like Volunteermatch.org can be very useful in finding the perfect fit for you.

- **Alumni associations** are great for rekindling relationships that may have once been a part of your immediate radials. Alumni associations instantly bond you with alumni from many graduating classes located in geographic areas around the world whose professions represent a wide spectrum. It is a great way to find a mentor, referrals, and job considerations, and to stay posted on your educational institution's progress and advanced resources.

- **Social/niche organizations'** primary purpose is to link individuals who have a common interest other than looking for a job. Such networks can be for the purpose of dating or sharing hobby, travel, or other leisure interests. Other niches may include working moms, retired persons, or individuals of a certain income bracket. While the express purpose is not to find job-search leads through such associations, there is a fine line between social and professional networking, and it is not out of the realm of possibility to find access to a job-search tip through this type of network.

- **Organized networks** are networks formed for the specific purpose of exchanging leads. Attendance requirements are much more structured, and meeting times are consistently set (usually once a week). Such networks typically have local chapter meetings with national or international networking capabilities. Typically, these networks require substantial membership fees to weed out casual or flippant involvement, and meetings have a very clear objective: to create a network that will be your eyes and ears to specifically help you grow one or more streams of income as you reciprocate the deed toward fellow members of your group.

- **Resource networks** such as trade publications; business information newspapers, magazines, and journals; and company and informational Web sites can help you learn about companies' history and financial data. Such networks are useful for information gathering and preparing for interviews.

▪ **Personal networks** include private parties, picnics, and events at friends' homes or catered venues. Think of all interactions through personal networks as potentials for growing your network.

Other Hidden Networks

Even in a good market, many jobs are not advertised. In a shaky job market, the number of hidden jobs increases, as employers can truly afford the luxury of being extra-selective. Discover hidden jobs by:

▪ **Consulting or temping:** Companies that don't readily have approval for permanent positions will hire consultants or temporary employees to fulfill job requirements. If you prove to be a productive and reliable employee, you may be considered over an outside candidate once budgets allow for a stable opportunity.

▪ **Volunteering or interning:** This is also a great way for recent college graduates, re-entrants into the job market, and change-of-career employees to land an on-the-job interview to prove their capabilities.

▪ **Researching relocated companies:** Access companies that have moved to a desired work location near you, as many times such companies do not retain all of their employees because of commuting conflicts. Look for such companies in the commercial real estate section of a newspaper or a local business information publication.

▪ **Using staffing and search firms:** How could I omit the portal that has been my source of livelihood because of clients' loyal trust in having me find them the very best talent for jobs that would be too time-consuming to recruit for if posted online. Staffing and search firms have established relationships with their clients based on past proven success. Being submitted by a search professional can save you months of aggravation of trying to get through the door without a trusted endorsement behind your candidacy.

▪ **Attending open houses and job fairs:** Open houses and job fairs give potential employers a chance to meet you without the expectation of having to formally interview you. These situations may entice exploratory interviews. Exploratory interviews are worth pursuing, as they give you a preliminary advantage over your competition by putting you in front of the recruiter before a job even opens up.

Networking is truly a process that takes patience, organization, and endurance to master. The possibilities are endless, but one thing is for sure: Its results are much more successful when integrated as part of your lifestyle. You can't expect to find yourself looking for a job and magically have one of your networks immediately come to the rescue. You need to put in your time. You need to have given before you ask to receive.

16

Write It Up
Cover Letters, Résumés, Thank-You Notes, and Other Correspondence

What is written without effort is in general read without pleasure. —*Samuel Johnson (English poet, critic, and writer)*

WRITE IT UP! This is what recruiters say shortly after an offer has been accepted and a start date has been confirmed. However, before achieving this great feat, as you well know by now, the search process is a lengthy and intense one. Whether I am actively seeking candidates or screening submissions, my decision to pursue them is greatly impacted by their written correspondence. As an image consultant, my intuition formulates opinions on how the 3-D version of the written word will look, act, and sound before the person actually comes in. Cover letters, résumés, executive summaries, and thank-you notes are like advertisements in a magazine or banner ads on your computer screen. They are the coming attractions of a full-length movie. I, along with many of my recruiting colleagues and in-house recruiting managers, as discerning audience members, will not give further consideration to someone if we don't like the preview.

The best advice I can give you is to be truthful about everything you write down, to the best of your recollection, of course. Do not embellish the facts, because even if it gets you through the door, a savvy and experienced interviewer will unmask you in no time. Even when you think you've "gotten one over," you will be found out in the end, when you've lived and survived the interviewing process and you think you are off the hook. Just when you're about to resign from your present job or about to figure out the start date for your new job, you will be haunted by the results of your background check. If you have not been truthful, this will be the time you will be busted. That is an unfortunate and embarrassing situation to be caught in.

Getting back to your written correspondence, you must be extra-meticulous about spelling and grammar, awkward phrasing, and carelessness in presentation and delivery, because they will not only undermine your credibility but they also will be the writing on the wall to future negligence on your part should you be chosen for the job in spite of such glaring clues.

Remember the Five Cs as guidelines to writing interview correspondence:

▪ **Clarity:** Spell-check will take you only so far, as it will not pick up spelling errors such as confusing "to," "two," and "too." To all of you smarty-pants mathematical geniuses, reading, grammar, and punctuation still count, even if you are looking for a numbers-related job. As far as tenses, only your current job should be described in the present tense. All previous jobs should be described in the past. Keep the vocabulary simple and clear of unnecessary technical mumbo jumbo.

▪ **Coherence:** Write sentences that are well thought out and logical. You don't want to sound like you were under the influence of something that won't make it past the drug screening, so pay close attention to this.

▪ **Compelling:** Don't be afraid of selling yourself to the recruiter. Be persuasive and confident, yet be mindful of sounding cocky. A lot of candidates let the opportunity to be compelling pass them by. It's a bit tricky because you don't want to sound like a braggart. Think of this part as the one where matching your credentials and skills to the job description will do you good.

• **Correctness:** I cannot stress this one enough: Pay special attention to details such as the title of the person you are addressing and the title of the position you are seeking (if you know the title), and make sure that all names are spelled properly. Also, make sure the address on the envelope is correct, with the correct floor, so that your correspondence reaches the right hands.

• **Character:** Presenting your disposition, performance, and trustworthiness will most likely come in the form of reference letters. Include such letters with your résumé or carry them with you during an interview. If you don't have letters handy, have names and contact information ready to divulge.

The Cover Letter

The cover letter does just what its name implies. It serves as the cover or outerwear that protects and shields the main outfit, otherwise known as the résumé. The cover letter is meant to entice the screener to keep reading the rest of the information that is enclosed. You will want to show how your assets, such as your personality, your capabilities, and your credentials, are a good match for the job (if you have read the job description ahead of time) or, at the very least, how they are compatible with the corporate culture of the company where you are submitting your résumé.

Time is precious, so keep your cover letters brief. I often receive cover letters that repeat *everything* that is on the résumé that accompanies it. It's not only redundant and time-consuming to read two versions of the same thing, but it also causes me to quickly move on to the next résumé. Instead, transfer information from your résumé that most relates to the job description (see "Job Description Sample") to show that you are a perfect match. The one thing you can't reiterate often enough is your contact information. In the event that your cover letter and résumé are ever separated, a hiring manager should be able to pair them by the contact information. However, the main goal of a cover letter is to highlight your point of difference.

The tone of your cover letter should be proactive, not reactive. While you have a choice of business letter layout, my personal favorite is the full-block style, as it is the easiest one to remember. You really can't go wrong with it because everything is flush with the left margin, and tabs are non-existent. It is professional, neat, and businesslike. There is also the modified block style where the date, return address, complimentary closing, and signature are to the right of center, while the body of the letter is aligned at the left margin. Candidates with longer cover letters like to use the modified block for its "breaks," so the words don't appear overly crowded on the page. Regardless of which layout you choose, the margins should be between 1" and 1.5" and start around six to ten lines from the top of the paper.

As a precaution, avoid taking the liberty of having your salutation read, "Dear Mike" when the person you are addressing is named "Michael Lane" and you haven't even met him. In this case, if you know the recruiter's name, your salutation would be "Dear Mr. Lane" or "Dear Mr. Michael Lane," followed by a colon (:). If the name of the addressee is top secret (as per their receptionist), then it is appropriate to address the recipient by his or her title, such as "Dear Human Resources Director." As far as the closing that precedes your signature, it should be businesslike and respectful, such as "Sincerely," Sincerely yours," or "Cordially yours."

Lastly, keep your current salary and the salary you are seeking out of the picture for now. Salary is something that is best discussed in person, during the interview (preferably during your first meeting). Most job requisitions have a salary range, and you may be doing yourself a great disservice by pigeonholing yourself into a particular number early on, when in fact you could get more once you have been interviewed for the job.

JOB DESCRIPTION SAMPLE

Position: Retirement Services Director

Direct Report To: CEO

Synopsis: Mega investment bank's Retirement Services business producing $1.5 billion in revenues through a combination of individual account sales as well as selling and advising 401(k) plan sponsors is searching for a senior-level executive to bring the existing business to new heights. This thriving business is offering a talented individual with the proper credentials an opportunity to further increase growth by integrating firm-wide efforts to deliver a distinctive solution to its client sectors.

Responsibilities:
- Establish cross-synergy through team building and leading.
- Define business strategies for a wide range of client groups (middle class, affluent, and high net worth).
- Develop marketing and promotional programs that effectively reach clients at various life stages.
- Promote awareness of the Retirement Services team capabilities internally and externally to leverage prospective opportunities.
- Establish a cutting-edge technology infrastructure and procedures to track key metrics and manage 401(k) rollovers and transactions.

Credentials:
- Similar professional experience required, with a minimum of 18 years in retirement services.
- Expertise in retirement strategies, product development, and financial management analysis.
- Proven ability to simultaneously manage and lead several large professional teams.
- Strong "hands-on" client interaction with ability to create incentive-driven client experiences.
- MBA degree "a must."

SAMPLE FORMAL BLOCK-STYLE COVER LETTER
(use 1.5" margins on all sides)

Chris V. Brown (single line)

30 Main Road · Suburbs, New York 12345

914·123.0000 · cvbrown@nyc.com (two lines)

October 30, 2009 (four lines)

Patricia Garner (one line)

Director of Talent Management (one line)

Finance Incorporated (one line)

440 Madison Avenue, Suite 1600 (one line)

New York, New York 11111 (two lines)

Re: Director of Retirement Services Position (two lines)

Dear Ms. Garner: (two lines)

Upon researching Finance Incorporated's Web site, I learned of the available Director of Retirement Services position as posted on your "Employment Opportunities" section. The job specifications and requirements are remarkably comparable to my past and present work history as well as my educational credentials. This position would allow me to use and develop my 20+ years of experience in:

- Managing retirement service products within large financial institutions: 401(k) trust administration, rollovers, investments, and sales
- Building cross-functional team synergy
- Developing sales and marketing plans with proven multimillion-dollar revenue
- Creating innovative technological infrastructure to increase metrics and statistics used for mergers and acquisitions
- Discovering business models and procedures that focus on areas of improved profit, increased revenue, and performance and customer satisfaction (two lines)

I am submitting my résumé, which further delineates how my experience and qualifications would be of value to Finance Incorporated's Retirement Services Division. I am confident that my expertise, combined with my passion, drive, and commitment to excellence, will meet your expectations for the goals set within an unprecedented time frame. (two lines)

I welcome the opportunity to confidentially discuss my candidacy with you further at your convenience. Please feel free to contact me via the contact information provided above. (two lines)

Respectfully yours, (four lines)
Chris V. Brown (two lines)
Enclosures: (include your résumé or other addendums such as copies of sample work and specify the number of enclosures)
Cc: (write name[s] of anyone you are copying, such as an assistant)

Your Résumé

Résumé writing is an intimidating task even for someone who is not putting one together for the first time. Regardless, your résumé should be a written representation of who you are. That doesn't mean that you should go as far back to when you were the milk monitor in kindergarten. The rule of thumb that I, along with most recruiters, recommend is to list and describe jobs within 10 years of your work experience. I often suggest to candidates who have additional relevant experience past the suggested 10 years to simply list the names of companies along with the date and title held while employed. It is important to try to keep it to one or one-and-a-half pages long.

Beware of inflating your past or current titles, positions, responsibilities, and education because it will only embarrass you when an experienced corporate recruiter delves deeper into your history, only to find out you were flat-out lying. I'm not talking about finessing your title from Customer Service Clerk to Client Services Representative (and sometimes I'm even wary of doing that). I'm talking about trying to pose as an impostor by pretending to hold a job a level or two above you. The same goes for education. If you have not completed your degree, simply write the name of the academic institution, followed by the dates you attended or are currently attending or write "degree pending." Refrain from writing BA, MA, or MBA because it implies that you have attained the degree. Background-check results will confirm that, even if you haven't earned a BS, you sure are full of it.

Scanning your photo along with your résumé is another no-no, even if you think your looks are one of your best attributes. It is inappropriate and unnecessary to include your picture. Only performers enclose a headshot along with a résumé. Otherwise, it seems like you are looking for a date, not a job. If your experience can take you in many different directions, then you should start with an all-purpose résumé. Then create offshoots of the résumé with buzzwords that will attract recruiters from the particular industry in which you are seeking employment.

Haven't a clue where to start? Shop the competition. How are other candidates in your field structuring their résumé? You will most likely notice that junior candidates, such as recent college grads, place their education at the very top of their résumé, while more experienced candidates place it at the end. Take notes while you browse through them. Job sites like Monster.com and CareerBuilder.com are good places to take a gander. Start with the easiest part of structuring your résumé at the top center of the paper with your name, address, e-mail, and home and cell phone numbers. Second, decide which of the résumé formats—chronological or functional—you are most comfortable with and understand when an executive summary is useful.

The Chronological Résumé

This is my personal favorite. Why? It is straightforward and easy for me to read. Whenever I'm reading hundreds of résumés for one job, I appreciate when candidates make my life easier. A chronological résumé has your most recent job experience first and then works backward toward former jobs. Bold-faced, one- or two-word headers separate each section, such as experience, affiliations, extracurricular activities, awards, and education. I also recommend writing things in bullet-point style, as it helps the reader pick up your information at a glance.

In the example of Chris Brown's résumé that follows, you can see the progress she's made throughout her career. Chris has a nice, solid, and consecutive background. The bullet-point format really separates all of the strengths of her background and accomplishments. She uses exact numbers and percentages to show how her work has impacted her employer's growth. She highlights her current position by offering the most information, since it is also the position she has held for the longest time within her career. She is a senior executive, so although she attended top schools, they remain at the bottom of her résumé. In addition, her qualifications, credentials, and education suit the Retirement Services Director job description well. On paper alone, Chris seems like a very viable candidate for the role of Retirement Services Director.

As a candidate, you must be realistic about your background and match it properly to the specifications of a job. Additionally, it is next to impossible for you to cross over from another industry without the retirement services background into this position, even if you have the marketing, sales, and promotions background or an MBA. Moreover, if you currently hold a more senior position to the one that is available, it is also impossible to convince potential employers that you are willing to take a step backward to take two forward. There are many valid reasons why someone would take a cut in salary and title (such as advancing within a larger, more prestigious firm), but employers can't afford to be burned. Many see this as a desperate fix, especially if you are unemployed during a tough economy. They believe that as soon as something better comes along, you will fly the coop.

SAMPLE CHRONOLOGICAL RÉSUMÉ

Chris V. Brown
30 Main Road· Suburbs, New York 12345 · 914·123.0000 · cvbrown@nyc.com

OBJECTIVE
Seeking an executive-level position within the Retirement Services Division of a mid- to large-size financial institution.

PROFESSIONAL EXPERIENCE

Global Financial Services, New York, New York   **January 1999–present**

Senior Vice President—Business Development
- Senior executive responsible for developing long-term strategies used to redefine brand image and attain new market position within the company's Retirement Services sector.

- Increased annual revenue from $500 million to $900+ million.
- Leader of marketing and public relations campaigns that have successfully heightened internal and external consciousness of new and existing retirement products.
- Handle product development and relationship management initiatives to increase revenue and margin by 45%. Fostered strategic relationships with top financial institutions such as AmeriFunds, LV Funds, Sherrill Lynch, Silverman Sachs, IBEX, and Lyndheimer Funds.
- Key contributor to three acquisitions and mergers totaling $1 billion in revenue and 12,000+ retirement plans. Successfully integrated sales teams, corporate culture, and products.
- Work closely with other department leaders within the firm such as the Corporate Client Group, Global Wealth Advisory Group, and the Investment Advisory Group to leverage potential synergies.
- Collaborate with the firm's Chief Technology Officer to improve technological communications necessary for tracking participant information.
- Awarded "Most Valuable Executive" recognition in 2006, 2007, and 2008.

Sherman Advisors, New York, New York　　　　　**September 1992–December 1998**

Vice President, Regional Retirement Services Manager (1996–1998)
- Executed sales and promotion of all retirement products in the Northeast and Mid-Atlantic regions.
- Achieved sales level of $250 million in 1998.

National Sales Manager (1994–1996)
- Supported senior management with creating 401(k) sales plan and new product development.
- Developed sales and marketing training materials that increased overall company profitability by 30%.
- Traveled throughout Maryland, Delaware, Virginia, and Washington, D.C., territories to manage and provide on-site sales training.
- Managed a staff of 10 sales professionals and 2 sales assistants.

Sales Manager (1992–1994)
- Responsible for tri-state territory (New York, New Jersey, and Connecticut) sales of 410(k) plans and packaged retirement plan products.

- Maintained and increased relationships with 12 institutions, with a strong focus on customer service, producing marketing plans, and bringing assets under management.

World Manhattan Bank, New York, New York   **August 1988–September 1992**
Trust Administrator—Pension Trust Security Services (1990–1992)
Assistant to Trust Administrator (1988–1990)

PROFESSIONAL LICENSES
Series 6 and 63

PROFESSIONAL AFFILIATIONS
National Pension Fund Association, Board President, 2007–present
Corporate Employee Retirement Services of America, Member, 1999–present

EDUCATION
Columbia Business School, New York, New York
Master of Business Administration, 1998

Wesleyan University, Middletown, Connecticut
Bachelor of Arts in Economics, 1988

The Functional Résumé

Change-of-career candidates and re-entries to the job force gravitate to the functional résumé. As a recruiter, I am leery of what a functional résumé is trying to hide. They are written with the purpose of highlighting the most pertinent work experience first as opposed to the most current related experience. Since the majority of résumés are written in the chronological format, whenever I come across a functional résumé, it breaks my reading pattern and slows me down. Functional résumés are sometimes written without sequence in order to conceal job-hopping and unexplained gaps in dates. While functional résumés can be written in bullet-point format (as shown in the Functional Résumé Sample), when written in wordy paragraph form they appear convoluted. As a result, buzzwords and catchphrases are often lost, making it appear as if you are deliberately trying to conceal information in your background.

As you can tell, I am not partial to the functional résumé, though it is perfectly acceptable to use if it suits your needs. Just know that recruiters and interviewers are savvy enough to uncover holes in your background regardless of your preferred format.

Qualification Summaries and Their Real Objective

A career objective on a résumé is something I recommend if you want to market yourself into a very specific job, such as Retirement Services Director. Otherwise, it is a one-track heading on your multifunctional résumé. It often strikes me as a "life support" tactic used to revive a skill-starved résumé with egocentric adjectives that go on and on and on: "Talented, goal-oriented professional possessing excellent organizational and communication skills with exceptional ability to multitask and prioritize seeks a position with ample opportunity for career advancement."

Résumé gurus have replaced the Objective section, or sometimes added a Qualifications Summary, which is a lengthier written text regarding your abilities, career skills, and accomplishments located right below the Objective section (so much for keeping your résumé to a page or page and a half). Qualifications Summaries can be appropriate if you are an experienced candidate trying to avoid having your résumé look like a novel. On the other hand, candidates with light experience will use a Qualifications Summary as a clever way of padding a résumé. They may also be helpful if your candidacy is accepted for further consideration among higher-ranking officers within a firm. Often, the first round of interviewers will pass your information along to a senior officer (such as a CEO) who only has time to see the highlights of your results-driven accomplishments in a particular area that correlates to the job you are interviewing for.

In essence, Qualifications Summaries recap your strengths and accomplishments. They may be used in your cover letter, résumé, thank-you note, or follow-up letter. Think of it as your personal commercial advertising you using an "at-a-glance" format (see the Functional Résumé Sample for an example).

FUNCTIONAL RÉSUMÉ SAMPLE

Chris V. Brown

30 Main Road· Suburbs, New York 12345
914·123.0000 · cvbrown@nyc.com

OBJECTIVE

Seeking an executive-level position within the Retirement Services Division of a mid-to large-size financial institution.

QUALIFICATIONS SUMMARY

- Senior executive within the financial services industry with a concentration in retirement services, 401(k) trust administration, investments, and sales.
- Strategic force behind business models and procedures that focus on areas of improved profit, increased revenue, performance, and customer satisfaction.
- 20+ years of implementing cross-functional team synergy, sales and marketing plans with proven multimillion-dollar revenue increase, metrics and statistics used for mergers and acquisitions, product development and rollout, relationship management, strategic partnering, and innovative technological infrastructure.

PROFESSIONAL ACCOMPLISHMENTS

- Senior executive responsible for developing long-term strategies used to redefine brand image and attain new market position within the Retirement Services sector.
- Consistently increased annual revenue and exceeded goals by 30 to 50%.
- Leader of marketing and public relations campaigns that have successfully heightened internal and external consciousness of new and existing retirement products.
- Handled product development and relationship management initiatives to increase revenue and margin. Fostered strategic relationships with top-notch financial institutions.
- Key contributor to acquisitions and mergers. Successfully integrated sales teams, corporate culture, and products.
- Possess exceptional managerial, leadership, and mentoring capabilities.
- Ability to leverage potential profitable synergies by working closely with other department leaders within an organization. Collaborate with company Chief Technology Officers and Chief Information Officers to improve technological communications necessary for tracking participant information.
- Awarded "Most Valuable Executive" recognition in 2006, 2007, and 2008.
- Available to travel throughout domestic and international territories to manage and provide on-site sales training.
- Strong focus on customer service.

PROFESSIONAL WORK HISTORY

Global Financial Services, New York, New York   January 1999–present
Senior Vice President—Business Development

Sherman Advisors, New York, New York   September 1992–December 1998
Vice President, Regional Retirement Services Manager (1996–1998)
National Sales Manager (1994–1996)
Sales Manager (1992–1994)

World Manhattan Bank, New York, New York   August 1988–September 1992
Trust Administrator—Pension Trust Security Services (1990–1992)
Assistant to Trust Administrator (1988–1990)

PROFESSIONAL LICENSES

Series 6 and 63

PROFESSIONAL AFFILIATIONS

National Pension Fund Association, Board President, 2007–present
Corporate Employee Retirement Services of America, Member, 1999–present

EDUCATION

Columbia Business School, New York, New York
Master of Business Administration, 1998

Wesleyan University, Middletown, Connecticut
Bachelor of Arts in Economics, 1988

Thank-You Notes

The value of a simple yet well-crafted thank-you note is frequently under-estimated by job seekers. What candidates fail to realize is that often the thank-you note can be what makes or breaks the decision to extend an offer. Thank-you notes are not only gestures of good etiquette and appreciation, but they also provide concrete evidence that you have strong follow-up skills and real attention to detail.

Just when is a thank-you note appropriate to send? Anytime someone has given you time, advice, information, updates, or referrals. Generic thank-you letters come across as if you are just going through the motions. Be specific and indicate why you are thanking the recipient. Poorly written or unwritten thank-you letters are a leading cause of not getting the offer. I encourage my candidates to cite something the recruiter has described about the position, the company, or the person the position reports to. Then clearly define how and why you are the perfect match for the position. It not only shows what may be an obvious connection, but it also indicates that you paid attention during the interview and remember details about your conversation.

Don't get sloppy or lazy about writing a thank-you note, even if you are not interested in the position, because it will come back to haunt you. Human resources managers and directors have a funny way of ending up, years down the road, at another company where you would kill to land a job. You would be surprised how long a bad impression can last. It can follow you for years. If you are interested in the position, then a thank-you note is sure to keep you on the decision makers' minds. You need to literally dot your i's and cross your t's.

Be sure you ask for the recruiter's card before you leave the interview so you can verify the correct spelling of her name and the exact title of her position. Don't make the mistake of sending a thank-you to just one of the people who interviewed you in the hopes that she will pass it along to everyone else who took the time to meet with you. See to it that each and every person who interviewed you receives a letter of appreciation and insert something about what you discussed with each of them. This way, the thank-you note comes across in a more personal way. Candidates falsely believe that because human resources professionals, office managers, and the like are hired to interview candidates, they are not necessarily expecting to be thanked for their time. The truth is that while their key responsibility may be screening, interviewing, and hiring, they have other responsibilities and meetings, so thanking them for their time is not only appropriate—it is necessary!

By the way, I am partial to handwritten notes on crisp white correspondence cards. I find them to be gracious and personal yet still appropriate for business. They should be delivered within 24 hours of your initial contact. I use the thank-you letter as a huge litmus test for hiring for my company or referring on to a client. Experience has proven that if the thank-you note is weak or altogether missing but I choose to hire a candidate in spite of it, I always end up disappointed.

Sample "Thank You" Note in Modified Block Form
(typed on letterhead or handwritten on fine stationery)

Chris V. Brown (single line)
30 Main Road · Suburbs, New York 12345
914·123.0000 · cvbrown@nyc.com (two lines)
October 30, 2009 (four lines)

Patricia Garner (one line)
Director of Talent Management (one line)
Finance Incorporated (one line)
440 Madison Avenue, Suite 1600 (one line)
New York, New York 11111 (two lines)

Re: Director of Retirement Services Position (two lines)

Dear Ms. Garner: (two lines)

Thank you so much for allowing me to share my background for the Director of Retirement Services position. As much as I was interested in the position prior to the interview, having spoken with you makes me realize that this opportunity would truly be a perfect next step in my career. I believe my relationship management skills and my team-building ability would be invaluable assets toward the growth of the Retirement Services Division. As discussed during our meeting, this can be a timely and mutually beneficial situation for all of us. (two lines if typed)

Once again, thank you for your time and consideration. Though you mentioned you are at the beginning stages of your search, I do hope to hear from you soon regarding my status. It sounds like your plans to expand this particular area are pivotal to the overall growth and expansion of the firm. I know I can apply my 20+ years of experience to help you achieve such efforts. (two lines if typed)

Please let me know if I can supply you with additional information that will help you market my candidacy to other decision makers within your team, including the CEO. I will gladly furnish you with such details. If you need to contact me for any other reason, I prefer you do so either via cell, 914·123.0000 or e-mail at cvbrown@nyc.com. (two lines if typed)

Sincerely, (four lines)
Chris V. Brown

Enclosures: 1
Cc: Ms. Sarah Wolfe

The Follow-Up Letter

Just like the thank-you note, the follow-up letter keeps you a heartbeat away from the recruiter's mind. Follow-up letters are essential when you are not being represented by a third-party agency or recruiting firm. These letters also show that your level of interest is still as strong as when you first met.

I like to make follow-up letters more about giving the recruiting manager a status update of where you are in the interviewing process and where your head is in the whole thing. If a particular company is your first choice, then say so in your follow-up letter. Let the recruiter know that other companies are pursuing you, but that since his company is your first choice, you would like to know where you stand in the process before you make any decisions. Certainly, you don't want to end up with nothing. Therefore, if your candidacy is not strong, you would appreciate notice of this so you can weigh your other options accordingly. Most human resources professionals appreciate this, as it is straightforward and not pushy.

Sample Follow-Up Letter in Modified Block Form

Chris V. Brown (single line)
30 Main Road · Suburbs, New York 12345
914·123.0000 · cvbrown@nyc.com (two lines)
October 30, 2009 (four lines)

Patricia Garner (one line)
Director of Talent Management (one line)
Finance Incorporated (one line)
440 Madison Avenue, Suite 1600 (one line)
New York, New York 11111 (two lines)

Dear Ms. Garner: (two lines)

I am writing you pursuant to our interview on November 12 for the Director of Retirement Services position. You mentioned that you would be contacting candidates for second- and third-round interviews after completing your initial candidate meetings at the end of the week. Within the past two weeks, I too have continued my search, and while many opportunities sound enticing, none seem as perfect of a fit as the one with Finance Incorporated. In fact, just today I learned of a job offer made to me by another large financial institution. (two lines)

The reason for this letter is to let you know my current status and to find out if you could kindly provide me with any insight regarding my candidacy at your firm. You are undoubtedly my first choice, and I am willing to waive my current offer if I am still a viable candidate for the available position within Retirement Services. Therefore, any information you can provide for me would be greatly appreciated. (two lines)

Since our last conversation, I have had a chance to give the requirements and responsibilities further thought, and the prospect of spearheading this type of endeavor truly motivates me. I am optimistic about completing the interviewing process at your firm and ultimately gaining the opportunity to take on this exciting venture. As usual, I may be contacted via the information located at the top of this letter. (two lines)

Sincerely, (four lines)
Chris V. Brown

Enclosures: 1
Cc: Ms. Sarah Wolfe

Deliver with Style
Deliver

While the bulk of résumés are submitted via e-mail, some are still faxed, mailed by snail mail, or delivered in person. If your goal is to distribute your résumé in bulk to reach multiple human resources departments within a large company (where human resources is not centralized within one department) or to scores of different companies throughout, then e-mail is the most efficient distribution method. Timeliness, convenience, and urgency (as when you are given no notice or severance) are other reasons for choosing e-mail as your means of circulating and marketing yourself. Yet another reason for using e-mail is to come across as someone who is modern with the times, computer-literate, and savvy. A recent college grad will usually e-mail his résumé, while a returning mom or retiree will choose to mail her typewritten résumé, raising concerns that she is not comfortable with word processing or e-mail.

Faxing has quickly become "so yesterday." Unless you are specifically asked by a recruiter to fax your résumé, I would not recommend doing so, because faxed résumés have a funny way of not ever making it into the right hands. Fax machines that are not regularly monitored can have loads of documents sitting on them. Sometimes, the résumés will slip right off the machine as the breeze from an open window blows in. In addition, fax machines run out of toner quicker than you know in a busy office, so the quality is often fuzzy, with weird lines spilling through your priceless credentials.

Believe it or not, there are times when snail mail is the most appropriate way to submit your résumé. Mailing your résumé works when you are gainfully employed and therefore submitting your résumé to test the waters or grab a pulse on how marketable you are at the moment. Some candidates will mail their résumé as a clever way of camouflaging it into recruiters' first-class mail. I will admit that I always open a résumé submission via mail, though it doesn't guarantee I'll bring the applicant in.

In-person résumé submissions are bold and can sometimes do the deed. If you do decide to exercise this method, be sure to look as sharp as if you were going in for a scheduled interview. You should not assume that you will be seen or even have the opportunity to have the recruiter come out to give you a quick handshake. However, should the recruiter happen to pass by the front desk, overhear his name, and look over at you as you hand your unfolded cover letter and résumé in a large envelope to the receptionist, you had better not look like something the cat dragged in. You should not only look your best but also be in the frame of mind to be interviewed on the spot. Hand-delivering résumés is time-consuming and tedious. I would reserve this method for your first-choice company. If you do so, realize that it will not guarantee you an interview, though it is the most proactive approach.

Style
Details such as font style, point size, ink color, and stationery (paper, envelope, size) all give your interview correspondence loads of personality.

There is no one designated font I recommend, though the best font is one that is simple to read. The most commonly used font is Times New Roman (which is the one I'm using to write this book), but any font that has a little curve, known as a serif, at the end of each letter will do. Serif font styles are easier to read when lots of words are grouped together in a text. Choose any of these suggested fonts: Book Antiqua, Bookman Old Style, Century Schoolbook, Garamond, Palatino, Linotype, or Perpetua. Plenty of candidates determine that using one of these fonts is boring and then experiment with funky stencil, calligraphy, or script fonts. Don't get caught up in fancy schmancy fonts. As far as point size, stick to 11-point or 12-point depending on the font style you choose for résumés and correspondence.

Your contact information should be bold, centered with your name written in caps, and up to two points larger in size than the rest of the text. Résumé correspondence should be free of bright- or neon-colored fonts. Instead, it should be written in varying values of black, using the darkest and boldest for headings. If you have custom letterhead stationery, the ink color could be a color other than black as long as it is a dark value. Keep in mind, however, that colors will appear different when viewed on different computer monitors, so it is safest to go with black.

You may choose to have your résumé professionally typeset, but for those of you who are cost-conscious, as you well may be, using color laser printing really does the job. For hard copies of your résumé or other interview correspondence, 24-pound writing stock and a slight texture add a touch of elegance and finesse. Keep in mind that while watermarks give paper prestige, they do not always transfer well when copied or scanned. The color palette should be subtle, traditional, and professional, consisting of linen white, pearl, bone, eggshell, or ecru. Coordinating envelopes and correspondence cards further help harmonize and brand your image. If you do decide to mail your business correspondence, remember the following:

- Use proper names, titles, and company name.

- Include your name and return address on the back flap.

- Place the right amount of postage.

- Neat handwriting is preferred over having addresses printed on the envelopes (it shows more of a personal touch). Printed address labels are in bad taste.

You may, however, choose to save some trees by leaving the envelope and cover letter behind if you are on an actual interview. In that case, offer the recruiter just the résumé shortly after shaking hands. I do not like to fuss with a résumé that has been folded over twice and keeps trying to stay curled up, so storing copies in a portfolio is preferred. You can also be socially responsible by using paper that is Green Seal- and FSC-certified, recyclable using a high percentage of post-consumer fiber, and is acid-, lignin-, elemental-, and chlorine-free.

17

Virtually Yours
Netiquette

No matter how well you know the rules of netiquette, you will eventually offend some- one who doesn't. —Don Rittner (American historian, archaeologist, and author)

TECHNOLOGY IS progressive, informative, and often addictive. Today, you can do everything with the touch of a button—from shopping to dating— while simultaneously pursuing a job search (talk about multitasking). Since technology has become such an attainable amenity, abusing techno- logical privileges is among the most common causes of being dismissed as a viable candidate. You must not be deceived into thinking that your pro- fessional "e-image" is not under close scrutiny at all times.

The fact is that the netiquette you use to connect with a potential employer during an interview process and the discretion you show in han- dling the "e-gadgets" that facilitate such communication *will* influence how far along you get in the process—that is, if you even enter the process. For instance, if you drink, eat, and sleep with a wireless Jawbone in your ear, you are apt to step out of an elevator and into the reception area of an interview with it still clipped onto your ear. You will be none the wiser to the fact that an hour interview quickly turned into a five-minute "go see," just because of this careless oversight.

There are also issues of misusing the technical devices. This is sure to exhibit poor judgment and credibility as either the initiator or recipient of virtual information. Your voice, gestures, and body language will all be interpreted with the flip of a switch, without visual clues to support them. For this reason, I highly recommend assessing and finessing your netiquette skills, as their absence will magnify blunders a zillion times over.

Widget-Free

Wireless electronic communication devices make us accessible 24/7, making them our lifeline. Many of these state-of-the-art doodads can be easily stimulated with mere voice activation. I won't question the convenience and functionality these tools provide, but when it comes to interviewing, their presence can be downright rude, distracting, and unprofessional. Consequently, all portable instruments, such as cell phones, BlackBerrys, PDAs, iPods, MP3 players, and the like are to be kept out of sight and sound during any type of interview. Even a laptop should be kept off the premises unless it is to be used for the purpose of enhancing your interview by showing graphs, charts, or illustrations that are pertinent to selling your competence for a particular job. The same applies for accessories sticking out of your head, behind your neck, and inside your ears (e.g., wired ear buds, ear clips, and wireless headsets). Forget that they may be the latest and greatest with cutting-edge capabilities. Flaunting them, even if left dormant, is self-indulgent; displaying and engaging in their use during a time when your sole purpose is to communicate with a potential employer is utterly deplorable.

Touchtone Matters
When You Are the "Initiator" of Phone/Cell/Voice-Mail Communication
In a perfect world, you would have enough information about each potential interviewer to determine which source of communication would be

most suitable. Unfortunately, most often, you know very little about the recipient's schedule and communication preference, in which case, it is your personal inclination that will dictate the channel you choose. Initiating an introduction to your candidacy or even following up on a résumé via phone is the most proactive approach. You're playing Russian roulette when you choose the phone as your preferred method since you don't know what to expect from the recipient on the other end. Timing is everything, and as long as you're prepared for the worst-case scenario (a hang-up), you may be pleasantly surprised when your call turns out to open a golden opportunity. Here are some simple guidelines to help you maximize your phone encounter with a sought-after decision maker:

▪ **Introductions:** Remember to introduce yourself using your first and last name, and state the reason for your call. Is the recruiter or assistant still there? Assure yourself by asking a question that requires an answer: "Good morning, my name is Chris Brown and I'm calling regarding the Director of Retirement Services position I saw on your Web site. Are you the person handling this search or can you refer me to the appropriate person?" By asking a question that requires an answer after the introduction, you are soliciting information about more than just the response to the question. The voice on the other end will indicate whether your call is welcomed or not based on the manner, tone, and immediacy with which it is answered.

As far as leaving a voice mail with your introduction, it can be looked at in one of two ways: You either lose control or gain control. For instance, if you don't pique the recruiter's interest enough to have your call returned right away, you are in essence giving up control, since you can't call too soon after. However, a voice mail can also be looked at as the icebreaker that establishes your candidacy. If you do opt to leave a voice mail, follow all directions provided by the recipient. This will be the first opportunity to show that you are willing and able to follow directions well.

▪ **Interruptions:** Turn off speaker features on your phone that produce echoing noises that obstruct effective communication. Dedicate a time and place to make productive phone contacts with potential employers.

Avoid all outside disturbances found within a hectic workplace or busy home life. Disregard all incoming phone calls by disarming your call-waiting feature. Instead, activate a call-forwarding feature so that other calls can be retrieved once you're done with your introductory call. Also, limit all other activities such as eating, drinking, driving, and using bathroom facilities—all of which hinder your level of alertness and produce distracting background disruption.

▪ **Strategies:** Get a sense of the recruiter's schedule by asking the company receptionist or an assistant within human resources. If you are faced with overly tight-lipped assistants, then experiment by calling at different times during the day without leaving a voice mail until you get a live voice. I have found that recruiters are more apt to be engaged in conversation at either the beginning or the end of the day. At the beginning of the day, a recruiter has a clear mind and is able to better focus on informational calls. At the end of the day is when many terminations occur, and your timing may be perfectly suitable to fill one of the open requisitions. In addition, planned terminations often take place at the end of the week or before a holiday weekend. Therefore, calling on a Monday or a Tuesday after a holiday weekend could work in your favor.

To combat the possibility of your mind going blank when you finally get the person you've been yearning to speak to on the phone, have a script prepared with some bullet points highlighting the gist of what you want to say and how you want to sell yourself.

▪ **Turnoffs:** Let's face it, there are times when you replicate the textbook introductory call only to have a nasty, self-righteous recruiter deflate every expectation you ever had of being a viable candidate. I've known many recruiters who remain fixtures at large corporations, sitting on a high horse for years while turning away perfectly qualified and well-mannered candidates who do pretty much everything right. If you encounter one of those recruiters, move along to the next prospect quickly. However, if you keep encountering the same negative reaction, it could very well be that you are at fault, exhibiting blatant turnoffs.

Sometimes a turnoff can fall under the guise of having an entitlement issue. In other words, you act as if recruiters are there for your purpose and your purpose only. In your mind, a recruiter's job is merely to search for talent, so why isn't she giving you the time you deserve? That is a major turnoff! Understand that recruiters have many other duties besides looking for talent. Many conduct orientation training, handle internal employee conflicts and harassment, and administer benefits, vacations, and exit interviews. Therefore, even if you hear a trace of an attitude, use a neutral tone, articulate your words, monitor your volume, and phrase your sentences in a way that makes you sound like you are in control of your emotions. You are not desperate (even if you feel desperate, never show it) or beaten by rejections. You are optimistic, full of positive energy while keeping a smile on your face as you speak, which will reflect such emotions. Who would pass up an opportunity to meet the voice behind such cheerful discourse? Even if the job was just filled, recruiters may still want to meet you as a possibility for their active candidate file.

- **Follow-ups:** Plot a course of action toward achieving your final goal—gaining an in-person interview. While you may personally prefer the comfort of a virtual interview, a face-to-face encounter means you are making progress. Theoretically, a physical interview increases your likelihood of convincing the recipient that you are perfect for the job. If you are unsuccessful at securing a one-on-one interview, ask for a recommendation on how best to stay on top of the available opportunities at the company. (You may be referred to the company Web site or a third-party recruiting firm that does the screening.) Ask whether she can be a point of reference for you or if she has an assistant whom you can refer to. The point is to make a connection that you can go back to and with whom you can start building a virtual relationship.

When You Are the "Recipient" of Phone/Cell/Voice-Mail Communication

You spend time, energy, and money on the production of your cover letter and résumé, and then circulating it throughout the companies you hope will consider you. When one of your top choices finally notices you within the mounds of applicants, you shoot yourself in the foot by having your first virtual impression scare talent-acquisition scouts away. It's one thing to alienate telemarketers, but this is your future we're talking about. Compose a professional-sounding outgoing recording that persuades potential employers to leave a message. Designate a phone number with a message box that will not clog up with personal messages. Building your e-presence sets the tone for positive results in getting you through to the first round of interviews or further along as a feasible contender at the later stages of competition. Aim for the following:

■ **Accessibility:** Don't make it difficult for a screener or recruiter to reach you. For starters, you might consider setting up your outgoing voice-mail greeting to begin after no more than one to three rings. Programming your message to begin after too many rings may frustrate a recruiter into thinking that you don't have voice mail set up, causing her to move on to her next prospect. Another accessibility obstacle that is a major pet peeve of mine is when candidates add a call-intercept feature to their phone. It leads me to believe you have collection agencies breathing down your neck and that maybe that's why it's so difficult to get to you.

To further help the process along, your outgoing message should instruct the caller to have you paged or to use a different means of communication for a given day, such as e-mail if you happen to be at a site with limited access to voice mail. Be careful not to end up being the candidate who's missing in action during a crucial time, such as when references are required or when you must unexpectedly go meet one final person who is available only at a certain time and date. The message conveyed when you are inaccessible is that you are evasive and unreliable. Stay on top of your important messages by checking your dedicated voice mail every hour on the hour. It will guarantee you return the message within the 24-hour window of professional protocol.

■ **Professionalism:** Strange or cutesy messages are high on my list for disregarding candidates who may have initially been appealing on paper. I listen for clues, such as how you pronounce your name or whether you even include your last name (as you should). Neutralize your tone to sound pleasant, though not overly chummy. Avoid background music of any sort, as it tends to compete with your spoken words. Refrain from having your adorable child record the outgoing message, as it adds an element of informality.

• **Authenticity:** You are the real deal and you have but a small window to prove it. Speak with conviction to validate your words. Also, be prepared for an on-the-spot pre-interview. What may seem like an unofficial response to your submittal can turn out to be a discerning phone screening. That means that if you are not in a position to speak freely (making you sound tentative), you should request permission to reach the caller within a specified period of time. Be sure to call back at the precise time you agree on to show accuracy and dependability.

• **Sensibility:** It may seem obvious but it's better said than unsaid: Under no circumstances should you ever place a person on hold who is calling in response to your becoming a potential employee. There is nothing more infuriating than taking time out of a busy screening process to call someone, only to be put on hold. This applies to answering call waiting, another line extension, or a land phone if you're on your cell (no one needs to hear your other conversation). Instead, be gracious and appreciative for the recruiter's interest and treat her with kid gloves. In addition, be sensible about the phone number you disclose as a contact number. The last thing you need is to be contacted via your present job's phone line and let the entire office and boss know you're looking—unless of course you're hoping to blatantly expose your job search and purposely want to be released of your work duties.

E-Matters

E-mail can be a far more comfortable medium of communication for some because it allows you to say your piece without interruptions from the party on the other end. It is a less invasive method, since both participants have the freedom of retrieving and answering the message at will. It is also much more cost-effective than calling or express-mailing samples of your work to several hiring officials located halfway across the world. Time-effectiveness is another advantage to using e-mail, as you can cut, paste, insert, and delete information from your letters of introduction, résumés, and other documents in just minutes to customize the criteria of multiple job searches. However, its productiveness clearly correlates with the efficiency with which it is used. Used thoughtlessly and irresponsibly, it can sever a professional relationship before it even begins.

- **Address to impress:** Choose an e-mail address that is specifically designated for job searching and is privately accessed from home. Too many times I've had to console candidates whose misuse and abuse of company e-mail for the purpose of looking for a job has landed them instant termination. Therefore, you can never be too cautious. If for some reason your first and last name combination is not available in any form, choose something that is professional sounding, such as LVJobsearch@yahoo.com rather than Tanbod@yahoo.com or Hoochymamma@gmail.com. Your e-mail will set the tone as to the level of seriousness and professionalism you bring to the table. While on the subject of "addressing," be sure your recipient's e-mail address is correct and free of misspellings so that your e-mail reaches him.

- **Modern mistakes:** Writing a business e-mail requires a more structured set of guidelines than writing to your college bud. It should reflect the same level of professionalism as all of your nonvirtual business correspondence. Unfortunately, job seekers trying to gain exposure will make blatant e-mail blunders that in fact move them to the bottom of the pile. Here are 10 best practices to follow in order to stay current while avoiding modern mistakes.

1. Update your subject line to reflect the current purpose of communication.

2. Avoid sending your résumé, cover letter, and other business correspondence as a mass e-mail. Personalize bulk mailings by entering

names and e-mail addresses onto a spreadsheet that can be used through the mail merge function, which then personalizes your e-mail with individual names. Investing in an e-mail marketing service is also an option for distributing your résumé in mass quantities.

3. Know who and when to include other recipients to your cc: (i.e., carbon copy). You may want to include a recruiter's assistant who has access to the recruiter's Outlook calendar. On the other hand, if two recruiters have interviewed you, it would be best to address each of them separately.

4. Learn that the bcc function (i.e., blind carbon copy) makes recipients anonymous. Candidates who enter multiple recruiter e-mails in this area will achieve confidentiality but will lose the personal aspect by having to write a generic greeting such as "Dear Sir" or "To Whom It May Concern."

5. Use a greeting, closing, and signature on your first encounter of the day. If a conversation develops, you may start subsequent e-mails as if you were engaged in verbal conversation.

6. Keep the body of your e-mail brief and remember to check for spelling, grammar, and clarity. Longer documents should be included as attachments.

7. Avoid the usage of abbreviations that may not be comprehensible to everyone, such as BTW (by the way) or FOA (first of all).

8. Refrain from using graphic symbols that represent emotions, known as emoticons. These include :) to show a happy face or :(for a sad face or : to show boredom. They may be sweet among friends, but they are killers in business.

9. Abstain from using certain key functions that reflect anger: capitalized letters, bold text, underlining, and exclamation points.

10. Respond within 24 hours of e-mail receipt.

Worlds Apart—Instant Messaging (IM) and Faxing

Let me make myself clear: Instant messaging is intrusive. I don't care for it on a social level, and on a professional level it's intolerable. Who wants to have you meddling in the middle of a busy workday? Reserve instant messaging for chitchatting with friends (I just hope I'm not one of them). I know people addicted to instant messenger who have forsaken using e-mails altogether, opting to bypass e-mail server delays and malfunctions. What do I say to those people? "Hold your horses." I'm all for a sense of urgency, but instant messenger is truly overstepping your boundaries when it comes to connecting with a decision maker.

Then there's faxing. Truthfully, I can't remember the last time I received a faxed résumé or cover letter. This method of communication is taking a backseat to other methods (including even snail mail), since very often the quality is compromised. In addition, privacy is often a concern. So in order to combat the issue of discretion, advance notice is required for me to leave my desk and barricade the area that surrounds the fax machine. First, the cover *sheet* may spew out, then the cover *letter,* and then slowly and blotchily (check the toner) the résumé finally churns out. Honestly, who has the time? Besides, contributing to a paperless environment should be your way of showing a progressive and altruistic side.

For most of us, nothing beats a face-to-face meeting, but the e-alternatives are sometimes more accommodating to busy work schedules. As long as you realize that you cannot hide behind electronic devices, your netiquette skills should reflect the innovative and forward-thinking "you."

18

Vocalize This!
Voicing Your VIP Status

Words mean more than what is set down on paper. It takes the human voice to infuse them with shades of deeper meaning. —Maya Angelou (American poet)

THERE ARE VOICES that, for better or worse, stick with you for a lifetime. Some voices are soothing and pleasant to the ear, while others are brassy, raspy, or nasally, striking you like nails on a chalkboard. What many candidates fail to realize is that your voice is a powerful natural instrument that paints a mural of your inner thoughts and emotions. So if your voice does not coincide with your professional image, it may very well be a contributing factor to losing out on a job opportunity.

The sound of your voice, in addition to how you use it to shape your words, particularly over the phone, where there are no other visual clues to escort it, forecasts clues about your character traits: shy, nervous, arrogant, sophisticated, intelligent, energetic, sluggish, professional, or polished. For that reason, aligning your voice and speaking style to either accentuate or camouflage the personality and physical characteristics you want to convey is essential for building your overall business image. Perhaps you stand six feet tall and you find yourself being interviewed by someone who is nearly a foot shorter than you. In this case, a softer more approachable voice would work in your favor. Or maybe you're interviewing for a position within a fast-paced, competitive environment; a strong voice with an engaging style would be more fitting.

To help me clarify the physiological components of the voice, I reached out to Dr. Craig Zalvan, MD, FACS, medical director at the Institute for Voice and Swallowing Disorders at Phelps Memorial Hospital Center, located in Sleepy Hollow, New York. My initial conversation with Dr. Zalvan was over the telephone, upon the return of a message I left with his receptionist. He possessed a voice that was warm, friendly, yet authoritative in the area of laryngology (the study of voice disorders). As demanding as his schedule is with clinical appointments, planned and unplanned surgeries, and membership and advisory board positions within professional associations, his enthusiasm and willingness to share his knowledge were evident through his phone voice.

We worked on securing a time and date that was mutually convenient, and in the midst of conversation we discovered we live a few houses away from one another and that our daughters travel on the same school bus each day. The local coffeehouse was to be our meeting place. It turns out I unexpectedly gave birth just six days before our meeting. Rather than rescheduling our talk, Dr. Zalvan was kind enough to pay me a house call. His appearance and disposition were every bit as warm as his voice had been on the phone. Then, over afternoon coffee and banana bread, he explained the inner workings of the voice we all produce to verbally communicate our ideas during an interview and beyond. He characterizes the voice as having four core components:

• **The Generator,** which is where the voice originates its power, is found within our lungs and abdomen. For optimal performance, it is important to maintain a posture without slumping or constriction of the chest cavity. Doing so can limit the amount of air intake, which will decrease the volume of exhaled air. Insufficient breath support will inevitably produce inferior vocal production as well. Skintight clothing and restrictive shape wear also obstruct inhaled air from fully reaching the generator, yet another reason to leave your circulation-cutting garb out of the picture.

▪ **The Vibrator,** akin to a reed of a precious woodwind instrument located inside our throats, refers to our vocal folds. These are sheltered inside a cartilage box called the larynx, which rests on top of the passages that messenger air from your lungs to your nose and mouth. Individuals who are chronic smokers have vocal paralysis or develop polyps, nodules, and cysts and will end up with vocal folds that generate a dysfunctional vibration, causing the sound we hear to be husky, hoarse, or gravelly. Though in chronic cases surgical measures may be necessary to restore vocal deterioration, less severe situations can be alleviated with vocal exercises, voice rest, and/or medical therapy prescribed by a voice pathologist or therapist and/or a laryngologist.

▪ **The Resonance** is created by the size and shape of the human body's chambers. Thus, the sound you hear when you speak aloud is the echo that literally ricochets off the cavities in your skull, the sinuses, the oral cavity, oropharynx, and throat. This is precisely why you may be oblivious to housing a voice that is completely grating, annoying, too soft, or too loud; you are used to the resonant sound that you produce. Though partial deafness, earwax buildup, and even cultural upbringing may contribute to a skewed perception of your resonance, the best way to accurately assess how the outside world hears you is by recording your voice. You will be surprised at what you hear, enticing you to work on what until now has been a blatant deterrent in landing a job.

▪ **The Articulators**—your tongue, cheeks, teeth, and lips—all contribute to the formation of words using the proper sound and accent. Often, candidates can sound like they have a mouthful of marbles, and it is predominantly because one or more of the articulators is out of proportion or being misused. Most articulator problems stem from developmental, cultural, behavioral, and possibly neurological issues. Some are also due to anatomic problems such as jaw misalignment, muscle weakness, and anything that changes the anatomy of the oral cavity. The challenge of shaping your words is often due to idle tendencies getting the best of you. If that's the case, then this is probably a good time for you to step in front of a mirror and evaluate whether that wide, toothless gap you've been procrastinating on having fixed is at all contributing to you not sounding as professional as you would like. Voice therapists can help train your articulators to produce a voice that is more fluent, understandable, and pleasing to others.

As we continued our conversation, Craig (we established a first-name-basis rapport) enlightened me on the types of surgical techniques he uses to correct particular voice disorders that contribute to poor voice quality. I recorded the ones that pertain to the recurring voice issues candidates face while on interviews.

▪ **Weak, frail, and "breathy" voices:** This type of voice may be the result of a paralyzed vocal fold, which can sound weak and breathy with occasional coughing or choking. To confirm this, a laryngologist would examine your vocal cords with a stroboscope—a tool that allows slow-motion evaluation of the vocal folds. In this case, vocal fold injection medialization surgery would be an option, whereby the vocal folds are injected with material to push them together. Thyroplasty, a procedure using a small incision in the Adam's apple, places an implant next to the vocal fold, which helps push paralyzed vocal folds toward the midline to provide adequate closure, another solution for this difficulty.

▪ **Deep, raspy, rough, gravelly, and throaty voices:** Cysts, polyps, and nodules are some of the lesions found in the voice box that affect the smooth quality of its sound, producing voice breaks, cracks, and range restriction. Microlaryngoscopy, a treatment using a surgical micro flap, removes the offending lesions from the affected vocal fold, leaving the majority of healthy tissue behind to vibrate normally, thus improving vocal quality.

▪ **Fatigued, strained, and crackled voices:** Consistent misuse and abuse of your voice can age your vocal folds to such extremes that there is great disparity between the sound of your affected vocal folds and your external, professional appearance. To restore the youth and clarity of your voice, voice therapy could be instrumental in returning a more fluent, smooth sound to your voice. Vocal hygiene, change in behaviors, and avoidance of vocal abuse can also restore a more youthful sound to your voice. There are also procedures to help improve vocal quality by providing better closure of the voice box or removing lesions of the vocal folds. Not smoking can greatly improve your vocal quality, not to mention help avoid the development of laryngeal, or voice box, cancer.

Amazingly, there are an abundance of advanced procedures available to optimize a vocal quality that has been afflicted by organic distress. For those of you who use friends or colleagues to record voice-mail greetings on your behalf because you loathe the sound of your own voice, there are attainable solutions for you.

We each took our last sip of coffee and proceeded to wrap up our chat, not a moment too soon, as my newborn decided to use his voice to wail for his feeding. He sure knows how to use his "generator." It was somewhat of an expedited good-bye, but one not without a handshake and some parting words from the doctor: "The first thing your readers need to have is self-awareness. Only then can the problem be addressed." "Thank you so much for your help!" I replied. "I'll see you at Family Fun Night coming up."

He gave me the name of a colleague who would be instrumental in volunteering information regarding habitual voice challenges. I thanked him one last time for stopping by, for his words of wisdom, and for his referral. The baby's cry was amplified throughout the double-entry foyer. As soon as I closed the door, I switched into "Mom" mode and in my sweetest falsetto voice I sang one of my favorite lullabies as I rushed toward the nursery to satiate my baby's hunger. All my years of voice lessons were finally paying off. There was no time to nap once the baby fell back to sleep. Time was marching on, and a sleeping baby meant a free moment to contact Craig Zalvan's referral.

Leah Ross-Kugler, MS, CCC-SLP, works alongside Dr. Zalvan to rehabilitate people with vocal problems. Leah, a former opera singer, is a certified speech-language pathologist with specific training and experience in voice disorders. She helps individuals eliminate harmful vocal behaviors, change the manner of their voice production, and help with vocal fold tissue healing following injury, including surgery. To change the way a voice is produced, she may help adjust volume for emphasis and auditory interest, to vary inflection to eliminate a monotonous voice, or to "unload" muscle tension in a strained-sounding voice.

As a general speech pathologist, she assists those with speech difficulties such as stuttering or "cluttering" (similar to mumbling) or articulation errors like lisping. She has also helped those who desire accent modification. I called Leah as soon as the baby closed his eyes and I was able to safely return him to his crib. She had been expecting my call but with back-to-back appointments, Sunday morning seemed like a more relaxing time for us to speak over the phone.

Bright and early in the morning, Leah's voice was full of expression and personality. We immediately connected as we shared anecdotes about the types of voices I've encountered during my interviewing years and the ones she's worked with throughout her 12 years as a voice therapist and speech pathologist. I correlated the most memorably jarring ones I've come across with popular icons who possess similar voice types. This is assuming that there are no organic or neurologic causes to the voice productions, as Leah reminded me; these voices are due to behavioral or habitual causes. Following are my descriptors along with her assessments and suggested solution:

▪ **The Fran Drescher "Nanny" voice:** This whiny, nasally voice full of exaggerated inflections may be interpreted as being high maintenance and difficult to please. High-maintenance employees require extra handholding and constant reassurance, so hiring managers may choose to steer clear of a candidate with this voice.

Response: If the hypernasal resonance in the voice is minor, it can be helped by increasing the area of the oral cavity to allow for more oral resonance.

- **The Marilyn Monroe voice:** The soft, breathy quality of this voice comes across vulnerable and frail with a sexy, wannabe connotation. This voice may be construed as lacking substance and credibility for a position that requires authority and expertise.

Response: Make sure both posture and breath support are adequate. Vocal function exercises (similar to exercises that singers perform called "vocalese") may also strengthen the voice. Increasing vocal volume without strain may also help to decrease breathiness.

- **The Joan Rivers voice:** This loud, raspy voice sounds like the candidate is cramming the entire interview into one breath. Running out of breath before finishing phrases and sentences may result in lost messages.

Response: The power supply for the voice is the exhalatory cycle of breathing. Therefore, if you are running out of air when you speak, it's similar to driving a car on empty. That's why the voice sounds strained. Decreasing speech rate and/or increasing replenishing breaths will help, so that the candidate doesn't put too many words in one breath. Occasionally, speakers can exhibit a lack of coordination between breathing and speaking, so that they exhale too much before an utterance. Replenishing breaths and effective breath pauses can remedy this.

- **The Rod Stewart voice:** While this voice is a great fit for rock 'n' roll, it can be especially harsh and rough for a corporate environment. It could come across as overly forceful and brash during an interview.

Response: A chronically harsh voice may be a sign of laryngeal pathology (i.e., swellings or bumps on the vocal folds). A laryngological examination can confirm this. Treatments vary according to the cause of the growths. You can reduce the hoarseness by speaking, shouting, and singing less; performing gentle vocal warm-ups; or changing the resonance by placing the voice "in the mask" as singers describe.

- **The Ethel Merman voice:** Piercing and loud, this voice can make a person sound pompous and self-absorbed, especially when confined to a small interview venue.

  Response: Ethel Merman had a unique belting voice that vibrated "in the mask." A comparable speaking voice can carry easily without having to yell or speak loudly. Some self-awareness exercises to decrease vocal volume can help, while maintaining an animated, forward focus.

- **The James Earl Jones voice:** This bold voice may be considered overly authoritative and intimidating, depending on the role or level of position being sought.

  Response: The candidate could benefit from softening the quality. This can be achieved by decreasing volume, increasing "melody" or intonation contour, or speaking with an even style of smooth and connected speech.

- **The Michael Jackson voice:** This voice's childlike quality may discredit your proficiencies and capabilities. It may hinder you from being considered for a high-profile or leadership position as it may come across as too innocent and naive to handle matters of conflict resolution.

  Response: It may be that the power supply (respiration) is suboptimal, so increasing breath support could help strengthen this voice. Adding more melody or inflection would vary the pitch more, to produce a variety of low-, mid-, and high-modal tones. In rare cases, there is a disorder called "puberphonia," where a patient maintains the childlike quality of the voice beyond puberty. A voice therapist trained in treating this disorder can help this.

Articulation/Enunciation/Diction

Bear in mind that when sounds are interchanged, distorted, or omitted, it can make speech difficult to understand. For instance, you may substitute the letter "w" for the letter "r," making the word "run" sound like "won"; distort "s" or "sh"; or omit certain sounds by pronouncing the word "fool" as "foo." However, "errors" may also be considered a cultural or dialectical variant, as found in African American Vernacular English (AAVE) or some regional New York accents, whereby "d" sounds may be substituted for "th" sounds, making "this" sound like "dis." An "accent," whether regional or "foreign" (as a nonnative speaker of English may speak), can be modified if it presents difficulty in being understood, if it detracts from the context of your message, or if it makes you feel uncomfortable speaking in business settings, especially during an interview. Altering vowel and consonant pronunciation as well as varying the stress, rhythm, and inflection of your speech can modify accents.

Mumbling can be a result of a motor speech disorder or it can be a habitual way of speaking. Among the suggested methods for improving mumbling are slowing the rate of speech, moving the articulators more, or using more melody in the voice. If there is a motor weakness, some exercises can increase strength, precision, and range of motion.

"Actually, It's Like, Um, You Know"

Paralanguage refers to vocalizations like whistling, snorting, giggling, and other fillers such as "um," "uh," and "ah," which can greatly impede fluency during an interview. In addition, interjections such as "like," "you know," "basically," and "actually" may alter the flow of a conversation, which is also distracting during an interview. Self-awareness is a fundamental step toward correcting habitual speech patterns. Consequently, Leah recommends audio- or videotaping yourself in a mock interview to heighten your self-awareness. Focusing on your breathing by taking replenishing breaths between phrases can help reduce speech fillers. As a cue for a habitual giggler who wishes to eliminate such behavior, Leah uses a technique of wearing a designated bracelet or wristwatch on the hand that is not routinely used; it can act as a reminder to avoid nervous laughter. Also, substituting a positive behavior, such as smiling, instead of giggling is helpful.

Pace

Speaking too quickly or too slowly will hamper your verbal communication. Candidates who cram everything into one breath are difficult to understand. They may show signs of being overly nervous or having cluttered thoughts. Alternatively, those who have overly slow speech patterns may come across as weak and powerless. Besides mirroring the rate of your interviewer's speech, concentrating on phrasing is another solution for modifying your pace. Phrasing involves visualizing what you're saying as you would if you were reading written text, by acknowledging commas, periods, and colons for pausing.

You don't have to be a world-class singer or motivational speaker to possess a healthy, well-trained voice that delivers crystal-clear messages. However, for many of us who make it a priority to practice and improve our voice and speech skills, the rewards are indicative of our labor. Use the warmth and intensity of your voice to add value and color to your speech. Also, be sure to follow a regimen of good oral hygiene. You will undeniably be heard even in the noisy and competitive arena of finding the perfect job. Access laryngologists, voice therapists, and speech pathologists in your area through the American Speech-Language and Hearing Association (www.asha.org).

LEAH'S TIPS FOR MAINTAINING A HEALTHY VOICE (VOCAL HYGIENE)

- Drink plenty of water.

- Avoid excessive or loud talking and yelling.

- Get enough sleep.

- Rest the voice if feeling strain or fatigue.

- Avoid colds and upper respiratory infections.

- Reduce or avoid alcoholic and caffeinated beverages that can be drying to the vocal folds.

- Don't smoke.

Open Mouth, Insert Foot
Appropriate Q&A for Interviewing Success

There are no foolish questions and no man becomes a fool until he has stopped asking questions. —Charles P. Steinmetz (German-born engineer and inventor)

DON'T WE ALL wish we had access to a crystal ball that would guide us through the perfect question-and-answer interview session? Unfortunately, such a futuristic device does not exist, so we must rely on our discretion and intuition. But who's to say that your interview will even be a dialogue? Many times, from the moment you sit in your chair, the one-sided interrogation begins. However, even in that type of extreme scenario, the interviewer will allow you a question or two at the end of the cross-examination. Therefore, you must prepare on some of the broadest and most common topics that you should feel confident asking about and answering while in the hot seat.

One thing is certain: Not asking questions during an interview will make you appear disinterested, unprepared, timid, and unmotivated. It may also be indicative of your personality being too proud to ask questions on the job, greatly increasing the possibility for error at the company's expense. Answering questions to the best of your knowledge in a straightforward, creative, theoretical, or analytical manner are sure ways to score points in your favor—transporting your candidacy closer to the finish line.

Interview Flair

The interviewer's method of asking questions may be a reflection of his personal preference or be based on the type of industry for which he is interviewing. For your preparations, expect questions asked of you, as well as questions you will ask (if given the opportunity), to be formed in one of four ways:

1. Conventional

2. Behavioral

3. Situational/stress

4. Case managerial

Conventional interviews are traditional, straightforward questions. This style of questioning can really make an interview move along quickly, because there's no hidden agenda behind what is being asked of you. A recruiter or hiring manager may ease into an interview with conventional questions to break the ice. Junior candidates such as interns, recent college grads, administrative candidates, temporary employees, and returnees to the workforce can expect entire interviews composed of conventional questions. Among the most common traditional questions asked of candidates are:

Q: So, what can you tell me about yourself?

This is a typical question for switching gears from casual small talk about the weather or such into formal interview mode. It is *such* an open-ended question that you must be careful not to be overwhelmed by it. As simple as it sounds, where does one begin to summarize oneself? Do you start way back when you were the milk monitor in kindergarten? The best way to prepare for this common question is to be ready with three adjectives to describe yourself, three verbs (action words), and three adverbs that describe the how, when, and where.

A: Well, I am loyal, enthusiastic, *and* self-motivated. *(Three adjectives) I* work (1st verb) **well** (1st adverb) *with others,* resolve (2nd verb) *issues* quickly (2nd adverb)*, and* always *(3rd adverb)* respond (3rd verb) *to constructive criticism.*

Q: Why are you on the job market at this particular time?

This is where the hiring manager is doing his due diligence in finding out whether you've been fired, want more money, or are just plain window shopping for a job. If you're unemployed, state the truth without reservation, and if you are employed you never want to go into a tirade about how you're undervalued, underappreciated, and underpaid. You will come across as a shallow, money-hungry complainer who will make the interviewer get into a bidding war when it comes down to accepting an offer. You might also come across as someone who, when the chips are down, will accept a counteroffer.

A: I've really gotten to the top of my learning (not earning) *potential and I find that my skills are not being used to their optimum potential.*

Q: You've been at your present company for nine months, and before this job you were at your job for less than a year. What are your reasons for such short tenures at both of your most recent jobs?

Companies want to be sure that you will be a reliable employee if hired. Nothing makes a potential employer more hesitant than a "jumpy" background. They will be investing time and money to get you on board, and the last thing they want or need is to have their effort and resources wasted. My best advice is to be truthful and consistent about your reasons because sooner or later the truth is always revealed. There are many valid reasons why you may be forced to leave a job, and all you can do is explain them with honesty and candor. Hopefully, you will have other qualifying and compelling assets that will keep you in the running.

A: The reason why I've been with my present company for only nine months is because the person I report to retired and his replacement is bringing her own team. Before my current position, I was with that employer for less than a year because I followed my current boss (the one who's retiring) from his last job.

Q: Where do you see yourself in five years?

This question gets many candidates in trouble. While you don't want to sound like you are not goal-driven, you also don't want to sound like you have unrealistic aspirations. A tactful way of answering such a question is by assuring them that you see yourself within their company, in a role that allows you to use your existing skills, learn new skills, and take on additional challenges. This answer does not show any expectation of upward mobility, though it does show a desire for lateral mobility.

A: I see myself working here in a role that further challenges my sales and management capabilities.

Q: You currently work for our main competitor. What makes our company a more appealing choice for you?

Be prepared to earn brownie points by indicating the positive assets within the company where you are interviewing, but not at the expense of bashing your present company. If you're prepared with up-to-date background information on the company you are hoping will be your next employer, then you don't have to knock the one that is still signing your paycheck or give away hush-hush information to validate your point. Being prepared helps you answer questions with concrete examples to substantiate your responses. Highlight what the company you're interviewing with has to offer without undermining what your current company lacks.

A: I understand that your company has a top-notch, state-of-the-art technological infrastructure. As a systems engineer, this is a great source of attraction for me.

Behavioral interview queries are used throughout different industries and levels of interviewing. However, this style of interviewing is reserved for questions that are asked in the middle or at the end of an interview rather than at the beginning. Behavioral questions focus on former work experiences, with the assumption that candidates, being creatures of habit, will repeat their behavior in the new position that they are seeking. The following are some of the most common behavioral questions asked by interviewers:

Q: Tell me about a time during your career when prioritizing was absolutely necessary.

Slightly more sophisticated and moderately more thought-provoking, this question forces you to think back not just to your current or last job but to your entire career. Come on, think, and think fast. It is important for companies to know that you are good at prioritizing, because in a fast-paced, ever-changing work environment, what was priority five minutes ago can rapidly be put on the back burner until further notice. Potential employers want to know that you can quickly change gears and "get with the program."

A: Prioritizing is one of my biggest assets. Coincidentally, just the other day my direct report was away on business for two weeks and left me an agenda of items that needed to be tended to while she was gone. As it turns out, our biggest client called to request an urgent meeting regarding our latest campaign, and I had to reshuffle many of the items on the list to accommodate a week's worth of work for this client. My boss and our client were very impressed with my sense of urgency and my ability to move things around for the benefit of our client while still fulfilling all of the items on the original agenda.

Q: Can you think of an example where you had to make a difficult work decision?

Your ability to make decisions on an everyday basis is of extreme importance to a company. Difficult decisions are scrutinized even more, for if you're caught like a deer in headlights, the results can impact the company gravely. Even if you're not being hired for a leadership role where decision making is imperative, companies still want to know they will be hiring someone with sound judgment who is independent enough to make resolutions.

A: I recently had to fire an employee whom I liked a great deal. Unfortunately, he was consistently unable to come to work on time or respect our attendance policy. After several talks with him and many false promises assuring change, I had to take a deep breath and terminate his employment.

Q: Can you specify a time when you dealt with a new policy or procedure with which you did not agree?

This question's intention is really to find if you are the type of employee who "rocks the boat." Even though companies want to hire progressive-thinking and independent individuals, when procedures are replaced because of new management or restructuring, they want to make sure that they are not hiring the one bad seed that will contaminate the crop. If you start getting into the time you were at the forefront of a company-wide upheaval, it will not come across as a positive attribute in your favor. At the very least, describe how you tried to embrace the new system or principle and even give kudos if the new procedure turned out to be a better one than what you were used to. Remember, the goal is to remain positive.

A: Last summer our company decided to withdraw its summer casual dress policy. I had been instrumental in implementing the policy five years ago, so naturally I was not in favor of this. I did confidentially suggest that employees be awarded a stipend to subsidize the expense of building a corporate wardrobe. Much to my surprise, my recommendation was accepted, prompting a morale increase. Once the new dress policy was enforced, I noticed that the increase in morale also boosted productivity.

Q: Describe how you've handled positions of leadership or authority in the past.

The way you answer this question can divulge your strengths and weaknesses as a chief, manager, or principal. Are you a micromanager who tends to look over everyone's shoulder and correct everything, or do you delegate responsibilities with a more consultative approach? Neither is technically incorrect, though one may prove to be more productive than the other.

A: I regulate my leadership style according to the individual personalities within my group. Some individuals, regardless of the level of experience, require more guidance than others who are just entering the job force. I evaluate the strengths and weaknesses within my group, and I do my best to match everyone's skill set to a particular project. Typically, I reserve any comments until the end of a project if there is ongoing progress. My teams are all well aware that I am available for guidance at all times.

Q: Could you describe a circumstance or encounter that has influenced you into the career path you're presently seeking?

This question is often geared at recent college grads or change-of-career candidates who may not have the work history to prove they are committed to a specific industry. Hiring managers and recruiters want to assure themselves that you have a compelling reason for choosing to start in a designated field. They also want to make sure that you are not caught up in the grandeur of a glamorous environment and come in with unwarranted expectations. In other words, you must prove your case.

A: Last summer I interned at a fashion magazine where I learned what it takes to succeed in the industry. I learned that it is a very competitive, challenging, and unpredictable environment. I now understand how my work-life balance may be compromised, but I'm ready for the challenge.

Situational/stress interviews focus on extracting sensitive information from you by using a hypothetical and/or intimidating approach. Behavioral and situational/stress interviews are similar in that they force you to be more analytical than when answering traditional questions. However, note that behavioral questions require you to dig deep into scenarios that have taken place, whereas situational questions require you to be a bit more imaginative and look into that crystal ball to visualize the scenario and base your answer on the theory of it actually happening.

Q: If you were to be offered this position, what would be your first undertaking?

This question can be really daunting, especially if you haven't yet met all of the players involved (superiors and subordinates). What recruiters want to find out with this question is whether you have the confidence, initiative, and leadership ability to infuse change. A smart way to handle this question early in the interview process is to ask more specific questions about why the position is vacant and the challenges that exist within the department. Perhaps there is a discipline issue within a group that you would be managing, or maybe revenue has declined because of low morale. Get to the root of the problem in order to give an educated answer. If indeed there is a morale issue, and you feel that is the crux of the malfunction, choose that as your first order of business and support it with similar challenges you have overcome during a similar experience where you had to prioritize to organize. This is where asking whether you can take notes at the beginning of the interview can prove to be helpful in recollecting information that can help you answer this type of question.

A: Based on our discussion so far, it sounds like the main cause of chaos within the group I'm being considered for is lack of direction. Therefore, that sounds like the sensible place to begin.

Q: If I were to ask your current boss what your greatest weakness is, what would she say?

This question can be tricky because although you want to be honest, you don't want to come up with a weakness that is such a turnoff that it ruins your chances of being considered for a job. Surely, you have weaknesses that can be viewed as positives from an employer's point of view. For instance, you may be someone who never says no to a coworker who needs help, even if helping is not within your jurisdiction. Another weakness could be you're always the last person to leave the office just to catch up on work. Whatever you do, don't make your weakness be that you're always late to early-morning departmental meetings.

A: I believe she would say I don't know when to stop perfecting things. No matter what task, it can always stand additional tweaking. Though the final outcome will always exceed the requirements, I will often overthink things.

Q: If you witnessed a coworker performing an illegal act while on company time and premises what would you do?

This question is just plain nasty, but interviewers do ask it. Other than putting your back against a wall, this question tests your loyalty and your judgment. So which will you be: a whistle-blower or a traitor to the company? Neither one is pretty, but the one thing you can do is present it in such a way that it helps the company by knowing and the employee by learning from the repercussions of you telling. Hopefully, you'll never be caught in that type of situation and it will remain a hypothetical situation.

A: It would be my duty as an employee of the firm to report any situation that compromises the moral values, privacy, and reputation of the firm. I would have no choice but to confidentially alert the administration of such an occurrence.

Q: How would you handle your direct supervisor's request to work extended hours outside of the scope of the usual and customary schedule?

Who said interviewing isn't nerve-racking? This question's goal is clearly to get to the bottom of how you handle unexpected overtime, business travel, and entertaining requests. However, this can be a learning experience for you too, as it can clear up any reservations you might have concerning the work schedule before committing to the position. Be open and flexible; however, if heavy travel and unexpected commitments will be a big part of this position and that is an inconvenience for you because of other engagements, it's better to find out sooner than to be surprised later. Be honest.

A: I don't consider myself a clock-watcher. However, I am available for extended commitments to fulfill this position on a (regular, occasional, or rare) basis. Any advance notice is greatly appreciated. I hope this does not hinder my chances of being hired.

Q: If you had an opportunity to delete any experience or skill off your résumé and replace it with one you wished you had, what would it be?

Do you have any regrets? This is the question that brings any misgivings out in the open. This shows interviewers a sense of how strong your self-evaluation skills are. This question will compel you to examine and discuss any career decisions that, left unexplained, may otherwise hinder your chances of being hired. Perhaps it's as simple as swapping out a past job that does not correlate with your current goals but offered exceptional financial rewards or a job that you were overqualified for but accepted out of desperation, which now places you in a lower compensation range.

A: I wish that instead of French, I had taken Italian, which would help me with the overseas markets, and I would replace the creative role I had six years ago for a more quantitative position, as it seems to have type-cast me into similar types of positions.

Case managerial interviews are primarily used in management consulting firms in order to retain the crème de la crème, though they are quickly making their way into other discerning industries. The questions are similar to analytical questions found in college entrance standardized tests, though the overall goal is to grade the thought process rather than the conclusion. Case managerial interviews may be administered verbally or in written form, and most often the questions are not even related to the industry in which you are seeking employment. Sometimes time is factored into the evaluation, and other times you may be permitted to dissect it as you would a take-home test, with the added convenience of being able to research information. The steps you take to solve the case(s) are analyzed with the following criteria in mind: critical thinking, resourcefulness, creativity, spontaneity, inquisitiveness, focus, stress management, and organizational and quantitative skills.

In addition, the format may be one or a combination of any of the following:

- **Guesstimations:** How many gallons of water do Americans consume each month?

- **Pictorial interpretations:** Deciphering charts, graphs and other types of illustrations.

- **Hypotheseis:** A 10-person company must generate $30 million in sales during one year. How would you go about executing this as the leader of the firm?

- **Brain exercises (riddles, puzzles, sequential math):** Why is the sky blue?

Wait Your Turn . . .

Regardless of the style and length of the interviewer's questions, at some point he or she should have the interview etiquette to ask, "Do you have any questions?" This is your moment to find out what you've been patiently hoping will come up during conversation. Whatever you do, *do not* allow the interview to end without asking a minimum of one question. If your mind draws a complete blank during this moment, here are five questions to show you the type to keep in mind.

Q1. I read in the *Wall Street Journal* yesterday that the company has expanded by 40 percent because of mergers and acquisitions across the United States and Canada. Will the company's recent growth directly impact XYZ department?

This sort of question shows you did your homework and prepared for your interview. You are "in the know" about what's going on within the company, and this automatically designates you as being interested enough and sharp enough to be invited back for a second or third round of interviews. You may also follow the question with one that addresses how the growth specifically affects your position. Organizational changes due to expansion could mean additional responsibilities not listed on the original job description that was composed prior to the recent change.

Q2. How far along are you in the interview process, and do you have a time frame to fill it?

This is a fair and important question to ask a hiring manager because it will give you an idea of what the sense of urgency is. Many times there is no sense of urgency because the person who is being replaced is being transferred or promoted into another department, giving the company the luxury of extending the search. Other times the position is red hot because the department manager is requesting the position be filled as priority business. Either way it is important for you to know what you're up against, as it will help you make decisions about other opportunities that may be offered to you in the meantime. Also, this question will clarify whether you are the first or fifth person they've seen for the job. Sometimes it's to your disadvantage to be the first person seen, because the hiring manager has no basis of comparison and will not move the process along to the next level until she has accumulated enough viable candidates to present to an internal department.

Q3. In addition to the duties and responsibilities listed in the job description, are there any other anticipated requirements or commitments I should know about?

This question allows you to protect yourself from surprises in your work schedule down the road. If there is an annual conference that you must travel to as part of your job description and it happens to fall on the date of your wedding anniversary *every year,* then this is the time to evaluate whether the financial rewards will be enough to upgrade your spouse's gift to ease the disappointment of not being together each year during your special day, or whether this annual commitment will add unnecessary conflict to your relationship. It's best to factor such work conflicts or commitments into your lifestyle early on, in order to set your expectations and the expectations of your loved ones straight from the get-go.

Q4. Can you tell me how I can improve my chances of getting this position and offer any guidance in terms of the personalities of those I will be working with?

This question not only communicates your high level of interest, but it also shows flexibility on your part to go the extra mile. It basically says, "I'm willing to take direction, just show me the way." The second part of the question can uncover interesting information regarding the dynamics of the group or department you would be working with. Perhaps the person you would be reporting to is a stickler for timeliness and detail, or maybe someone in the group has long-standing seniority and likes to take on a mentoring role. This is all useful information gathering.

Q5. Do you think I'm well suited for this position?

This is a very direct question and one that you should ask if, in your mind, this job is your top choice. If it is your top choice, then it is to your benefit to get a better sense of whether the interviewer agrees with your sentiment. Most times, interviewers are very forthright when answering this type of question. While they're not promising you the job, it does confirm you're on the right track to being invited back or ending up on the short list of finalists.

TEN INTERVIEW-KILLER QUESTIONS

1. What sorts of growth opportunities does this company offer?

Growth opportunities are influenced by your proven work performance. Therefore, it is difficult to answer this question since you haven't yet demonstrated your worth.

2. What types of bonuses or perks are there associated with this position?

Asking about bonuses or perks is similar to having a waiter or waitress ask how much you will be tipping before you sit down.

3. Who is your medical and dental insurance carrier and what are my co-pays?

Your goal is to show that you are interested in learning about the job and its duties and responsibilities instead of getting ahead of yourself by asking questions that are more appropriate once you're offered the job.

4. What is your sick day policy?

If this one of your most pressing questions, it might be assumed that you are either a hypochondriac or love to head to the beach in 90-degree weather.

5. Is it really necessary for me to fill out this application since everything is explained on my résumé?

This is just the "writing on the wall" to all of the other policies and procedures you will try to circumvent. Don't be difficult; follow instructions and stop complaining about the print being too small.

6. How much lead time do I have before the drug test screening?
Are you kidding? Can you be a little less obvious?

7. What day of the week does everyone get together for happy hour?
Okay, you social bee, this is really telling of just how much of an extrovert you are. Will you take over as the office chatterer and gossipmonger? Remember, you're being hired to work, not to socialize. Even if it's after hours, the fact that you're asking about happy hour gives the impression that it's a criteria for choosing your next job.

8. Is there a waiting period before I am eligible for vacation time?
You haven't even started and you're already thinking about taking time off? This question is even more absurd when asked by someone who is currently unemployed. This question is liable to extend your unemployment vacation more than anything else.

9. How do I know your company won't be closing its doors in a year's time?
This is such a confrontational question, and, by the way, as I said earlier, who has a crystal ball to know such things?

10. Is this a female- and minority-owned company? I've never seen so many in one company.
Talk about sounding politically incorrect and ignorant. Keep any such observations to yourself even if you're in favor of working in a diverse environment.

Illegal Questions

If you've interviewed enough, surely you've come across at least one company representative who is imprudent, oblivious, or both to questions that are not only inappropriate, but also illegal. Questions that are illegal are intended to somehow uncover information about particular group members that will hinder employment in certain institutions. However, some questions may be rephrased to obtain information that specifically pertains to a requirement of the job. If you are asked an illegal question, you may choose to handle it one of three ways:

- **Submissive:** You don't want to rock the boat, and who cares if you disclose such information. You have nothing to hide and you're proud of your background.

- **Passive-aggressive:** You subtly make mention that given the fact that it's an illegal question, you don't want to compromise their hiring decision by answering it; perhaps ask whether the question can be rephrased.

- **Aggressive:** Stop the interview and firmly state you will not answer illegal questions.

Protected Groups

The U.S. Equal Employment Opportunity Commission (EEOC) oversees, enforces, and regulates all the federal Equal Employment Opportunity (EEO) laws that prevent job discrimination among protected groups:[1]

- Title VII of the Civil Rights Act of 1964 (Title VII), which prohibits employment discrimination based on race, color, religion, sex, or national origin.

- The Equal Pay Act of 1963 (EPA), which protects men and women who perform substantially equal work in the same establishment from sex-based wage discrimination.

- The Age Discrimination in Employment Act of 1967 (ADEA), which protects individuals who are 40 years of age or older.

- Title I and Title V of the Americans with Disabilities Act of 1990 (ADA), which prohibit employment discrimination against qualified individuals with disabilities in the private sector, and in state and local governments.

- Sections 501 and 505 of the Rehabilitation Act of 1973, which prohibit discrimination against qualified individuals with disabilities who work in the federal government.

- The Civil Rights Act of 1991, which, among other things, provides monetary damages in cases of intentional employment discrimination.

- The Uniformed Services Employment and Reemployment Rights Act of 1994 (USERRA 38 U.S.C. 4301–4335), which protects civilian job rights and benefits for veterans and members of Reserve components.

- The Genetic Information Nondiscrimination Act of 2008 (GINA) includes two titles. Title I (effective May 21, 2008), which amends portions of the Employee Retirement Income Security Act (ERISA), the Public Health Service Act, and the Internal Revenue Code, addresses the use of genetic information in health insurance. Title II (effective November 21, 2009) prohibits the use of genetic information in employment, prohibits the intentional acquisition of genetic information about applicants and employees, and imposes strict confidentiality requirements.

Individual state and local laws protect other groups, such as persons in different age groups, those who are smokers (ERISA §510 and State Privacy Law), those who have had previous arrests, or those with a particular sexual orientation. For a more complete listing of state employment protection laws, you may access information at http://hr.blr.com.

IT'S ALL IN THE DELIVERY—
ILLEGAL QUESTIONS REPHRASED WITH A PURPOSE

- What is your height and weight? (Gender/sex discrimination, Title VII) *Rephrased:* Are you able to carry 75-pound boxes for a distance of 30 feet throughout three one-hour intervals during a workday?

- What is your date of birth? (Age discrimination, ADEA) *Rephrased:* Are you 18 years of age or over?

- Are you a U.S. citizen? (National origin, Title VII) *Rephrased:* Do you have authorization to work in the United States, and can you provide valid documentation upon offer acceptance?

- Are you married? (Sex, Title VII, or sexual orientation)
Rephrased: Are there outside obligations that would prevent you from maintaining a designated work schedule?

- Do you have any disabilities or have you participated in any type of genetic testing that classifies you as a high risk for developing any specific diseases, disorders, or future disabilities? (ADA and GINA)
Rephrased: Can you handle the duties and responsibilities of the position I've just described with (or without) modifications?

- What type of military discharge were you given? (USERRA)
Rephrased: How do you think the training and education you received while in the military prepared you for this type of position?

- Are you a smoker? (ERISA §510)
Rephrased: In addition to time taken for lunch, we allow two additional breaks during the work hours.

- Have you ever been arrested? (Innocent until proven guilty)
Rephrased: Have you ever been convicted of theft or fraud?

- Are your salary requirements flexible because of your change of career? (Equal pay, EPA)
Rephrased: Are you aware that this position's salary ranges from $60K to $75K per year?

- Do you have any religious affiliations? (Religion, Title VII)
Rephrased: Are there any professional associations or networks that would help you gain visibility within this industry?

Conclusion

The great end of life is not knowledge but action. —*Aldous Huxley (English novelist and critic)*

CONCLUDING THE writing of this book to which I've dedicated so much time and energy is both exhilarating and saddening. I feel enormous pride to have accomplished this lifelong goal during a time when so much else around me could have deterred me or taken precedence. It's taken a great deal of self-discipline to disassociate myself from external realities that might have otherwise discouraged my objectives. Throughout my writing, disheartening headlines have been the subjects of trepidation, all in agreement that unemployment numbers have soared to record highs in more than two decades. Even a multibillion-dollar stimulus law has been slow to curtail the major economic recession we are currently experiencing.

In the midst of such a recession, it seemed pointless to write about image, as its importance appeared trivial by comparison. If there aren't any jobs available, there are no employers around to see what you're wearing, how you behave, or how you communicate. You just can't squeeze water out of a rock. Optimistically, I continued with my mission, as I believe that there is a light at the end of the tunnel. So when things do turn around, you should be prepared to bask in the glow. Current reports project that more than half a million jobs will be saved and created throughout the months to come—a small confirmation that progress is being made. I sincerely hope that by the time this book reaches you, the economic crisis has at least started to turn around. History has shown that restoration eras are a time for reestablishing fresh ground, leaving room for new beginnings that encourage change as a means of improvement and development. Improvement and development are what image is about, so this book is timely after all.

Speaking of change, as I thumb through each of these chapters, I'm reminded of meaningful events that have inspired change in my own life during the creation of this book. The first was discovering the joyful news of becoming a mother for a second time after eight years of having a single child. As elated as I was to be able to experience motherhood again, I knew what it would mean in terms of my writing. Early in my pregnancy, writing late at night was nearly impossible, since my eyes and mind would shut down by 8 P.M. My days were filled with other work, responsibilities, and infinite bathroom trips. Still, by my second trimester, I managed to increase productivity, and by my third trimester I managed to have increased my weight by a whopping 50-something pounds. Let's just say it wasn't easy to write about appearance when mine was beyond camouflaging.

All kidding aside, I balanced the pregnancy and book writing pretty well, if I do say so myself. That period became a sort of self-reflecting nesting period for me, where most of my time was spent nurturing my "twins," the baby and the book. Delivering three weeks early was a blessing, but it meant three fewer weeks of quiet writing time. The next change was learning to juggle a baby boy, a daughter, a husband, and the book—and the pressure was on to balance my act. While the broken sleep made it challenging to concentrate during the day, I managed to get myself on a healthy action plan, a plan that fueled my mind and melted away the pounds as quickly as they had been piled on. Suddenly, by eating "volumized" meals, drinking plenty of water, and moving my body again, I found my vigor and strength. I was right back on track and on a mission to rebuild my own image as a working mother, author, and motivator of career and image.

Writing a book can make it feel like you're living in a vacuum. The isolation was challenging for me, being the extrovert that I am, but what it forced me to do was become self-reflective. Self-reflection is the crux of establishing your image. In the process of my self-reflection, I not only shed some weight, but I also shed new light on the things that are most important in my life: family, health, and career. For the first time in a long time, I was able to appreciate and acknowledge how far I've come in my life through some of the autobiographical anecdotes I shared throughout the book. It was refreshing to experience my own "rebirth."

We spend so much time measuring our success by how high we've climbed the corporate ladder. If you don't bother to stop and look down, you never gain a full perspective of how far you've gotten. I urge you to look down and around, to take inventory of your accomplishments, and to give yourself credit for *all* of your successes. To bring it back to shopping terms, you need to know what you have in your closet before you can start to rebuild your wardrobe, and sometimes you can even get lucky and find a treasure that just needs some sprucing up. The same concept applies with achieving self-discovery and assessing where to begin your image journey.

I've provided you with the information. Now it's up to you to take action. It's one thing to know what to do, but it's a whole other thing to actually do it. Today's employment market requires you to be a chameleon: open to different ideas and flexible to new approaches. Companies and positions are being revised and reinvented to fit the boundaries of the budgetary constraints. Finding a comfort zone within your image is a time-consuming process. Use this time to reflect and devise an action plan that is right for you. Perhaps you need to reach out to your network of contacts, rework your résumé, or revamp your look. The possibilities are endless. All you need is to develop a focus, and the rest should follow. Start slow and steady if you need to, but push yourself to the finish line.

As much as I've harped on the subject of saying thank you, my conclusion would not be complete without thanking you for choosing my book as a viable option toward achieving your career goals. Let it guide you through the process of finding a job that is challenging, satisfying, and profitable. I really don't like long-winded good-byes so I will just say so long and leave you with these last parting thoughts: Accentuate your goals, balance your emotions, and communicate by executing.

Best of luck!

END NOTES

CHAPTER 3

1. Cotton Incorporated, "The Classification of American Pima Cotton,"
http://www.cottoninc.com/ClassificationofCotton/?Pg=7

2. International Wool Textile Association, "Wool Is Best: Wool Explained,"
http://www.iwto.org/

CHAPTER 5

1. A. Flusser, *Dressing the Man: Mastering the Art of Permanent Fashion* (New York: HarperCollins, 2002)

2. Shoe-Design.Com, Glossary of Shoes,
http://shoe-design.com//glossary-footwear-definitions.html

3. *New York Times,* July 25, 2005

CHAPTER 6

1. Gillette.com, "Gillette Grooming Glossary,"
http://www.gillette.com/en-US/#/grooming/glossary/en-US/circlebeard.shtml/

CHAPTER 7

1. Craig C. Freudenrich, "How Sweat Works," *How Stuff Works,* Jan. 10, 2008,
http://health.howstuffworks.com/sweat.htm

2. Unilever Australasia, Understanding Deodorants & Antiperspirants,
http://www.unilever.com.au/ourbrands/beautyandstyle/Understanding_deodorants_and_antiperspirants.asp

3. Jay Marks, MD, "Intestinal Gas (Belching, Bloating, Flatulence)," http://www.medicinenet
.com/intestinal_gas_belching_bloating_flatulence/article.htm

CHAPTER 9

1. David Lewis, *The Secret Language of Success: Using Body Language to Get What You Want.* (New York: Carroll & Graf Publishers, Inc., 1990)

CHAPTER 11

1. Shari Roan, "Chewing Gum Helps Raise Students' Math Scores," *Los Angeles Times,* April 27, 2009

CHAPTER 19

1. The U.S. Equal Employment Opportunity Commission, "Federal Laws Prohibiting Job Discrimination Questions and Answers," http://www.eeoc.gov/facts/qanda.html

APPENDIX: Useful Web Sites

To learn more about each web site listed below, please visit *www.lizandravega.com*, where you will find a detailed description of the services each site offers.

INFORMATIONAL WEB SITES
Career TV, *www.careertv.com*
Chamber of Commerce, *www.chamberofcommerce.com*
Hoover's, Inc., *www.hoovers.com*
Job-Hunt, *www.job-hunt.org*
Quintessential Careers, *www.quintcareers.com*
Weddles, *www.weddles.com*
ZoomInfo, *www.zoominfo.com*

GENERAL "MEGA" JOB-SITE WEB SITES
CareerBuilder, *www.careerbuilder.com*
Monster, *www.monster.com*
Yahoo! HotJobs, *www.hotjobs.com*

"HIGH ROLLER" JOB SITES
6FigureJobs, *www.6FigureJobs.com*
CEOExpress, *www.ceoexpress.com*
The Ladders, *www.theladders.com*

ADDITIONAL JOB SITES
CollegeGrad.com, *www.collegegrad.com*
Dice, *www.dice.com*
Diversity Jobs, *www.diversityjobs.com*
Hire Vets First, *www.HireVetsFirst.gov*
Retirement Jobs, *www.retirementjobs.com*

HOURLY AND PART-TIME JOB SITES
Guru, *www.guru.com*

Net-Temps, *www.net-temps.com*
Snag a Job, *www.snagajob.com*

CAREER NETWORKING WEB SITES
Career Fairs Global, *www.cfg-inc.com*
JobExpo, *www.jobexpo.com*
LinkedIn, *www.linkedin.com*
Networking for Professionals, *www.networkingforprofessionals.com*
Partner Up, *www.partnerup.com*
Ryze Business Networking, *www.ryze.com*

SOCIAL NETWORKING WEB SITES
Classmates.com, *www.classmates.com*
Facebook, *www.facebook.com*
Friendster, *www.friendster.com*
Twitter, *www.twitter.com*
YouTube, *www.YouTube.com*

GOVERNMENT SERVICE WEB SITES
DisabilityInfo.gov
GovBenefits.gov
MyMoney.gov
USA.gov
U.S. Department of Labor, *www.dol.gov*

NETWORKING ORGANIZATION WEB SITES
BNI International, *www.bni.com*
eWomen Network, *www.ewomennetwork.com*
ExecutiveMoms, *www.executivemoms.com*
National Association of Female Executives, *www.nafe.com*
Venture Street, *www.venturestreet.com*

GENERAL SEARCH ENGINES
Find a professional association or group by using any of the following:
http://groups.google.com
http://groups.yahoo.com
http://www.ysearchblog.com

ACKNOWLEDGMENTS

There aren't enough languages for me to express the gratitude I feel toward all who have contributed to the completion of this book.

Warm and special thanks to my dear friend Tricia Kenney Rubertone, the Godmother of this book. You have been my sounding board and confidante since the book's inception, and your professional opinion gave me the assurance to market my proposal before I had even secured a literary agent. Thanks to Richard Abate for your advice and to John Avila for editing my proposal, and to my wonderful literary agent, Grace Freedson, for believing in my script and for your hand-holding, which has gotten me through uncharted territory.

I am particularly grateful to Executive Editor Ellen Kadin at AMACOM Books for seeing the potential in my manuscript. Thanks for orchestrating and fine-tuning all of the necessary pieces that have made this the quality book I aimed to present to my readers. And thanks to: Managing Editor Andy Ambraziejus, for ensuring that every aspect of production went seamlessly; Senior Development Editor Barry Richardson, freelance editor Louis Greenstein, and copyeditor Chris Gage, for your comments and comprehensive work on the manuscript; and Editorial Assistant William Helms III for all of the behind-the-scenes administrative support on this project. I would also like to acknowledge and thank Creative Director Cathleen Ouderkirk for working so hard on the perfect cover for a book that is all about being judged by one's image.

Thank you to the Sales and Marketing team at AMACOM: Trade Sales Director Jenny Wesselmann Schwartz; Director of Trade Publicity and Sales Promotions Irene Majuk; Director of Rights and International Sales Therese Mausser; Publicist Alice Northover; and Vice President of Sales and Marketing Rosemary Carlough. I would also like to thank AMACOM President Hank Kennedy for welcoming me on my first visit to the company. Your warm and engaging personality is mirrored by that of your dedicated staff.

Thanks to everyone at Harrison Edwards Public Relations and Marketing: most especially Carolyn Mandelker, Laura Mogil, and Bobby Knight. Thanks to Bob Mogil for making the introduction to them.

To everyone at Perennial Resources International (PRI), thank you for your continued support in many facets of my personal and professional life: my business partners Bill Lewis, Joe Kelly, Michael Mazza, and Steve Brown. Thanks to Managing Director Joanne Nord-Montanez for keeping things going in the office. And my deepest appreciation to my assistant Katharine Katie Patterson, my technical guru. Thank you, Katie, for formatting, printing, delivering, and mailing various rounds of scripts, and for being the most reliable assistant one could ever have. I appreciate the efforts of all of the PRI employees who have worked so hard to weather the recession at our firm.

I would also like to acknowledge all of the experts who provided me with invaluable information or feedback in person, via e-mail, or by phone: Cheryl Forberg, Dr. Craig Zalvan, Leah Ross-Kugler, Deborah L. Rosenberg, Carol Davidson, and Melissa Gold Jelinek. A special thanks to those who contribute to my image enhancement: Richard Langiulli, D.D.S.; Dawn DeTrinca; and Ilene Goldman. And thank you to Barbara Levine for her insight on artwork and to my illustrator Monica Hellström, whose work visually underscores everything I write about.

To Theresa Dell'Ollio and Allison Murray, everyone at Young Wonders, and all the moms who helped out with rides while I was racing to make my submission deadline—I owe you all a huge thank you for lending a hand and giving me peace of mind.

Finally, to my family, to whom this book is dedicated. Mom and Dad, you inspire me to strive and persevere. Thank you for practically moving in to babysit round the clock during my last month of writing. To my two miracles, Julianna and Christian, I thank you for all of your hugs and kisses and for tucking me into bed whenever I fell asleep before you due to sheer exhaustion. To my husband, Stephen, as I refer to you after 5 pm, when you go from business partner to life partner, I appreciate your taking on more than your share of social and domestic responsibilities in order for me to complete the writing of my book. Thank you for dreaming big alongside me.

To every single one of you I say, "Merci, danke, grazie, gracias, mahalo, and thank you!"

INDEX

ABOUT THE AUTHOR

A graduate of Wesleyan University, Lizandra Vega cofounded Perennial Resources International, a full-service, boutique-staffing firm based in Manhattan. As the company's managing partner, she serves an elite roster of clients and has successfully coached thousands of job candidates on everything from career development to résumé writing and wardrobe planning, to interview techniques and business etiquette. She is recognized as one of the most respected recruiters in the New York staffing arena.

Ms. Vega completed the Fashion Institute of Technology's Image Consulting Certification Program to further hone her ability to enhance the personal attributes of her clients. She is a certified image consultant and a past board member of the New York/Tri State Chapter of the Association of Image Consultants International.

Lizandra Vega resides in Westchester County, New York, with her husband and two children. She can be reached at *www.lizandravega.com.*